PELICAN BOOKS

THE COMMON PURSUIT

Dr Frank Raymond Leavis, a University Reader in English from 1959 to 1962, was a Fellow of Downing College, Cambridge, from 1937 until 1962, and an Honorary Fellow for the following two years. Born at Cambridge in 1905 he was educated at the Perse School and Emmanuel College, where he read History and English. While engaged in University teaching he helped to start the well-known quarterly review *Scrutiny*, which he edited from 1932 until 1953, when it ceased publication. (Complete sets of the journal fetch as much as £100, and the whole has been reprinted in twenty volumes by the Cambridge University Press.) Among his publications are *Mass Civilization and Minority Culture* (1930), *New Bearings in English Poetry* (1932), *For Continuity* (1933), *Revaluation* (1936), *The Great Tradition: George Eliot, James and Conrad* (1948), *The Common Pursuit* (1952), *Two Cultures?* (1962), and *Anna Karenina and Other Essays* (1967). Dr Leavis, who was Visiting Professor at the University of York in 1965, is an Hon. Litt.D. of that university and of the University of Leeds. He is married and has two sons and a daughter.

THE
COMMON PURSUIT

F. R. LEAVIS

Penguin Books
in association with Chatto and Windus

Penguin Books Ltd, Harmondsworth, Middlesex, England
Penguin Books Australia Ltd, Ringwood, Victoria, Australia
Penguin Books Canada Ltd, 41 Steelcase Road West, Markham, Ontario, Canada
Penguin Books (N.Z.) Ltd, 182–190 Wairau Road, Auckland 10,
New Zealand

—

First published by Chatto & Windus 1952
Published in Peregrine Books 1962
Reprinted 1963, 1966, 1969
Reissued in Pelican Books 1976

—

Copyright © F. R. Leavis, 1952

—

Made and printed in Great Britain
by Richard Clay (The Chaucer Press), Ltd,
Bungay, Suffolk

For
MY WIFE

Contents

Preface

I TAKE the title of this book from *The Function of Criticism*, one of those essays of Mr Eliot's which I most admire. The immediately relevant passage runs:

Here, one would suppose, was a place for quiet cooperative labour. The critic, one would suppose, if he is to justify his existence, should endeavour to discipline his personal prejudices and cranks – tares to which we are all subject – and compose his differences with as many of his fellows as possible in the common pursuit of true judgement.

– 'The common pursuit of true judgement': that is how the critic should see his business, and what it should be for him. His perceptions and judgements are his, or they are nothing; but, whether or not he has consciously addressed himself to cooperative labour, they are inevitably collaborative. Collaboration may take the form of disagreement, and one is grateful to the critic whom one has found worth disagreeing with.

Most of the matter in this volume originated in a consciously collaborative enterprise – a sustained effort to promote the 'cooperative labour' of criticism. It appeared in *Scrutiny*, a review that, when the literary history of the past two decades comes to be written, may perhaps be found to have done more to vindicate and maintain the critical function in the English-speaking world than the very small amount of publicity accorded recognition would suggest. To the Editors of *Scrutiny* I am indebted for permission to reprint what first appeared there. 'Johnson and Augustanism' and 'Mr Eliot and Milton' appeared in *The Kenyon Review* and *The Sewanee Review* respectively, and I have to thank the Editors for permission to reprint those essays.

Five collaborators to whom I am especially grateful are Mr Quentin Anderson, Professor L. C. Knights, Mr George Santayana, Fr. A. A. Stephenson, s.j., and Professor René Wellek, critics to whom I am indebted for the peculiar advantage represented by a set critical exchange. The reader will recognize that, in so far as they are present in the essays of mine referring to them, they are present for my convenience, and that what they themselves have said is not fairly to be deduced from my references – any more than it is to be concluded that, given the opportunity, they would have nothing to rejoin.

Criticism, the 'pursuit of true judgement', is not, of course, a pursuit that one can count on finding very commonly practised or favoured. It was by way of countering the wrong meaning of 'common' that I picked my epigraphs from Henry James. The 'associational process' to which he refers (he is declining the offered chairmanship of the English Association) has become a much more formidable menace since his time; how formidable, I suggest in 'The Progress of Poesy', the last piece presented in the following collection. I have not included that piece and given it the salience of the final place out of wanton provocativeness. It seems to me that no one seriously interested can have failed to perceive that, where the critical function is concerned, what peculiarly characterizes our time in England is the almost complete triumph of the 'social' (or the 'associational') values over those which are the business of the critic.

Everyone can think of striking illustrations of what I am referring to. So striking are some of the most recent, and so obviously disastrous must this state of affairs be for literature, and consequently for so much else, that this discouraging moment is perhaps especially one when the explicit challenge may seem not altogether pointless. However that may be, a critic who has thought his pursuit worth his toil must feel that he is committed to taking the opportunity that offers, and to turning such attention as he can win – if he can win any – on the lamentable and unanswerable facts.

F. R. LEAVIS

Acknowledgements

I am indebted to Messrs Edward Arnold & Co. for kind permission to quote the extract from Professor Raleigh's *On Writing and Writers* in my essay on 'Sociology and Literature'; to the Oxford University Press for permission to quote the extract on page 190 from Cecil Sharp's Introduction to *English Folk-Songs from the Southern Appalachians*, and to The Society of Jesus and the Oxford University Press for permission to quote from Hopkins's letters and poems.

F. R. L.

For me, frankly, my dear John, there is simply no question of these things: I am a mere stony, ugly monster of *Dis*sociation and Detachment. I have never in all my life gone in for these things, but have dodged and shirked and successfully evaded them – to the best of my power at least, and so far as they have in fact assaulted me: all my instincts and the very essence of any poor thing that I might, or even still may, trump up for the occasion as my 'genius' have been against them, and are more against them at this day than ever. . . . I can't go into it all much – but the rough sense of it is that I believe only in absolutely independent, individual and lonely virtue, and in the serenely unsociable (or if need be at a pinch sulky and sullen) practice of the same; the observation of a lifetime having convinced me that no fruit ripens but under that temporarily graceless rigour, and that the associational process for bringing it on is but a bright and hollow artifice, all vain and delusive.

HENRY JAMES, *Letter to John Bailley,*
11 NOV. 1912

They are, in general, a sort of plea for Criticism, for Discrimination, for Appreciation on other than infantile lines – as against the so almost universal Anglo-Saxon absence of these things; which tends so, in our general trade, it seems to me, to break the heart.

HENRY JAMES, *Letter to W. D. Howells,*
17 AUGUST 1908

The Norwegian Society of Authors gave him a loving cup, but he asked them to scratch off the inscription and give it to somebody else.

Obituary notice of KNUT HAMSUN

At the end of my first term's work I attended the usual college board to give an account of myself. The spokesman coughed and said a little stiffly: 'I understand, Mr Graves, that the essays that you write for your English tutor are, shall I say, a trifle temperamental. It appears, indeed, that you prefer some authors to others.'

ROBERT GRAVES, *Goodbye to All That*

MR ELIOT AND MILTON

MR ELIOT'S paper on Milton, delivered in England as a British Academy 'Lecture on a Master Mind', and later broadcast in the Third Programme, was widely acclaimed as a classic of recantation – an authoritative and final piece of criticism, vindicating Milton against 'errors and prejudices' propounded by the same critic in his less discerning days, and slavishly taken up by his followers. On me, however, the paper has the effect of showing that Mr Eliot found himself unable to bring to Milton any but a perfunctory interest. And, as a matter of fact, I know of no evidence that his interest in Milton was at any time intense. In saying this I intend no score against Mr Eliot. In what I judge to have been his best days as a critic, the interest was adequate to his purposes, which were very effectually achieved, and it might perhaps be said that the recent paper shows him interested enough for the purposes of an address on Milton to the British Academy.

In it Mr Eliot recognizes two kinds of relevant critical competence: that of the practitioner of verse, and that of the scholar. He himself, of course, speaks as a practitioner. His own distinction as a critic no one today disputes; I cannot however acquiesce in his ascription of competence to the 'practitioner' as such without qualifying a great deal more than he does. But let me first say that the deference he exhibits towards the scholars seems to me wholly deplorable (they enjoy deference enough in any case). The questions discussed in this paper belong, in his own phrase, to 'the field of literary criticism'. For the purposes of criticism, scholarship, unless directed by an intelligent interest in poetry – without, that is, critical sensibility and the skill that enables the critic to develop its responses in sensitive and closely relevant thinking – is useless. That skill is not common among scholars. Of the 'champions of Milton in our time' who have rectified the 'errors' with 'vigorous hands' and who have opposed the 'prejudices' with 'commanding voices', is there one whose vigour takes effect as a vigour of relevance, or whose arguments command attention because they so unquestionably represent an intelligent interest in poetry?

If so, I haven't come across him. And no intimation of Mr Eliot's alters my own finding, which is that there can be little profit in arguing with these champions, since, confident as they are in their status as authorities, their critical education has so patently not begun: where poetry is to be discussed, they show themselves unaware of the elementary conditions of talking to the point. No doubt their learning sometimes has relevance to the understanding and judgement of Milton's poems – relevance they are themselves unable to enforce. No doubt, too, there is relevant knowledge that a critic must have in order to understand and judge. It is possible to argue plausibly that in such a case as Milton's the enabling knowledge will be very extensive. But nothing is plainer to me than that the learning of the scholars to whom Mr Eliot defers has not, in fact, enabled.

I feel called on to make the point with a certain indelicate bluntness, because, though I cannot claim to be either a practitioner of verse or a scholar, I confess to being a 'teacher' – that is, my business is to promote, according to my powers, the intelligent study and discussion of literature. And everyone whose business is the same knows that the academic world in general takes more readily to promoting the deferential study of the scholars, and that the kind of student who has the best chance of academic distinction finds it easier to acquire skill in showing familiarity with the 'work on' (say) Milton than the skill I have referred to above: the skill to develop in relevant thinking the responses of a trained sensibility to the work of the poet. The application of such skill will involve a recourse to scholarship, and the acquisition of knowledge; but it will involve also something quite different from a deferential attitude towards the scholars. Even intelligent students may waste much of their limited time and energy (literature is extensive and the critical lights rare) making a full discovery of the latter truth for themselves, and the teacher accordingly has his responsibilities.

As for the special critical competence of the 'practitioner', one can grant it, I think, only if one delimits one's practitioner very narrowly. Mr Eliot seems to me to be merely abetting confusion when he suggests that 'the criticism of the scholar will be all the better, if he has some experience of the difficulties of writing verse'. Had he said that the scholar would be a better critic if he were capable of becoming a poet of the kind of originality for which Mr Eliot is important in literary history, one would readily agree. But it would be more to the point to say that the scholar's criticism would be better worth attending to if he were critic enough to be able to acclaim an Eliot when he appears, instead of denouncing his verse as unscannable, and seeing the contemporary poetic achievement in a *Testament of Beauty*.

Mr Eliot's superiority as critic over the champions to whom he shows so misleading a courtesy has certainly the closest of relations to the creative genius manifested in his verse. As he himself has said, 'sensibility alters from generation to generation in everybody, whether we will or no, but expression is only altered by a man of genius'. The man of genius in our time has been Mr Eliot; he had the 'consciousness', and acquired the technical skill, to 'use words differently'. In such a creative achievement a distinguished critical intelligence has its inseparable part. (One may add, with immediate relevance, that Bridges' long experience of the difficulties of writing verse didn't make him an intelligent critic or, to all appearances, tend that way in the least.) More generally, the 'practitioner' who may be assumed to have advantages as a critic is the real poet, creative and original.

To become a major poet in Mr Eliot's time, when current poetic conventions and idioms afforded no starting point, so unadaptable to the needs of 'sensibility' were the inveterate habits of expression, required perception and understanding of a rare order. The author of *Portrait of a Lady*, *Gerontion* and *The Waste Land* was in the nature of the case qualified to write criticism as influential as any in literary history. Mr Eliot's best criticism, directed for the most part on the poetry of the past, is immediately related to his own problems as a poet – a poet confronted with the task of inventing the new ways of using words that were necessary if there was to be a contemporary poetry. The interest it shows Mr Eliot taking in his subjects is correspondingly restricted. But the restriction can be seen to be a condition of the extraordinary cogency of the criticism – the clean finality with which it does what was necessary for his essential purposes. Never was there a finer economy. About Milton directly he says very little; there was no need to say more. But the two or three passing observations transmit the force of a whole close context, the *ensemble* of essays, in which Mr Eliot, discussing predominantly qualities and effects that seem to him to call for appreciative study, maintains so sharp and consistent a relevance to his focal interest, the interest of the practitioner. 'The important critic', we read in *The Sacred Wood*, 'is the person who is absorbed in the present problems of art, and who wishes to bring the forces of the past to bear on the solution of those problems'. The measure of his own importance is the efficacity with which he served the function defined here. Though he says, in his influential criticism, so little about Milton, the result of his work as critic and poet was Milton's 'dislodgement'.

I put this last word in inverted commas because it is the one I used, a decade and a half ago, in a passage that has been a good deal cited for derision. The passage opens a discussion of Milton's verse that is to be found in my *Revaluation*. The deriders represent it as showing me in a posture of comically servile deference to authority: Mr Eliot, in his well-known pontifical way, says 'Milton's no good', and I, innocently supposing that to settle the matter, proclaim Milton's annihilation to the world. And now Mr Eliot goes back on his tip, leaving me exposed in my discomfiture for the amusement of his less snobbish – his judicious and real – admirers.

Actually, that passage states briefly certain historical facts, the recognition of which seems to me to be entailed in any intelligent response to Mr Eliot's poetry. The facts (as I saw and see them) are that, when Mr Eliot began to write, Milton had long been prepotent as an influence in taste and practice, and that, as a result of Mr Eliot's work, he ceased to be. That, at any rate, is what the passage says. The brief statement has for support, in other parts of the book, a good deal of particular observation and analysis, illustrating the ways in which the Miltonic 'prepotence' is manifested. Mr Eliot himself, in the paper under discussion, explicitly recognizes that his achievement in poetry entailed as an essential condition a critical attitude towards Milton. What I object to in that part of his argument is the way he puts the case: 'the study of Milton could be of no help: it was only a hindrance'. The frank and simple statement seems to me insidious. And, as I shall explain, I

associate it with an attitude about Milton's influence in the past
that amounts, I think, in its poised liberality, to a surrender of the
function of criticism: 'we can never prove that any particular poet
would have written better poetry if he had escaped that influence'.

What, however, I have to turn to immediately is Mr Eliot's
account of the Miltonic fact – I mean, his analysis of Milton's own
characteristic use of language. Perhaps 'analysis' may be judged to
be the wrong word for what Mr Eliot gives us; but his undertaking certainly commits him to offering an analysis, and what he
does offer is not only surprisingly superficial, but also vitiated by
familiar confusions and fallacies. He recognizes a 'fault' in Milton,
a 'weakness of visual imagination' that is apparent in his imagery.
This weakness, however, mustn't be accounted a disadvantage: it
is offset by a strength of which we can see it to be a condition – a
strength of 'music'. And Mr Eliot in developing his case proceeds
to work the time-honoured abuse of 'music' and 'musical' with
an apparent wholeness of conviction that I find astonishing in so
distinguished a critic – and in the author of his poetry.

We must, then, in reading *Paradise Lost*, not expect to see clearly; our
sense of sight must be blurred, so that our *hearing* may become more
acute. *Paradise Lost* like *Finnegans Wake* (for I can think of no work
which provides a more interesting parallel: two great books by musicians, each writing a language of his own based upon English) makes
this peculiar demand for a readjustment of the reader's mode of apprehension. The emphasis is on the sound, not the vision, upon the word,
not the idea; and in the end it is the unique versification that is the most
certain sign of Milton's intellectual mastership.

I don't know whether Mr Eliot is a 'musician' or not, but in
discussing *Four Quartets* it would be very much to the point to
adduce the poet's evident interest in music. But has 'musicians' in
the parenthesis above any function but that of supporting, illegiti-
mately, the pretensions of 'music' and 'musical', as he employs
them, to be respectable instruments of criticism, and not mere con-
fusing substitutes for the analysis he leaves unperformed? It is true
in suggestion to say that, in Milton's use of language, the
'emphasis is on the sound', but if one aims at advancing the
business of critical thinking one must insist that this 'sound' is an
entirely different thing from the musician's. Milton's interest in
sound as a musician was an entirely different thing from his

interest in 'sound' as a poet, and a man may appreciate the 'music' of Milton's verse who hasn't ear enough to hum *God Save the King*!

'The emphasis is on the sound, not the vision, upon the word, not the idea' – that simple antithetic use of 'sound' and 'vision' seems to me pregnant with fallacy; and I find it odd indeed that the author of *Burnt Norton* should have been content to leave us in that way with the word 'word' on our hands. What is the 'word'? It is certainly not the pure sound – no poet can make us take his verbal arrangements as pure sound, whatever his skill or his genius. And once we recognize that meaning must always enter largely and inseparably into the effect, we see that to define the peculiarities that make Milton's use of language appear to be a matter of specializing in 'verbal music' isn't altogether a simple job.

We might start by challenging a proposition of Mr Eliot's: 'in reading *Paradise Lost* . . . our sense of sight must be blurred, so that our *hearing* may become more acute'. This proposition illustrates the insidiousness of the fallacy inherent in 'sound', when the term is used for critical purposes as Mr Eliot uses it. To say that in responding to the Miltonic 'music' our hearing becomes specially acute is to suggest that some kind of sharp attentiveness is induced in us, and this seems to me the reverse of true. The Miltonic 'music' is not the music of the musician; what our 'hearing' hears is words; and the sense in which Milton's use of words is characterized by a 'musical' bias can be explained only in terms of a generally relaxed state of mind he induces in us. We say that the 'emphasis is on the sound' because we are less exactingly conscious in respect of meaning than when we read certain other poets – say Mr Eliot, or the Wordsworth of *The Ruined Cottage*, or the Yeats of *Sailing to Byzantium*; not because meaning doesn't give the 'sound' its body, movement and quality: it is not only our 'sense of sight' that is blurred. The state induced has analogies with intoxication. Our response brings nothing to any arresting focus, but gives us a feeling of exalted significance, of energetic effortlessness, and of a buoyant ease of command. In return for satisfaction of this order – rhythmic and 'musical' – we lower our criteria of force and consistency in meaning. In order to apply our normal criteria we have to check our response. That is what Mr Eliot meant when, some years ago, he said that 'we have to read

Milton twice, once for the sound and once for the meaning' –
implying that the two kinds of reading cannot be given at the same
time. In the recent paper he notes the tolerance of inconsistency.

He quotes, as showing 'Milton's skill in extending a period by
introducing imagery which tends to distract us from the real
subject', this:

> Thus Satan talking to his neerest Mate
> With Head uplift above the wave, and Eyes
> That sparkling blaz'd, his other Parts besides
> Prone on the Flood, extended long and large
> Lay floating many a rood, in bulk as huge
> As whom the Fables name of monstrous size,
> *Titanian* or *Earth-born*, that warr'd on *Jove*,
> *Briarios* or *Typhon*, whom the Den
> By ancient *Tarsus* held, or that Sea-beast
> *Leviathan*, whom God of all his works
> Created hugest that swim th'Ocean stream:
> Him haply slumbring on the Norway foam
> The pilot of some small night-founder'd Skiff,
> Deeming some Island, oft, as Sea-men tell,
> With fixed Anchor in his scaly rind
> Moors by his side under the Lee, while night
> Invests the Sea, and wished Morn delayes:
> So strecht out huge in length the Arch-fiend lay
> Chain'd on the burning Lake . . .

Mr Eliot comments:

There are, as often with Milton, criticisms of detail which could be
made. I am not too happy about eyes that both blaze and sparkle, unless
Milton meant us to imagine a roaring fire ejecting sparks: and that is
too fiery an image for even supernatural eyes. The fact that the lake was
burning somewhat diminishes the effect of the fiery eyes; and it is
difficult to imagine a burning lake in a scene where there was only
darkness visible.

These criticisms seem to me unanswerable, though, properly
understood, they amount to more than criticism of mere detail –
unanswerable, unless with the argument that if you read Milton as
he demands to be read you see no occasion to make them. Very
few admirers of Milton, I believe, have ever been troubled by
'sparkling blaz'd', or by the inconsistency that Mr Eliot notes.

Such things escape critical recognition from the responsive reader as they escaped Milton's – and for the same reason: response to the 'Miltonic music' (which, therefore, they don't disturb) *is* a relaxation of attentiveness to sense. And if we are to talk of imagery, we must note that it is more than a weakness of *visual* imagery that Mr Eliot calls attention to. To talk of 'imagery' with any precision is a critical undertaking of some difficulty, since the term covers such a variety of things; so I will make my point with a quotation:

> Season of mists and mellow fruitfulness!
>   Close bosom-friend of the maturing sun;
> Conspiring with him now to load and bless
>   With fruit the vines that round the thatch-eaves run;
> To bend with apples the moss'd cottage-trees,
>   And fill all fruit with ripeness to the core;
>   To swell the gourd, and plump the hazel shells
>   With a sweet kernel . . .

The strength that distinguishes Keats so radically from Tennyson can be localized in the un-Tennysonian 'moss'd cottage-trees'. The imagery going with that strength cannot be easily classified. It is more than merely tactual, though the distinctively tactual 'plump' clearly owes its full-bodied concreteness to the pervasive strength in the use of words represented by 'moss'd cottage-trees' (as does 'swell the gourd', the simple statement that is so much more than a statement in the Keatsian context).

This strength cannot be taken stock of in any Sitwellian analysis of 'texture'. It is a matter, among other things, of the way in which the analogical suggestions of the varied complex efforts and motions compelled on us as we pronounce and follow the words and hold them properly together (meaning, that is, has from first to last its inseparable and essential part in the effect of the 'sound') enforce and enact the paraphrasable meaning. The action of the packed consonants in 'moss'd cottage-trees' is plain enough: there stand the trees, gnarled and sturdy in trunk and bough, their leafy entanglements thickly loaded. It is not fanciful, I think, to find that (the sense being what it is) the pronouncing of 'cottage-trees' suggests, too, the crisp bite and the flow of juice as the teeth close in the ripe apple. The word 'image' itself tends to encourage the notion that imagery is necessarily visual, and the visualist fallacy (we have it in Imagism – it is present in Pound's 'phano-peia' and 'melopeia') is wide-spread. But if we haven't imagery – and non-visual imagery – in the kinds of effect just illustrated, then imagery hasn't for the critic the importance commonly assigned to it.

And to take from Keats one more illustration of an un-Miltonic effect, it seems to me that we have a very obvious non-visual image here:

> And sometimes like a gleaner thou dost keep
> Steady thy laden head across a brook . . .

As we pass across the line-division from 'keep' to 'steady' we are made to enact, analogically, the upright steadying carriage of the gleaner as she steps from one stone to the next. And such an enactment seems to me properly brought under the head of 'image'. This effect, I say, is un-Miltonic: the rhythmic habit of Milton's verse runs counter to such uses of stress and movement.[1] And Milton's preoccupation with 'music' precludes any strength in the kinds of imagery that depend on what may be called a realizing use of the body and action of the English language – the use illustrated from Keats. It may be said that apart from such a use there may be a strength of visual imagery. But this is just what, with unanswerable justice, Mr Eliot denies Milton. What then has he?

He has his 'music'. In this 'music', of course, the rhythm plays an essential part – the Grand Style movement that, compelling with its incantatory and ritualistic habit a marked bodily response, both compensates for the lack in the verse of any concrete body,

---

1. So that the expressive felicity of the versification in the Mulciber passage (Bk. I, l. 738) is exceptional:

> and how he fell
> From Heav'n, they fabl'd, thrown by angry Jove
> Sheer o're the Chrystal Battlements: from Morn
> To Noon he fell, from Noon to dewy Eve,
> A Summers day; and with the setting Sun
> Dropt from the Zenith like a falling Star
> On Lemnos th'Aegaean Ile . . .

such as is given by strength in imagery, and lulls the mind out of
its normal attentiveness. It is the lack of body – 'body' as I have
illustrated it from Keats – that, together with the lack, in the
sense, of any challenge to a sharp awareness, makes us talk about
'music' – makes us say that the 'emphasis is on the sound'. Again,
it is 'upon the word, not the idea': that is, we have the feeling that
the 'medium' is for the poet what musical sound is for the com-
poser; our sense of it as something that employs (and flatters) the
skill of the vocal organs, and gives that order of satisfaction,
remains uppermost. We remain predominantly aware of eloquence and declamation; our sense of words as words, things for
the mouth and ear, is not transcended in any vision – or (to avoid
the visualist fallacy) any *realization* – they convey.

'Declamation', significantly, is the word Mr Eliot uses for the
Miltonic mode:

> It may be observed also, that Milton employs devices of eloquence
> and of the word-play in which poets in his time were practised, which
> perpetually relieve the mind, and facilitate the declamation.

The passage Mr Eliot quotes in illustrating his point provides a
good opportunity for questioning his earlier proposition that
'Milton's poetry is poetry at the farthest possible remove from
prose'. If it is so far removed from prose it is not so (it seems to
me) in the sense of exhibiting in concentration the distinctively
poetic uses of language. If called upon to instance poetry at the
farthest possible remove from prose I might reasonably adduce Mr
Eliot's *Marina*, in reading which, if one supposes oneself to be
faced with something at all in the nature of the prose uses of
language, one will be defeated. The use of language is exploratory-
creative, nothing could be further removed (and in a com-
prehending approach to the poem one has to be aware of this)
from any process that can be thought of as one of 'putting' something – ideas or thoughts or a theme – 'into words'.

But the Miltonic mode, for all the 'maximal . . . alteration of
ordinary language' – 'distortion of construction', the foreign
idiom, 'the use of a word in a foreign way' and so on – presented
nothing radically alien or uncongenial to the eighteenth-century
mind. It is a mode, I have noted, that we naturally think of as
eloquence; the eloquence can, as the passage quoted by Mr Eliot

reminds us, take on without any disconcerting change a decided strength of declamation:

> My sentence is for open Warr: of Wiles
> More unexpert, I boast not: then let those
> Contrive who need, or when they need, not now.
> For while they sit contriving, shall the rest,
> Millions that stand in Armes and longing wait
> The Signal to ascend, sit lingring here
> Heav'ns fugitives . . .

In these speeches in Hell we have – it is a commonplace – a kind of ideal parliamentary oratory. It is also a commonplace that Milton's peculiar powers have found here an especially congenial vein. And it is safe to venture that no parts of *Paradise Lost* have been unaffectedly enjoyed by more readers. The fact that a mind familiar with *Paradise Lost* will, without making any sharp distinctions, associate the 'Miltonic music' – 'God-gifted organ voice of England' – with a mode of strong rhetorical statement, argument and exposition,[1] running to the memorable phrase, is of the greatest importance historically (I am thinking of the question of Milton's influence).

But I have to pursue my examination of the weakness; the weakness noted by Mr Eliot (though he won't call it flatly that) in the extract from him given above:

The fact that the lake was burning somewhat diminishes the effect of the fiery eyes; and it is difficult to imagine a burning lake in a scene where there was only darkness visible. But with this kind of inconsistency we are familiar in Milton.

Earlier Mr Eliot has said:

I do not think that we should attempt to *see* very clearly any scene that Milton depicts: it should be accepted as a shifting phantasmagory. To complain, because we first find the arch-fiend 'chain'd on the burning lake' and in a minute or two see him making his way to the shore, is to expect a kind of consistency which the world to which Milton has introduced us does not require.

1. Though in this mode too, as Mr Eliot notes, there is no sharp challenge to a critical or realizing awareness – there is the relaxation of the demand for consistency characteristic of rhetoric: 'It might, of course, be objected that "millions that *stand* in arms" could not at the same time "*sit* lingring".'

I have to insist that, in reading Milton, it isn't merely a matter of
our not *seeing* very clearly; the weakness of realization that he
exhibits can't be limited to the visual field. If we are not bothered
by the absence of visual consistency, that is because, while we are
submissively in and of Milton's world, our criteria of consistency
in general have become very unexacting. The kind of consistency
which that world 'does not require' turns out, when examined
with any attention, to be decidedly comprehensive. If the weakness of visualization becomes, when we consider it, an aspect of
something more general – a weakness of realization (a term the
force of which I have tried to make plain), this, in its turn, we
have to recognize as something more than a characteristic of
imagery and local expression: it affects the poet's grasp of his
themes, conceptions and interests.

The instances of visual inconsistency that Mr Eliot remarks are
drawn from Milton's Hell. What they illustrate is Milton's failure
to give us a consistently realized Hell at all. I will adduce on this
point the commentary of Mr A. J. A. Waldock (so finding an
opportunity to recommend his *Paradise Lost and Its Critics*[1] – it
seems to me by far the best book on Milton I have read). He points
out that, because of Milton's inconsistencies of conception and
imagination, his Hell 'loses most of its meaning'.

It is obvious that as the conclave proceeds Hell, for all the effective
pressure it exerts on our consciousness, has as good as vanished. The
livid flames become mere torches to light the assembly of the powers.
A little later, when there is leisure, Milton recollects his duty, resumes
his account of the infernal landscape and adds further items to his
(somewhat meagre) list of tortures. But as he had just proved to us in
the clearest way how little the rebels are inconvenienced by their situation, it is impossible for us to take these further lurid descriptions very
seriously. The plain fact of it, of course, is that Milton's Hell is very
much a nominal one . . .
Yet conditions, even while the action is in progress, are (theoretically) bad enough: 'torture without End still urges' (I, 67); 'these rag-
ing fires Will slack'n, if his breath stir not their flames' (II, 2); in spite
of which organized field sports are possible. The reason for these and
other vaguenesses in the picture is fairly evident: Milton was trying his
best to accomplish two incompatible things at the same time . . . Hell

1. Published by the Cambridge University Press.

therefore as a locality has to serve a double duty: it is a place of perpetual and increasing punishment in theory; and it is also in the practice of a poem, an assembly ground, a military area, a base for operations. The two conceptions do not very well agree . . .

All this amounts, I cannot help thinking, to a radical criticism of *Paradise Lost* – a more damaging criticism than Professor Waldock himself recognizes (my main criticism of him is that he doesn't draw the consequences of his findings). It cannot be disposed of with the explanation that Milton's work doesn't require visual consistency. The inconsistency plainly touches essence, and touches it most seriously; for surely, in such an undertaking as that of *Paradise Lost* the conception of Hell must be, in a major way, significant – if the poem attains to significance at the level of the promise. The weakness, so far from being merely a 'limitation of visual power', is – to take up a word that Mr Eliot offers us with an odd insistence – intellectual.

The emphasis is on the sound, not the vision, upon the word, not the idea; and in the end it is the unique versification that is the most certain sign of Milton's intellectual mastership.

One can only comment that it may be the most certain sign, but that, as a justification for attributing *intellectual* mastership, it surely doesn't amount to much. Mr Eliot himself notes that it is the nature of the 'versification' to induce a relaxed concern for meaning – for 'the idea'. He illustrates the point (though he doesn't say so) in a footnote to a line of the long simile he quotes (the one reproduced above):

The term *night-founder'd*, which I presume to be of Milton's invention, seems unsuitable here. Dr Tillyard has called my attention to the use of the same adjective in *Comus*, l. 483:

Either someone like us night-foundered here

where, though extravagant, it draws a permissible comparison between travellers lost in the night, and seafarers in extremity. But when, as here in *Paradise Lost*, it is transferred from travellers on land to adventurers by sea, and not to the men but to their *skiff*, the literal meaning of *founder* immediately presents itself. A *foundered* skiff could not be *moored*, to a whale or to anything else.

The weakness is profoundly characteristic, and it would be easy to find other instances demanding similar comment. And I myself see Mr Eliot's instance as being significantly *of* the passage to which it belongs – the simile of which he says:

> What I wish to call your attention to is the happy introduction of so much extraneous matter. Any writer, straining for images of hugeness, might have thought of the whale, but only Milton could have included the anecdote of the deluded seaman without our wanting to put a blue pencil through it. We *nearly* forget Satan in attending to the story of the whale; Milton recalls us just in time. Therefore the diversion strengthens, instead of weakening, the passage.

The force of that 'therefore' seems to me illusory, and I find the logic specious. To say that the diversion *strengthens* anything is inapt and misleading; Miltonic similes don't focus one's perception of the relevant, or sharpen definition in any way: that, surely, is the point to be made about them. If they represent 'imagery', then it is the kind of imagery that goes with the 'Miltonic music'. We are happy about the introduction of so much extraneous matter because the 'Miltonic music' weakens our sense of relevance, just as it relaxes our grasp of sense. But

> this [musical] mastery is more conclusive evidence of his intellectual power than is his grasp of any *ideas* that he borrowed or invented. To be able to control so many words at once is the token of a mind of most exceptional energy.

We have to remind ourselves that Milton's control of words manifests itself in the looseness about meaning illustrated by his 'night-founder'd', and that, if he unquestionably exhibits great energy, 'mind' is an ambiguous word. In fact, it seems to me that Mr Eliot is unconsciously exploiting the ambiguity, the impulsion towards doing so deriving from an uneasy awareness (betrayed in that insistence on 'intellectual') of criticism to be brought against Milton that, if duly considered, would make Mr Eliot's present claims for him look odd.

> Other marks [of Milton's greatness] are his sense of structure, both in the general design of *Paradise Lost* and *Samson,* and in his syntax; and finally, and not the least, his inerrancy, conscious or unconscious, in writing so as to make the best display of his talents, and the best concealment of his weaknesses.

That 'inerrancy' (I will leave aside for the time being the 'sense of structure') is to me an astonishing proposition. Mr Eliot makes plain (in the next paragraph) that he covers with it the choice of subject: 'the complete suitability of *Paradise Lost* has not, I think, been so often remarked' [as that of the subject of *Samson*]. Yet the subject of *Paradise Lost* meant for Milton, inevitably and essentially, the undertaking to

> assert Eternal Providence
> And justify the wayes of God to men.

One doesn't need to go to the argumentative speeches of God the Father in order to make the point that such an undertaking was one for which Milton had no qualifications. Those speeches do indeed exhibit him as (considering his offer) ludicrously unqualified to make even a plausible show of metaphysical capacity. But it is in the 'versification' everywhere that the essential inaptitude appears: the man who uses words in this way has (as Mr Eliot virtually says) no 'grasp of ideas', and, whatever he may suppose, is not really interested in the achievement of precise thought of any kind; he certainly hasn't the kind of energy of mind needed for sustained analytic and discursive thinking. That is why the ardours and ingenuities of the scholars who interpret *Paradise Lost* in terms of a supposed consistency of theological intention are so absurd, and why it is so deplorable that literary students should be required to take that kind of thing seriously, believe that it has anything to do with intelligent literary criticism, and devote any large part of their time to the solemn study of Milton's 'thought'.

What the choice of subject illustrates is that lack of self-knowledge which gives us such obvious grounds for saying that in Milton we have to salute character rather than intelligence – for character he indisputably has: he massively is what he is – proud, unaccommodating and heroically self-confident. The lack of self-knowledge meets us, in *Paradise Lost*, in many forms. The choice of subject presents it in other ways than that which I have specified. Professor Waldock seems to me unanswerable when he says that 'Milton's central theme denied him the full expression of his deepest interests'. More, the theme cut clean against them:

He can read the myth (or make a valiant attempt to do so) in terms of Passion and Reason, the twin principles of his own humanistic thinking; but with all that, the myth obstinately remains, drawing him away from what most deeply absorbs him (effort, combat, the life of the 'wayfaring Christian') to the celebration of a state of affairs that could never have profoundly interested him, and that he never persuades us does.

The result, or concomitant, is discrepancy between theory and feeling; between the effect of a given crucial matter as Milton presents it, and the view he instructs us to take of it. His handling of the central episode of the myth provides notable illustration. After rendering Adam's fall with affecting pathos he gives, as Professor Waldock shows (it would be obvious enough in any case, if one read Milton at full cock of attention) a false account of it; Adam himself gives a false account of it to the Son; the Son accepts it, and it becomes the official account. The inconsistency can hardly be dismissed as not mattering in the 'world to which Milton has introduced us', and it occurs at the centre of the poem, which, as Professor Waldock says,

requires us, not tentatively, not half-heartedly . . . but with the full weight of our minds to believe that Adam did right, and simultaneously requires us with the full weight of our minds to believe that he did wrong.

The Miltonists, of course, don't see the problem in this way; they busy themselves (and it would be an amusing spectacle if one didn't know that they were authorities to whom thousands of students are expected to apply themselves deferentially) with determining, if a word can't be found to cover both Adam and Eve, just what Adam's sin is to be called – gregariousness, levity, uxoriousness, pride or lust.

Conflict between feeling and theory is not the only way in which a radical lack of integration manifests itself in *Paradise Lost*. The weakness meets us in a characteristic that everyone has noticed – the personal quality that obtrudes itself in a good number of passages, some of them among the most admired. Professor Waldock illustrates the weakness (without calling it that) here:

At no point in the poem is Milton himself more thoroughly *with* Adam than at this; he is bitterly, weepingly with him. It is as if the two, author and character, coalesce, and whose voice it is in that final exasperated indictment we hardly know:

> Thus it shall befall
> Him who to worth in Women overtrusting
> Lets her Will rule; restraint she will not brook,
> And left to herself, if evil thence ensue,
> She first his weak indulgence will accuse.
>
> (IX, 1182)

Again:

> Milton seems to us often, as he writes of [Satan] to be giving of his own substance, but he can give of his own substance everywhere. In those altercations, for example, between Satan and Abdiel in Books v and vi we feel Milton now in the lines of the one, now in the lines of the other, but chiefly, without any doubt, in the lines of Abdiel.

In these passages, where he seems 'to be giving of his own substance', we have the clear marks of Milton's failure to *realize* his undertaking – to conceive it dramatically as a whole, capable of absorbing and depersonalizing the relevant interests and impulses of his private life. He remains in the poem too much John Milton, declaiming, insisting, arguing, suffering, and protesting.

The best known example of his 'own substance' getting the upper hand and becoming a problem is in Satan. Not that the great Satan of the first two books isn't sufficiently dramatized; the trouble is quite other:

> It would be hard to quarrel with what Dr Tillyard has to say about Satan. Dr Tillyard is not with the 'Satanists', but he does not see 'how we can avoid admitting that Milton did partly ally himself with Satan, that unwittingly he was led away by the creature of his own imagination': and he feels (to my mind with perfect rightness) that 'it is not enough to say with Saurat that Satan represents a part of Milton's mind, a part of which he disapproves and of which he was quite conscious'. The feeling of most readers would surely be with Dr Tillyard that there is more than conscious recognition, more than conscious disapproval, in all this. The balance *is* disturbed; the poem, instead of being on an even keel, has a pronounced list, and Satan is the cause of it.

And Professor Waldock points out that the Satan of the first two books appears no more, the Satan of the address to the Sun near the beginning of Book iv being a different one – different in conception. But, not satisfied that this substitution restores the proper balance of sympathy, Milton, as Professor Waldock shows in detail, intervenes constantly to incite a disparaging view of Satan – to 'degrade' him, the extreme instance of the 'technique of degradation' being the pantomime trick in Book x by which the infernal host, breaking into applause, are made to hiss.

What radical 'consistency', what wholeness, do these criticisms, which Professor Waldock enforces with minute observation and analysis, leave to *Paradise Lost*? Milton has so little self-knowledge and is so unqualified intellectually, that his intention (the intended significance of the poem) at the level of 'justifying the ways of God to Men', and what he actually contrives as poet to do, conflict, with disastrous consequences to both poem as such and intention. Satan, a major element in the poem, gets out of hand (and a closely related misfortune overtakes God the Father), with the result that the 'balance *is* disturbed' – and very badly. As a result of the conflict between feeling and theory Milton's treatment of the Fall is such that Professor Waldock has to conclude: '*Paradise Lost* cannot take the strain at the centre, it breaks there, the theme is too much for it'. And yet he seems to think that Milton can be credited with 'architectonic' – just as Mr Eliot speaks of Milton's 'sense of structure'.

Words used in that way seem to me to have no meaning. The attribution looks to me no better than a mere inert acquiescence in convention: 'architectonic' power has always been taken to be the mark of the Miltonic genius. But it is perhaps worth asking what gives the idea its plausibility – what makes it possible for Professor Waldock to say:

Nothing of this . . . can, it seems to me, make much difference to the obstinate fact that *Paradise Lost* is an epic poem of singularly hard and definite outline, expressing itself (or so at least would be our first impressions) with unmistakable clarity and point.

That 'epic poem', I think, gives the clue to a large part of the explanation: *Paradise Lost* is a classical epic – it is epic, classical and monumental: a strong traditional suggestion of qualities goes with those words. Actually, the undertaking to treat the chosen theme in an epic on the classical model illustrates very strikingly the peculiarities of the Miltonic genius that made strongly against clarity and outline (at least, in any complex whole), and made for inconsistency, muddle and vagueness. To put it in a positive way, it illustrates the peculiarities that lead us to say that the word for Milton is 'character' rather than 'intelligence'. On the one hand there was his heroic self-confidence, his massive egotism and his conviction that nothing but the highest enterprise was worthy of him: for the Renaissance poet and scholar the form must be the epic; for the dedicated voice of the chosen English people the theme must be the greatest of all themes. On the other hand, only a great capacity for unawareness – unawareness in the face of impossibilities, his own limitations, and the implicit criticism incurred by his intentions in the attempt to realize them – could have permitted him, after pondering such an undertaking, to persist in it.

When he came to the war in Heaven even Milton, as Professor Waldock observes, seems to have had some difficulty in persuading himself that he was taking it seriously. Yet the war in Heaven is an essential part of the epic conception, and to foresee the absurdity of the part would have been to forswear the whole.

Having elaborated his criticisms, Professor Waldock, in the 'Conclusion' to his book, says that the poem 'has enough left, in all conscience, to stay it against anything we can do'. But what has it left? There are the first two books, which are of a piece and grandly impressive, and, in the others, numbers of 'beauties' major and minor. But, surely, whatever is left, it cannot justify talk about 'architectonic', 'hard and definite outline', or Milton's 'sense of structure'. And if more is to be said by way of explaining illusions to the contrary, the Miltonic character may be invoked: it certainly suggests massiveness and a 'hard and definite outline', and in reading *Paradise Lost* we are rarely unconscious of the author. And it is natural to associate our sense of the whole characteristic enterprise with our sense of the character.

The paradoxical association of this 'character' with a use of language that tends to the reverse of 'hard and definite outline' has much to do with the strength of Milton's influence in the nineteenth century – his prepotence in taste and practice in the period of English poetry to which Mr Eliot's work put a decisive end. That his own technical preoccupations as a poet entailed a critical attitude towards Milton, Mr Eliot, in his recent paper, admits. I challenge his way of putting things because it seems to me, as I said, insidious – calculated, that is, *not* to promote critical light. 'And the study of Milton could be of no help: it was only a hindrance'. – As if it were a matter of deciding *not* to study Milton! The problem, rather, was to escape from an influence that was so difficult to escape from because it was unrecognized, belonging, as it did, to the climate of the habitual and 'natural'. Mr Eliot, who 'had the consciousness to perceive that he must use words differently' from Tennyson and Swinburne, had at the same time the consciousness that enabled him to name Milton for immediately relevant criticism. (That didn't mean, of course, that he had to give Milton much of his critical attention.)

Along with this misleading formulation goes what I can only call a speciously judicial refusal to judge –

And we can never prove that any particular poet would have written better poetry if he had escaped that influence. Even if we assert, what can only be a matter of faith, that Keats would have written a very great epic poem if Milton had not preceded him, is it sensible to repine for an unwritten masterpiece, in exchange for one which we possess and acknowledge?

What we can say, and must, in so far as we are bent on getting recognition for Keats's greatness, is that, if he hadn't been capable of putting the beautiful first *Hyperion* behind him, with the re-mark that 'Milton's verse cannot be written but in an artful, or rather, artist's humour', he wouldn't have been capable of the qualities that are the strength of the ode *To Autumn* and of the induction to the revised *Hyperion*, that constitute the proof of his major genius, and that make Tennyson's, put side by side with his, a decidedly minor one.

The reference to Tennyson has much point. For there is some-thing decidedly Tennysonian about the handling of the medium in *Hyperion*, any representative passage of which, as I have noted elsewhere (*Revaluation*, pp. 267–8), offers the critic, in its way of being at the same time Tennysonian and Miltonic, an admirable way of bringing home the fact of Milton's predominance in the Victorian age – for in Tennyson we have the Victorian main current. Milton in Tennyson, as in Keats, is associated with Spenser, and Tennyson had his specific original genius: 'he knew', says Mr Eliot, 'everything about Latin versification that an English poet could use' and had a 'unique and unerring feeling for the sounds of words'. Tennyson himself defined his ambition as being to bring English as near to the Italian as possible, and his 'music' ('the emphasis . . . on the sound, . . . upon the word, not the idea') has a highly distinctive quality. But he, like Milton, had other than musical preoccupations; he aspired to be among 'the great sage-poets of all time'. In the ease with which he reconciled the two bents we see the Miltonic inheritance – as in the readiness with which the nobly-phrased statement of 'thought' and moral attitudes in sonorous verse (the 'emphasis . . . on the sound') was accepted as the type of serious poetic expression.

It would take a long separate essay to provide the historical backing for these last suggestions (obviously valid as they appear to me) in an examination of the Miltonic influence as it passes through the eighteenth century, appears in varied forms in the great poets of the Romantic period (it asserts itself plainly in Wordsworth, Coleridge, Shelley, Keats and Byron), and emerges from that period to a subtle predominance in the Victorian age. It must be enough here to adduce the case of Matthew Arnold. Arnold was not an original poetic genius; he was a very intelligent man with a talent of the kind that provides evidence of what cultivated people in a given age feel to be 'natural' in modes of poetic expression. The Tennysonian Palace of Art had no attractions for him, and he states in his criticism a view of the function of the poet that postulates something very different from the poetry of the Victorian 'otherworld':

every one can see that a poet . . . ought to know life and the world before dealing with them in poetry; and life and the world being in modern times very complex things. the creation of a modern poet, to be worth much, implies a great critical effort behind it. . . .

But Arnold's characteristic poetic achievement may fairly be represented by *The Scholar-Gipsy*. This is a charming poem, but the significance it holds for us is that Arnold so clearly intended it to be much more than charming. He offers the Scholar, with unmistakable moral unction, as the symbol of a spiritual superi-

ority; a superiority that makes him an admonition and an ideal
for 'us', who, in this 'iron time', suffer

> the sick fatigue, the languid doubt,
> Which much to have tried, in much been baffled, brings.

The Scholar-Gipsy, we are insistently told, had 'one aim, one
business, one desire'; his powers were 'firm to their mark'. But it
is mere telling; the 'aim' and the 'mark' are mere abstract
postulates: 'thou hadst – what we, alas, have not'. And that is
clearly all that Arnold knows about it. He exhibits the Scholar as
drifting about the Oxford countryside in an eternal week-end.
'For early didst thou leave the world' – and what the poem
actually offers is a charm of relaxation, a holiday from serious
aims and exacting business.

And what the Scholar-Gipsy really symbolizes is Victorian
poetry, vehicle (so often) of explicit intellectual and moral intentions, but unable to be in essence anything but relaxed, relaxing
and anodyne. Arnold himself was an adverse critic of the prevailing tradition, but he was not the 'man of genius' by whom
alone 'expression is altered'. He has his own personal style, it is
true; but the notion of distinctively poetic expression that informs it is quite normally and ordinarily Victorian. Various
influences are to be seen in the diction and phrasing of The
Scholar-Gipsy, but the significant clue is to be seen in such obvious
reminders of Milton as this:

> Till having used our nerves with bliss and teen,
> And tired upon a thousand schemes our wit,
> To the just-pausing genius we remit
> Our worn-out life, and are – what we have been.

Significant clue, I mean, when we are considering the question:
How can so intelligent a man as Arnold have been capable, when
writing verse, of such weak confusion, such intellectual debility,
as The Scholar-Gipsy exposes? He exemplifies with peculiar
force the general habit and tendency of Victorian poetic. For him,
poetry, while being a medium for intellectual statement – for the
presentment of 'thought' such as might have been expressed in
prose, differs from prose (we can see) in not imposing any strict
intellectual criterion. The inferiority, in rigour and force, of the

intellectual content is compensated for by nobility, sonority and finish of phrasing. But the compensating cannot be clearly distinguished from a process that combines exaltation and an effect of heightened significance with an actual relaxing of the mind, so that the reader, though conscious of an intellectual appeal, doesn't notice any need for compensation; for the nobility and sonority go with a subtly 'musical' use of language – the 'emphasis' is sufficiently 'on the sound' to save the 'idea' from close scrutiny.

Arnold, of course, had his own special exposure to Miltonic influence in his cult of Wordsworth. But his poetic was normally Victorian, and consideration of his case should bring home the force of the contention that, in Victorian poetic, we have to recognize the Miltonic influence. For in a tradition or habit – a use of language that seemed to the age 'natural' – which could do with a critic of Arnold's intelligence what the Victorian poetic did with him there is a potency that calls for a Milton to explain it. Milton's moral and intellectual prestige, and his power over the English mind, need not be enlarged on here. That prestige and that power had been refreshed by the great poets of the Romantic period, out of whose varied achievement emerged the Victorian poetic tradition, which favoured nobility, found the grand Wordsworth of the *Immortality* ode and the 'platform' sonnets more positively congenial than the Wordsworth of *Lyrical Ballads* and, at the same time, tended, as Mr Eliot himself has pointed out, to be essentially preoccupied with the evocation of a poetic 'otherworld'. The relevance of our earlier examination of Milton's use of language, for 'music' and yet for statement, should be plain.

Of course, it may be said that Milton cannot be held responsible for Victorian bents that made him congenial as an influence. But my point is that the critic has every ground for judging the Victorian poetic tradition to have been unsatisfactory in this and that way, and that consequently he has the duty so to judge. It was Mr Eliot who made us fully conscious of the weaknesses of that tradition, and he did so by 'altering expression'. And it seems plain to me that the altering could not have been done by a poet who hadn't arrived at the judgements about Milton expressed in Mr Eliot's early criticism, just as it seems plain to me that people who see in those judgements merely regrettably prejudices (now outgrown) don't, whatever they suppose, really appreciate Mr

Eliot's creative achievement. And there is, I am convinced, a clear significance in the association in that early criticism (which bore so closely on his technical preoccupations) of comments on the weaknesses of Victorian verse with the judgements on Milton and with the display of positive interest in poetry exemplifying 'the intellect at the tip of the senses'.

As for the possibility of Milton's becoming now a profitable study for poets, I should have been more shy about questioning such a suggestion when offered by Mr Eliot if he himself had appeared to offer it with any conviction. But the terms in which he phrases it are curiously large and general. And the lessons he proposes as the profit of frequenting Milton would, it seems to me, be more reasonably sought elsewhere. 'It [poetry] might also learn that the music of verse is strongest in poetry which has a definite meaning expressed in the properest words'. To recommend, where that lesson has been judged to be necessary, the study of Milton seems to me merely inconsequent. And I find it hard to believe that salutary lessons in 'verse structure' or in the avoidance of '*servitude* to colloquial speech' are likely to be learnt from a master in whom 'there is always the maximal, never the minimal, alteration of ordinary language' – who departs so consistently and so far from speech that the sensitiveness and subtlety of rhythm that depend on an appeal to our sense of the natural run are forbidden him. The lesson of 'freedom within form', I am convinced, would be better learnt from the study of Mr Eliot's own verse.

And that point suggests to me that an effective concern for the future of English poetry must express itself in a concern for the present function of criticism[1]; for it is the weakness of that function during the last twenty years that has permitted the most elementary and essential discriminations to pass unregarded, and the lessons to be ignored or unperceived.

---

1. Milton has been made the keep of an anti-critical defensive system. Replying, in a letter to the present writer, to the criticism passed on his *Paradise Lost and Its Critics* above, the late Professor Waldock said that of course he hadn't drawn the consequences of his findings: he daren't; he was afraid enough about what he *had* done.

IN DEFENCE OF MILTON

TODAY, when the quality of the literary studies encouraged or permitted at the academic places of education has an obviously important bearing on the prospects of literary culture (that is, of humane culture generally), it is correspondingly important, and certainly not less important than it has been in less desperate times, to defend literature – to defend the classics and the literary tradition – against the academic mind. The professional student of letters, the 'authority' – authority also, it must be remembered, in matters of curricula, instruction and examination at the high seats of learning – is rarely qualified in relation to his subject with one very relevant kind of authority (I had almost said the indispensable kind, but things are as they are), a kind that is not constituted, and need not be asserted or claimed: he is rarely a good first-hand critic – or even a good second-hand one. This is a truth we are often reminded of by the evident limitations of justly respected scholars: a man may do work that exacts the gratitude of us all as readers of poetry who yet betrays a lack of any developed sensibility, any fineness of perception and judgement.

So when Dr Tillyard[1] adduces Sir Herbert Grierson (in a large and varied company of supporters – Dr Tillyard seems to think that numbers strengthen his case and recruits even from the Sunday newspaper) as pronouncing with peculiar authority on the critical questions concerning Milton's verse and its influence, one can only reply that the genuine respect in which one holds the editor of Donne doesn't confer on him authority of that kind:

Professor Grierson has one peculiar advantage in writing on Milton. Having edited and praised Donne he cannot be suspected of giving untested allegiance to the old poetic hierarchy of the seventeenth century in which the Metaphysicals were accorded an inferior place. It is this that gives a peculiar force to his defence of Milton against modern defamation. The defence is admirable in itself: coming from the editor of

1. *The Miltonic Setting.*

Donne it may penetrate ears which had otherwise been quite sealed up against it.

I am obliged to comment that on Donne himself Professor Grierson speaks only with a limited kind of authority, the limitations being apparent in (to take a recent piece of evidence) this sentence from the Preface to the *Oxford Book of Seventeenth Century Verse*:

> Palgrave's chief and best guide was Tennyson, on whose fine ear the metres of the 'metaphysicals' must have grated as did those of his friend Browning; and a distinguished poet of our own day has in a recent lecture indicated clearly that his judgement is more in agreement with that of Tennyson than with that of the admirers of Donne.

If anyone should think that this remark, with the reference to A. E. Housman, is susceptible of something less disqualifying than the obvious interpretation I refer him to the Introduction (so valuable in various ways) to *Metaphysical Lyrics and Poems of the Seventeenth Century*, and especially to the passage (see p. xxxiii) in which Professor Grierson agrees with Professor Gregory Smith that 'the direct indebtedness of the courtly poets to Ben Jonson is probably . . . small.'

I do not recall these things wantonly, but in order to make, with all due respect to Professor Grierson, a necessary point. At the worst, perhaps, I shall be taken as returning the note of impatience and asperity perceptible in his comments on my own criticism. What is there to say, then, except that the scholar who commits himself to such pronouncements, distinguished authority on seventeenth-century matters as he certainly is, has no claim to be treated as a critical authority on the verse of the period – of any verse?

But I must add at once that Professor Grierson, who has all the scholarly virtues, is incapable of original critical extravagance or of any of the kinds of critical originality for which Dr Tillyard's book is remarkable, and he must, I imagine, if he has read the book, have been at least as surprised as myself when he came to p. 8 of it. We read there, after the appropriate quotation:

> That is the opening of *L'Allegro*, and it is one of the most puzzling passages in the whole of Milton; what possessed him that he should

write such bombast? By what strange anticipation did he fall into the manner of the worst kind of eighteenth-century ode? If Milton meant to be noble, he failed dreadfully. If, however, he knew what he was doing, he can only have meant to be funny. And if he meant to be funny, to what end? There is nothing in the rest of the poem that suggests humour – at least of the burlesque sort.

I must permit myself to comment, in defence of Milton, that these remarks, it seems to me, can only have the effect of discrediting the writer's very large critical pretensions. Did anyone ever before find that passage puzzling? I do not myself rank *L'Allegro* (or *Il Penseroso*) very high among Milton's works, but it never occurred to me to have doubts about his intention or touch in that opening paragraph, which seems to me, in relation to the change that follows, obviously successful. As for the 'strange anticipation' that Dr Tillyard descries, I can only say that the descrial makes the modesty that he expresses elsewhere about his qualifications to discuss eighteenth-century verse appear well-judged.

But it is no mere academic deficiency, no mere lack of ability to perceive, that can explain so fantastic an exhibition. The explanation comes when Dr Tillyard imparts his discovery that the themes of *L'Allegro* and *Il Penseroso* were derived from one of Milton's Latin *Prolusions*. If there had been no such discovery of a 'solution' would there have been any problem to solve? The answer is plain. The discoverer, that is, convicts himself of something worse than a deficiency, he exhibits a characteristic that has to be defined in terms of opposition to disinterestedness – a characteristic that we cannot imagine as impairing the scholarship of Professor Grierson, whom (as I have intimated) I take as representing the academic virtues.

The accumulation of scholarship – 'work on' – about and around the great things of literature is in any case, for all the measure one may recognize of the relevant and illuminating, a matter for misgiving. Dr Tillyard regrets, in his Preface, that he has had 'no room to refer to more than a fraction of the recent work on Milton' that has interested him. The problem, as a university teacher should be especially aware, is to ensure that the libraries and reading-lists of such work shall not, in effect, be the reverse of an aid and an encouragement to humane education and the vitalizing currency of the classics. In these conditions anything approaching the spirit that sets out to establish the indispensability of fresh impedimenta and seeks fresh impedimenta with a view to establishing, if possible, their indispensability, is peculiarly to be deplored. Dr Tillyard's interest in his projects shows, it seems to me, neither the critic's nor the scholar's disinterestedness.

A concomitant effect apparent in the book is that of his never really knowing what, in the way of discussible theme, he is offering to do. A major explicit undertaking is to unsettle the traditional notion of Milton as a lonely genius, maintaining in his age an aloof and majestic self-sufficiency. In so far as Dr Tillyard is likely to be influential (and that he is an accepted authority is a reason for discussing him) I think this aim deplorable. He supposes himself to be defending Milton, but it seems to me an odd defence that offers to rob the English tradition – for such is explicitly Dr Tillyard's aim – of that unique heroic figure. In fact, I must here come to Milton's defence (and tradition's) myself, and assert that Dr Tillyard nowhere produces anything that can be called a reason. He merely produces a Milton of his own – very much his own – and with a truly notable assurance commends him to us as the up-to-date substitute for the great Milton. For Dr Tillyard's Milton has no greatness, and is very much preoccupied with being up to date:

When Dr Leavis, after an excellent analysis of a passage in *Comus* proceeds to pillory the style of *Paradise Lost* as exhibiting a shocking decline in vitality and flexibility, he takes no account of what the changing ideas of the age demanded. Being likewise so insistent that poets should be 'aware of the contemporary situation', is he altogether just? If the changes Milton made in his style correspond to the general trend, ought he to be grudged the virtue of this 'awareness'? (p. 137.)

I should have been better pleased if Dr Tillyard had pointed out the blunder in my analysis. As for my alleged insistence that poets should be 'aware of the contemporary situation,' I assure him that, if (and the suggestion surprises me) I have indeed used the phrase, it was certainly without any suspicion of what it would look like in the context given it by him, and that I will make a point of leaving it alone for the future. To attempt to suggest what this virtue of 'awareness' is as Dr Tillyard conceives it and attributes it to Milton is to invite the charge of parody. I will confine myself to some representative quotations:

And when he comes to *Paradise Lost* he must needs once again bow to public opinion and write in a style remote from the virtuousness of his epitaph on Hobson. (p. 121.)

Anyhow the whole onus of choosing it (the style of *Paradise Lost*) is commonly thrust on Milton. If some readers can realize that he chose it for the very opposite reason, in order to be at one with his age, they may look on it with initial favour rather than with their present repugnance. (p. 122.)

Quite rightly he stuck to his own convictions [Dr Tillyard is dealing with Milton's failure to conform to fashion in the matter of the heroic couplet], but I am certain that he disliked going against the best contemporary practice. (p. 204.)

That 'best' and the certitude are admirable; the critic who aspires to awareness should ponder them and the ease with which the apparently discrepant criteria – that of the 'best' and that of the 'rightly' – are (time aiding) reconciled and glide into one. Milton went against the best contemporary practice, but he must (we do him the justice to grant) have felt that it was wrong to do so; and in any case, from the point of view of today's best contemporary opinion it is seen, not merely that he was right to stick to his convictions, but that his convictions were right. This is rather a complicated instance. Perhaps a simpler illustration is to be found in a modern poet who has been more immediately influential than Milton was. Mr Eliot, one gathers, is so important a figure in modern poetry because, in tackling his problems of style, he accepted contemporary opinion and, in each of his various changes of manner, bowed once again to public opinion in order to be at one with his age.

For all I know, Dr Tillyard will see nothing absurd in this suggestion, for Mr Eliot has been accepted by the age, which indeed has got as far as Mr Auden, and it is some years since the best opinion – the kind of opinion with which a critic practising in the spirit that Dr Tillyard applauds as Milton's would cultivate solidarity – has, for the most part, ceased charging Mr Eliot with literary Bolshevism. And a preoccupation with solidarity is something I have to insist on as a main characteristic of Dr Tillyard's criticism. It is so radical a habit that he tends to rest on it even in those places where his consciousness of applying, and even of showing a certain pioneering audacity in developing, the latest critical apparatus – of confounding the 'modern' critic with an ultra-modernity – is most apparent. For example, the essay in which he undertakes to confute my account of Milton's Grand Style by showing (with the support of Lascelles Abercrombie, William James, A. E. Housman, Gilbert Murray and Miss Maud Bodkin)[1] that Milton is, or may be plausibly argued to be, re-markable for 'primitive feeling', or 'a richer share than Donne of those fundamental qualities of mind that appear to have immediate contact with the forces of life'[2] – this essay begins (p. 43):

If you judged Shakespeare and Milton by the standards of Henry James and Virginia Woolf, there is no doubt that Shakespeare would fare the better.

What does this mean? Perhaps by dint of questioning and suggestion some discussible proposition could be elicited from Dr Tillyard. But such a sentence (and the formula is repeated more than once in the book) couldn't have been written and left standing if the author hadn't been more concerned with the response he was relying on than the thought he supposed himself to be expressing. Again, a few lines further on, he writes:

Dr Leavis (who is a better critic when he encourages us to read Carew or Pope than when he puts Spenser or Shelly on the index) . . .

This is Dr Tillyard's way of referring to the fact that I have criticized Shelley adversely and to the deduction that I set a lower value on Spenser than on Chaucer, Jonson, Pope, Blake, Crabbe, Wordsworth, Byron, Yeats and Eliot. It is a way that no self-respecting critic should permit himself; it should be left to the Sunday reviewers.

Dr Tillyard at the same time, in his assumption that it is praise-worthy to find reasons for recommending accepted authors (I

1. I hope Miss Bodkin's Archetypal Patterns are not going to become a part of the 'modern critic's' outfit.

2. Cf. 'A second primitive feeling may be deduced from the architectonic power which critics have so often praised in Milton. There is something quite uncommon, something alive and passionate, in the thorough manner in which Milton shapes and finishes off his plot,' etc. See p. 55.

cannot see why he should have been convinced by the reasons I give in favour of Carew and Pope) and reprehensible to criticize such authors adversely, seems to me to exhibit one of the most deadeningly academic traits of the academic mind. To his phrase about 'putting on the index' I might retort that Dr Tillyard pursues the steady aim of putting on the list of works that students must drudge through, and learn to admire, everything that he sees a chance of disinterring from literary history. This representative passage will suggest the spirit and manner of his book:

I am not especially attracted by the Miltonizing blank verse of the eighteenth century, but if I read it more assiduously I might like it better. So might others who have said hard things of it. And it may well be that, conditioned as it was, eighteenth-century poetry did well to model itself in part on Milton. Anyhow, I have not the slightest faith that by refusing to imitate Milton it would have developed powers that it does not now possess. However, this is not a topic I wish to pursue, and I will content myself with asking those who have condemned eighteenth-century Miltonics without having given the matter a great deal of attention to read (or re-read) Dr C. V. Deane's *Aspects of Eighteenth-century Nature Poetry* before they reiterate their condemnation. (p. 114.)

That a liking for the Miltonizing blank verse of the eighteenth century is (in spite of the generous inclusiveness of the project) not beyond Dr Tillyard's powers to achieve I am sufficiently convinced; he has, I think, supplied plenty of evidence of it in this book. For instance, he is capable of convincing himself, with a show of analysis (I am perhaps prejudiced here, since his account of Keats's ode affects me as being like a miscomprehending and ruinous adaptation of the analysis which I myself elaborated two or three years ago), that *Lycidas* and the *Ode to a Nightingale* are almost identical in structure and significance (though Milton

does not let his despairing emotions prey on him quite so thoroughly; indeed, he insists on blending with them a measure of dogma and a conscientious sense of literary tradition). (p. 36.)

Again, it is, as I and everyone I have consulted judge it, a fairly ordinary piece of stiff-jointed, pedantically-gaited Miltonic blank verse that, with enthusiasm, analysis and every appearance of con-

viction, Dr Tillyard, on pp. 132–4, pronounces superlatively remarkable for expressive sensitiveness of movement.

Outside Shakespeare and a few passages of the Elizabethan drama
such perfectly modulated blank verse is not to be found in English.

The truly monumental instance in this book of the tendency to
find new burdens for the literary student is Dr Tillyard's offer to
bestow on him an English Epic Tradition:

> Now in recent years there has been a distinct shift of opinion towards
> taking the *Faerie Queene* as something more than a pretty series of
> pageants and allowing it to speak for a whole civilization. With that
> shift I sympathize, and so sympathizing I should call the poem an epic.
> But what of *Arcadia*? Even if it attempts to be an epic, does it succeed?
> I answer that, for anyone who has the leisure and the patience to read it
> slowly, it does. . . . The unfailing vitality of the prose rhythms matches
> the unfailing enchantment of Spencer's metre. (p. 158.)
>
> Although the *Davideis* is a better poem than is usually allowed, only
> in one particular does it make any *vital* contribution to the English
> epic. (p. 162.)

There seems no point in arguing here. I will only state my own
view that if the English Epic, or the English Epic Tradition, became anywhere a recognized academic subject of study, anyone
who had furthered that end would have deserved ill both of the
literary student and of Milton.

And that there seems no point in arguing with Dr Tillyard is
what I have to say generally; between the unsatisfactory nature of
his interest in poetry and his concern for an ultra-modernity of
critical method he has, it seems, in the realm of criticism and
scholarship, lost all sense of what an argument properly is. One
can, of course, when he says (p. 118) that

> Milton (sensitive once more to the trend of advanced opinion in his
> own day) reacted against the riot of verbiage that makes the Eliza-
> bethans and Jacobeans so exhilarating,

and refers to 'the antiquated method of profusion', ask certain
obvious questions (Spenser, Shakespeare, Donne and Fletcher?
Marlowe? Ben Jonson?) and suggest that an argument about
style that starts comfortably with so large a feat of assimilation can
hardly be expected to lurch into closeness and acuity. But I will

not go on accumulating such annotations. I will merely, taking the above illustrations as a sufficient warrant, say that Dr Tillyard's arguments, when he undertakes to dispose of either Mr Eliot's views or my own about Milton's verse, seem to me to be elaborating merely an incomprehension of the issues. And perhaps, in case I should be thought to accept the views that Dr Tillyard seems to attribute to me (or 'the modern critic'), I had better add finally that I have nowhere complained 'that Milton did not write *Paradise Lost* in the style of Shakespeare' (p. 119), or (what seems to me a different thing) 'in a conversational style' or 'the tone of ordinary speech'; and that I have never, I think, given anyone any excuse for supposing that I hold the 'language of small talk' to be 'the basis of all good poetry' (p. 21); nor can I believe that any critic, modern or other, has held the 'sole object of art', or the object of art at all, to be

to bring into consciousness, to maintain in an unrelaxed awareness, the daily traffic of an intelligent mind with the world around it. (p. 43.)

or has urged it against Milton as a poet that he does

not show a simultaneous awareness of the four senses to what is going on in the street outside. (p. 48.)

One gets used, of course, to having attributed to one for demolition views one has never advanced and never held. Even Professor Grierson[1] performs at my expense a substitution, and does it in full view. Having said (p. 128) that a charge

brought today against Milton is that he has broken the tradition of English poetic diction,

he quotes this passage from me:

The predominance in various forms of Milton, from Thomson through Gray, Cowper, and Akenside to Wordsworth and, although allied with Spenser, through Keats and Tennyson ... must receive enough attention ... to bring out the significance of what we have witnessed in our time; the reconstitution of the English tradition by

3. *Milton and Wordsworth.*

the reopening of communications with the seventeenth century of Shakespeare, Donne, Middleton, Tourneur and so on.

He proceeds at once to comment:

This is a claim difficult to understand exactly. In his own age Donne was *not* regarded as a preserver of the English tradition but, by Drummond for example (as the late Professor W. P. Ker insisted), as an innovator. The tradition of English poetic diction as established by Chaucer had been renewed and enriched by Spenser . . .

And Professor Grierson goes on in this way, as if he were dealing with some proposition advanced in my paragraph. He has already, immediately before, having expressed himself unable to conjecture what I mean by talking about 'Milton's habit of exploiting language as a kind of musical medium outside himself', suggested (p. 127):

But Mr Leavis may mean that there are not the passionate ratiocinative subtleties of Donne's songs and elegies. But surely these would have been out of place, and surely there may be more than one kind of good poetry.

That I myself believe there may be more than one kind of good poetry might, I think, have been gathered from that paragraph of mine which Professor Grierson then quotes, and I cannot see what excuse he has for supposing me to make Donne the model and criterion: 'The seventeenth century of Shakespeare, Donne, Middleton and Tourneur', and, I might have added, of Ben Jonson, the Court poets and Marvell. These poets seem to me to exhibit between them a wide range of differences and to have written good poetry in a variety of manners. But all these manners have, in their different ways, a vital relation to speech, to the living language of the time. Milton invented a medium the distinction of which is to have denied itself the life of the living language. What I mean by this I still think I have made sufficiently plain; in any case, the fact seems to me plain in itself. And it is a fact that seems to me unaffected by any amount of arguing, in Dr Tillyard's vein, that Milton does not latinize as much as some people suppose, or that Shakespeare has latinizing lines and phrases.

What is meant by saying that Milton exploits language as a kind of musical medium[1] outside himself and that his influence predominates in the nineteenth century comes out clearly enough (as I tried to show) when we compare Keats's Miltonizing *Hyperion* with the induction to the revised version and with the *Ode to Autumn*, and when we note the close affinities between Keats's Miltonizing style and the Tennysonian. Professor Grierson, though he criticizes views he produces as mine[2] and quotes the passage reproduced above, does not consider that argument (which has a closely woven context) and Dr Tillyard's discussion of what Keats says in the Letters doesn't affect it.

1. 'Mr Eliot says that you have to read Milton twice: once for the sense, and once for the sound. Might not further readings yield a more unified result?' (*The Miltonic Setting*, p. 132). Mr Eliot makes the point admirably, giving a sufficient answer to Dr Tillyard's arguments (pp. 91–3) about the close of *Lycidas* and the passage from *Paradise Lost*; and Dr Tillyard's sally is, in its incomprehension, impertinent, following as it does on the suggestion that people who disagree with him about Milton do so because they haven't read Milton enough. Perhaps I had better put it on record that the pocket Milton I have referred to in writing this essay is falling to pieces from use, and that it is the only book I carried steadily in my pocket between 1915 and 1919.

2. He even seems to associate me (see p. 122) with the modern cult of Dryden, from which I have explicitly dissociated myself.

GERARD MANLEY HOPKINS

THAT Hopkins has a permanent place among the English
poets may now be taken as established beyond challenge:
academic scholarship has canonized him, and the love of 'a continuous literary decorum' has forgotten the terms in which it was
apt to express itself only a decade ago. It is now timely to ask just
what that place is. Perhaps, indeed, formal evaluation may be
judged a needless formality, the nature and significance of
Hopkins's work, once it has been fairly looked at, not being very
notably obscure. However, the centenary year of his birth seems
a proper occasion for attempting a brief explicit summing-up.

A poet born in 1844 was a Victorian: if one finds oneself
proffering this chronological truism today, when the current
acceptance of Hopkins goes with a recognition that something has
happened in English poetry since Bridges' taste was formed, it is
less likely to be a note of irony, invoking a background contrast
for Hopkins, than an insistence, or the preface to it, on the essential
respects in which Hopkins was, even in his originality, *of* his time.
His school poem, *A Vision of Mermaids*, shows him starting very
happily in a Keatsian line, a normal young contemporary of
Tennyson, Matthew Arnold and Rossetti – in the association of
which three names, it will perhaps be granted, the idea of 'Victorian poet' takes on sufficient force and definition to give that
'normal' its point. The elements of Keats in Hopkins is radical
and very striking:

> Palate, the hutch of tasty lust,
> Desire not to be rinsed with wine:
> The can must be so sweet, the crust
> So fresh that come in fasts divine!
> Nostrils, your careless breath that spend
> Upon the stir and keep of pride,
> What relish shall the censers send
> Along the sanctuary side!
> O feel-of-primrose hands, O feet
> That want the yield of plushy sward,

> But you shall walk the golden street
> And you unhouse and house the Lord.

These stanzas come from an 'Early Poem' printed by Bridges immediately before *The Wreck of the Deutschland*. A contemporary reader, if we can imagine it published at the time of writing, might very well have judged that this very decided young talent was to be distinguished from among his fellow Victorian poets by his unique possession, in an age pervaded by Keatsian aspirations and influences, of the essential Keatsian strength. Such a Victorian reader might very well have pronounced him, this strength clearly being native and inward, unmistakably a poet born – a poet incomparably more like Keats, the poet's poet (Keats was something like that for the Tennysonian age), than the derivatively Keatsian could make themselves. Actually, the body of the mature work – *The Wreck of the Deutschland* onwards – in which Hopkins's distinctive bent and his idiosyncrasy develop themselves, doesn't prompt us with Keats's name so obviously. Yet the same strength, in its developed manifestations, is there.

It is a strength that gives Hopkins notable advantages over Tennyson and Matthew Arnold as a 'nature poet'. This description is Mr Eliot's (see *After Strange Gods*, p. 48), and it is applicable enough for one to accept it as a way of bringing out how much Hopkins belongs to the Victorian tradition. Nature, beauty, transience – with these he is characteristically preoccupied:

> Margaret, are you grieving
> Over Goldengrove unleaving?
> Leaves, like the things of man, you
> With your fresh thought care for, can you?
> Ah! as the heart grows older
> It will come to such sights colder
> By and by, nor spare a sigh
> Though worlds of wanwood leafmeal lie;
> And yet you will weep and know why.
> Now no matter, child, the name:
> Sorrow's springs are the same.
> Nor mouth had, no, nor mind, expressed
> What heart heard of, ghost guessed:
> It is the blight man was born for,
> It is Margaret you mourn for.

Here the distinctiveness and the idiosyncrasy might seem hardly to qualify the Victorian normality of the whole (though Bridges couldn't permit the second couplet – see the improved poem that, modestly claiming no credit, he prints in *The Spirit of Man*). In

> What heart heard of, ghost guessed,

where the heart, wholly taken up in the hearing, becomes it, as the 'ghost' becomes the guessing, we have, of course, an example of a kind of poetic action or enactment that Hopkins developed into a staple habit of his art. As we have it, this use of assonantal progression, here, its relation to the sensibility and technique of

> Palate, the hutch of tasty lust

is plain. So too is the affinity between this last-quoted line and the 'bend with apples the moss'd cottage trees' in which the robust vitality of Keats's sensuousness shows itself in so un-Tennysonian, and so essentially poetic, a strength of expressive texture.

Hopkins was born – and died – in the age of Tennyson. This fact has an obvious bearing on the deliberateness with which Hopkins, starting with that peculiar genius, set himself to develop and exploit the modes and qualities of expression illustrated – the distinctive expressive resources of the English language ('English must be kept up'). The age in poetry *was* Tennyson's; and an age for which the ambition 'to bring English as near the Italian as possible' seems a natural and essentially poetic one, is an age in which the genius conscious enough to form a contrary ambition is likely to be very conscious and very contrary. That he was consciously bent on bringing back into poetry the life and strength of the living, the spoken, language is explicit – the confirmation was pleasant to have, though hardly necessary – in the *Letters* (to Bridges, LXII): 'it seems to me that the poetical language of the age shd. be the current language heightened, to any degree heightened and unlike it, but not (I mean normally: passing freaks and graces are another thing) an obsolete one'. His praise of Dryden (CLV) held by Bridges to be no poet, is well-known: 'His style and rhythms lay the strongest stress of all our literature on the naked thew and sinew of the English language'. This preoccupation, pursued by a Victorian poet intensely given to technical experiment, would go far to explain the triumphs of invention, the extravagance and the oddities of Hopkins's verse.

But this is not the whole story. His bent for technical experiment can be seen to have been inseparable from a special kind of interest in pattern – his own term was 'inscape'. Here we have a head of consideration that calls for some inquiry, though it can be left for the moment with this parenthetic recognition, to be taken up again in due course.

Meanwhile, demanding immediate notice there is a head the postponement of which till now may have surprised the reader. It is impossible to discuss for long the distinctive qualities of Hopkins's poetry without coming to his religion. In the matter of religion, of course, he differs notably from both Tennyson and Matthew Arnold, and the relevance of the differences to the business of the literary critic is best broached by noting that they lead up to the complete and staring antithesis confronting us when we place Hopkins by Rossetti. Here is Rossetti:

> Under the arch of Life, where love and death,
>   Terror and mystery, guard her shrine, I saw
>   Beauty enthroned; and though her gaze struck awe
> I drew it in as simply as my breath.
> Hers are the eyes which, over and beneath,
>   The sky and sea bend on thee – which can draw,
>   By sea or sky of woman, to one law,
> The allotted bondman of her palm and wreath.
>
> This is that Lady Beauty, in whose praise
>   Thy voice and hand shake still – long known to thee
>   By flying hair and fluttering hem – the beat
>   Following her daily of thy heart and feet, ·
> How passionately and irretrievably,
> In what fond flight, how many ways and days!

This very representative poem illustrates very obviously the immediate relevance for the literary critic of saying that religion in Hopkins's poetry is something completely other than the religion of Beauty. Rossetti's shamelessly cheap evocation of a romantic and bogus Platonism – an evocation in which 'significance' is vagueness, and profundity an uninhibited proffer of large drafts on a merely nominal account ('Life', 'love', 'death', 'terror', 'mystery', 'Beauty' – it is a bankrupt's lavishness) – exemplifies in a gross form the consequences of that separation of feeling ('soul' – the source of 'genuine poetry') from thinking which the Victorian tradition, in its 'poetical' use of language, carries with it. The attendant debility is apparent enough in Tennyson and Arnold, poets who often think they are thinking and who offer thought about life, religion and morals: of Arnold in particular the point can be made that what he offers poetically as thought is dismissed as negligible by the standards of his prose. When we come to the hierophant of Beauty, the dedicated poet of the cult, predecessor of Pater who formulated the credo, we have something worse than debility. And there is not only a complete nullity in respect of thought – nullity made aggressively vulgar by a wordy pretentiousness (Rossetti is officially credited with 'fundamental brainwork'); the emotional and sensuous quality may be indicated by saying that in Rossetti's verse we find nothing more of the 'hard gem-like flame' than in Pater's prose.

Hopkins is the devotional poet of a dogmatic Christianity. For the literary critic there are consequent difficulties and delicacies. But there is something that can be seen, and said, at once: Hopkins's religious interests are bound up with the presence in his poetry of a vigour of mind that puts him in another poetic world from the other Victorians. It is a vitality of thought, a vigour of the thinking intelligence, that is at the same time a vitality of concreteness. The relation between this kind of poetic life and his religion manifests itself plainly in his addiction to Duns Scotus, whom, rather than St Thomas, traditionally indicated for a Jesuit, he significantly embraced as his own philosopher. Of the philosophy of Duns Scotus it must suffice to say here that it lays a peculiar stress on the particular and actual, in its full concreteness and individuality, as the focus of the real, and that its presence is felt whenever Hopkins uses the word 'self' (or some derivative verb) in his characteristic way. *Binsey Poplars* provides an instance where the significance for the literary critic is obvious. The poplars are

All felled, felled, are all felled,

and Hopkins's lament runs:

> O if we but knew what we do
>   When we delve or hew –
> Hack and rack the growing green!
>   Since country is so tender
> To touch, her being so slender,
> That, like this sleek and seeing ball
> But a prick will make no eye at all,
> Where we, even where we mean
>   To mend her we end her,
>   When we hew or delve:
> After-comers cannot guess the beauty been.
>   Ten or twelve, only ten or twelve
>   Strokes of havoc unselve
>   The sweet especial scene,
>   Rural scene, a rural scene,
>   Sweet especial rural scene.

All the beauties Hopkins renders in his poetry are 'sweet especial scenes', 'selves' in the poignant significance their particularity has for him. Time 'unselves' them;

> Nor can you long be, what you now are, called fair,
> Do what you may do, what, do what you may,
> And wisdom is early to despair.

The Victorian-romantic addicts of beauty and transience cherish the pang as a kind of religiose-poetic sanction for defeatism in the face of an alien actual world – a defeatism offering itself as a spiritual superiority. Hopkins embraces transience as a necessary condition of any grasp of the real. The concern for such a grasp is there in the concrete qualities that give his poetry its vitality – which, we have seen, involves an energy of intelligence.

These qualities the literary critic notes and appraises, whether or not he knows any more about Duns Scotus than he can gather from the poetry. There is plainly a context of theological religion, and the devotional interest has plainly the kind of relation to the poetic qualities that has just been discussed. But the activities that go on within this context, even if they make Hopkins unlike Tennyson, Browning, Matthew Arnold, Rossetti, and Swinburne, don't do so by making him in any radical way like T. S. Eliot. It is a framework of the given, conditioning the system of tensions established within it, and these are those of a devotional poet. We can hardly imagine Hopkins entertaining, even in a remotely theoretical way, the kind of preoccupation conveyed by Eliot when he says: '. . . I cannot see that poetry can ever be separated from something which I should call belief, and to which I cannot see any reason for refusing the name of belief, unless we are to shuffle names altogether. It should hardly be needful to say that it will not inevitably be orthodox Christian belief, although that possibility can be entertained, since Christianity will probably continue to modify itself, as in the past, into something that can be believed in (I do not mean *conscious* modifications like modernism, etc., which always have the opposite effect). The majority of people live below the level of belief or doubt. It takes application and a kind of genius to believe anything, and to believe *anything* (I do *not* mean merely to believe in some "religion") will probably become more and more difficult as time goes on'. [*The Enemy*, January 1927.] The stress of the 'terrible sonnets' hasn't this kind of context. And Hopkins's habit is utterly remote from Eliot's extreme discipline of continence in respect of affirmation – the discipline involving that constructive avoidance of the conceptual currency which has its exposition in *Burnt Norton*. For Hopkins the truths are *there*, simply and irresistibly demanding allegiance; though it is no simple matter to make his allegiance real and complete (this seems at any rate a fair way of suggesting the difference).

His preoccupation with this frame is of a kind that leaves him in a certain obvious sense simple-minded:

> Here he knelt then in regimental red.
> Forth Christ from cupboard fetched, how fain I of feet
> To his youngster take his treat!
> Low-latched in leaf-light housel his too huge godhead.

It is the simplicity of the single-minded and pure in heart. Its manifestations can be very disconcerting, and we are not surprised to learn that as a preacher he was apt, in his innocent unconsciousness, to put intolerable strains on the gravity of his congregation. It appears in the rime of the stanza immediately preceding that just quoted (it will be necessary, because of the run-over of the sense, to quote the two preceding):

> A bugler boy from barrack (it is over the hill
> There) – boy bugler, born, he tells me, of Irish
>   Mother to an English sire (he
> Shares their best gifts surely, fall how things will),
>
> This very very day came down to us after a boon he on
> My late being there begged of me, overflowing
>   Boon in my bestowing,
> Came, I say, this day to it – to a First Communion.

It takes a Bridges to find all, or most, of Hopkins's riming audacities unjustifiable; they are often triumphant successes in that, once the poem has been taken, they become inevitable, and, unlike Browning's ingenuities, cease to call attention to themselves (that in the first of these two stanzas is a passable ear-rime). Nevertheless there are a fair number of the order of *boon he on-communion*, and it has to be conceded more generally that the naïveté illustrated has some part in the elaborations of his technique.

To say this, of course, is not to endorse Lord David Cecil's view that Hopkins is difficult because of his difficult way of saying simple things. It is relevant, but hardly necessary, to remark that for Hopkins his use of words is not a matter of *saying* things with them; he is preoccupied with what seems to him the poetic use of them, and that is a matter of making them do and be. Even a poet describable as 'simple-minded' may justify some complexities of 'doing' and 'being'. And if we predicate simplicity of Hopkins, it must be with the recognition that he has at the same time a very subtle mind.

The subtlety is apparent in the tropes, conceits and metaphorical symbolism that gives his poetry qualities suggesting the seventeenth century rather than the nineteenth. He can be metaphysical in the full sense; as, for instance, he is, triumphantly, in the first part of *The Wreck of the Deutschland*, notably in stanzas 4 to 8. The radically metaphorical habit of mind and sensibility that, along with concrete strength from which it is inseparable, makes his 'nature poetry' so different from Tennyson's and Matthew Arnold's, relates him to Herbert rather than to Eliot – it goes with the 'frame' spoken of above. It is a habit of seeing things as charged with significance; 'significance' here being, not a romantic vagueness, but a matter of explicit and ordered conceptions regarding the relations between God, man and nature. It is an inveterate habit of his mind and being, finding its intellectual formulation in Duns Scotus.

Of course, to be seventeenth-century in the time of Tennyson is a different matter from being it in the time of Herbert, Hopkins's unlikeness to whom involves a great deal more than the obvious difference of temperament. He is still more unlike Crashaw: his 'metaphysical' audacity is the expression of a refined and disciplined spirit, and there is no temperamental reason why it shouldn't have been accompanied by something corresponding to Herbert's fine and poised *social* bearing. But behind Hopkins there is no Ben Jonson, and he has for contemporaries no constellation of courtly poets uniting the 'metaphysical' with the urbane. His distinctiveness develops itself even in his prose, which has a dignified oddity such as one might have taken for affectation if it hadn't been so obviously innocent and unconscious.

Of the development of 'distinctiveness' in verse he himself says, in a passage that gives us the word:

> But as air, melody, is what strikes me most of all in music and design in painting, so design, pattern, or what I am in the habit of calling *inscape* is what I above all aim at in poetry. Now it is the virtue of design, pattern, or inscape to be distinctive, and it is the vice of distinctiveness to become queer. This vice I cannot have escaped. [See *Poems*, 2nd Edition, p. 96.]

Isolation, he might have added, would favour the vice. But the peculiar development of the interest in pattern or 'inscape' has, it may be suggested, a significance not yet touched on. We can't help relating it to a certain restriction in the nourishing interests behind Hopkins's poetry. It is as if his intensity, for lack of adequately answering substance, expressed itself in a kind of hypertrophy of technique, and in an excessive imputation of significance to formal pattern.

It may be replied that his concern for pattern in verse is paralleled by a concern for pattern (or 'inscape' we had better say, since the word associates the idea of 'pattern' with Hopkins's distinctive stress on the individuality or 'self' of the object contem-

plated) in the sights – a tree, a waterfall, a disposition of clouds –
that he renders from nature; renders in drawings as well as in verse
and prose. But his interest in nature – to call attention to that is
to make the same point again. In assenting, half-protestingly, to
Mr Eliot's description of him as a 'nature poet' one is virtually
recognizing that a significant limitation reveals itself when a poet
of so remarkable a spiritual intensity, so intense a preoccupation
with essential human problems, gives 'nature' – the 'nature' of the
'nature poets' – so large a place in his poetry. What is revealed as
limited, it will be said, is Hopkins's power to transcend the poetic
climate of his age: in spite of the force of his originality he is a
Victorian poet. This seems an unanswerable point. But even here,
in respect of his limitation, his distinctiveness comes out: the
limitation goes with the peculiar limitation of experience attendant upon his early world-renouncing self-dedication:

> Elected Silence, sing to me
> And beat upon my whorlèd ear,
> Pipe me to pastures still and be
> The music that I care to hear.
>
> Shape nothing, lips; be lovely-dumb:
> It is the shut, the curfew sent
> From there where all surrenders come
> Which only makes you eloquent.
>
> Be shellèd, eyes, with double dark
> And find the uncreated light:
> This ruck and reel which you remark
> Coils, keeps, and teases simple sight.
>
> *   *   *   *
>
> And, Poverty, be thou the bride
> And now the marriage feast begun,
> And lily-coloured clothes provide
> Your spouse not laboured-at nor spun.

(This is the remainder of the 'Early Poem', *The Habit of Perfection*,
from which, in the opening of this essay, stanzas were quoted in
illustration of Keatsian qualities.)

The force of this last point is manifest in the ardent naïveté with which he idealizes his buglers, sailors, schoolboys and his England:

> England, whose honour O all my heart woos, wife
> To my creating thought . . .

Meeting him in 1882, his old schoolmaster, Dixon, says: 'In so far as I can remember you are very like the boy of Highgate'. But this unworldliness is of a different order from the normal other-worldliness of Victorian poetry. Addressing Hopkins, Matthew Arnold might, without the radical confusion symbolized in his Scholar-Gypsy, have said:

> For early didst thou leave the world, with powers
>   Fresh, undiverted to the world without,
>   Firm to their mark, not spent on other things;
>   Free from the sick fatigue, the languid doubt . . .

The 'firmness to the mark' is really there in Hopkins's poetry; the 'mark' is not a mere postulated something that, we are to grant, confers a spiritual superiority upon the eternal week-ender who, 'fluctuating idly without term or scope' among the attractions of the countryside, parallels in his indolent poetical way the strenuous aimlessness of the world where things are done. To Hopkins it might have been said with some point:

> Thou hadst *one* aim, *one* business, *one* desire.

Yet this unworldliness, different though it is from Victorian poetical other-worldliness, does unmistakably carry with it the limitation of experience. And in his bent for 'nature' there is after all in Hopkins something of the poetical Victorian. It is a bent away from urban civilization, in the midst of which he spends his life, and which, very naturally, he regards with repulsion:

> Generations have trod, have trod, have trod;
>   And all is seared with trade; bleared, smeared with toil;
>   And wears man's smudge and shares man's smell: the soil
> Is bare now, nor can foot feel, being shod.
>
> And for all this, nature is never spent;
>   There lives the dearest freshness deep down things; . . .

And in *The Sea and the Skylark* he says:

> How these two shame this shallow and frail town!
>   How ring right out our sordid turbid time,
> Being pure! We, life's pride and cared-for crown,
>
> Have lost that cheer and charm of earth's past prime:
> Our make and making break, are breaking, down
>   To man's last dust, drains fast towards man's first slime.

Towards these aspects of human life his attitude – he is very much preoccupied with them – is plain. But they have little more actual presence in his poetry than 'this strange disease of modern life' has in Arnold's.

To come back now to his isolation – we have not yet taken full account of it. It is not merely a matter of his having had no support or countenance in accepted tradition, contemporary practice, and the climate of taste and ideas: he was isolated in a way peculiarly calculated to promote starvation of impulse, the over-developed and ingrown idiosyncrasy, and the sterile deadlock, lapsing into stagnation. As convert he had with him a tide of the élite (he could feel); as a Catholic and a Jesuit he had his communities, the immediate and the wider. But from this all-important religious context he got no social endorsement as a poet: the episode of *The Wreck of the Deutschland* – 'they dared not print it' – is all there is to tell, and it says everything; it came at the beginning and it was final. Robert Bridges, his life-long friend and correspondent, confidently and consistently discouraged him with 'water of the lower Isis': 'your criticism is . . . only a protest memorializing me against my whole policy and proceedings' (xxxvii). As against this we can point, for the last seven years of Hopkins's life, to the enthusiasm of Canon Dixon, a good and generous man, but hardly transmutable by Hopkins's kind of need (or Hopkins's kind of humility) into an impressive critical endorsement or an adequate substitute for a non-existent public.

To these conditions the reaction of so tense and disciplined an ascetic is the reverse of Blake's: he doesn't become careless, but – 'Then again I have of myself made verse so laborious' (LIII, to Bridges). (And here the following – from CIXVI – has an obvious relevance: 'To return to composition for a moment: what I want there, to be more intelligible, smoother, and less singular, is an audience'.) With the laboriousness goes the anguish of sterility registered in this sonnet – one of his finest poems:

> Thou art indeed just, Lord, if I contend
> With thee; but, sir, so what I plead is just.
> Why do sinners' ways prosper? and why must
> Disappointment all I endeavour end?
>   Wert thou my enemy, O thou my friend,
> How wouldst thou worse, I wonder, than thou dost
> Defeat, thwart me? Oh, the sots and thralls of lust
> Do in spare hours more thrive than I that spend,
> Sir, life upon thy cause. See, banks and brakes
> Now, leavèd how thick! lacèd they are again
> With fretty chervil, look, and fresh wind shakes
> Them; birds build – but not I build; no, but strain,
> Time's eunuch, and not breed one work that wakes.
> Mine, O thou lord of life, send my roots rain.

That there is a relation between this state of mind and his isolation, the absence of response, he himself knows: 'There is a point with me in matters of any size', he writes (CXXIX, to Bridges) 'when I must absolutely have encouragement as much as crops rain; afterwards I am independent'. The recurrence of the metaphor is significant, and the passage is clearly to be related to this other passage, itself so clearly related to the sonnet: 'if I could but get on, if I could but produce work, I should not mind its being buried, silence, and going no farther; but it kills me to be time's eunuch and never to beget' (CXXX). And again, he writes (CLVII): 'All impulse fails me: I can give myself no reason for not going on. Nothing comes: I am a eunuch – but it is for the kingdom of heaven's sake'. About the failure of impulse we are certainly in a position to say something.

It seems reasonable to suppose that if he had had the encouragement he lacked he would have devoted to poetry a good deal of the energy that (for the last years of his life a painfully conscientious Professor of Greek) he distributed, in a strenuous dissipation that undoubtedly had something to do with his sense of being time's eunuch and never producing, between the study of music, musical composition, drawing, and such task-work as writing a 'popular account of Light and Ether'.[1] For he was certainly a born writer. This is apparent in the Letters in ways we could hardly have divined from the poetry. Consider, for instance, the distinguished naturalness, the sensitive vivacity combined with robust vigour, the flexibility, and the easy sureness of touch of the representative passages that arouse one's anthologizing bent as one reads.[2]

Actually, of course, Hopkins did 'produce': there is a substantial body of verse, a surprising preponderance of which – surprising, when we consider his situation and the difficulties in the way of success – deserves currency among the classics of the language. His supreme triumphs, unquestionably classical achievements, are the last sonnets – the 'terrible sonnets' together with *Justus es*, the one just quoted, and that inscribed *To R. B.* (who prints it with the unsanctioned and deplorable substitution of 'moulds' for 'combs' in the sixth line). These, in their achieved 'smoother style', triumphantly justify the oddest extravagances of his experimenting. Technique here is the completely unobtrusive and marvellously economical and efficient servant of the inner need, the pressure to be defined and conveyed. At the other extreme are such things as *Tom's Garland* and *Harry Ploughman*, where, in the absence of controlling pressure from within, the elaborations and ingenuities of 'inscape' and of expressive licence result in tangles of knots and strains that no amount of reading can reduce to satisfactory rhythm or justifiable complexity. In between come the indubitable successes of developed 'inscape': *The Wreck of the Deuchsland* (which seems to me a great poem – at least for the first two-thirds of it), *The Windhover*, and, at a lower level, *The Leaden Echo and the Golden Echo*. *Henry Purcell* calls for mention as a curious special case. There can be few readers who have not found it strangely expressive, and few who could have elucidated it without extraneous help. It is not independent of the explanatory note by Hopkins that Bridges prints; yet when one approaches it with the note fresh in mind the intended meaning seems to be sufficiently *in* the

1. 'Popular is not quite the word: it is not meant to be easy reading' (xxxv, to Dixon).
2. See 'The Letters of Gerard Manley Hopkins' overleaf.

poem to allay, at any rate, the dissatisfaction caused by baffled
understanding.[1]

About Hopkins as a direct influence there seems little to say.
The use of him by Left poets in the 'thirties was not of a kind to
demand serious critical attention.

1944.

1. It may be worth comparing the note that Bridges prints in the *Poems*
with the explanation given by Hopkins in Letter XCVII:

The sonnet on Purcell means this: 1–4. I hope Purcell is not damned
for being a Protestant, because I love his genius. 5–8. And that not so
much for gifts he shares, even though it shd. be in higher measure, with
other musicians as for his own individuality. 9–14. So that while he is
aiming only at impressing me his hearer with the meaning in hand I am looking out meanwhile for his specific his individual markings and mottlings,
'the sakes of him'. It is as when the bird thinking only of soaring spreads
its wings? a beholder may happen then to have his attention drawn by
the act to the plumage displayed. – In particular, the first lines mean:
May Purcell, O may he have died a good death and that soul which I
love so much and which breathes or stirs so unmistakeably in his works
have darted from the body and passed away, centuries since though I
frame the wish, in peace with God! so that the heavy condemnation
under which he outwardly or nominally lay for being out of the true
Church may in consequence of his good intentions have been reversed.
'Low lays him' is merely 'lays him low', that is /strikes him heavily,
weighs upon him. . . . It is somewhat dismaying to find I am so unintel-
ligible though, especially in one of my best pieces. 'Listed', by the by,
is 'enlisted'. 'Sakes' is hazardous: about that point I was more bent on
saying my say than on being understood in it. The 'moonmarks' belong
to the image only of course, not to the application: I mean not detailedly:
I was thinking of a bird's quill feathers. One thing disquiets me: *I meant*
'fair fall' to mean *fair (fortune be) fall*; it has since struck me that perhaps
'fair' is an adjective proper and in the predicate and can only be used in
cases like 'fair fall the day', that is, *may the day fall, turn out fair*. My line will
yield a sense that way indeed, but I never meant it so.

THE LETTERS OF
GERARD MANLEY HOPKINS

THE irony of the process by which an original genius becomes a classic has been exemplified with peculiar force in the recent history of Gerard Manley Hopkins (the history that did not start till thirty years after his death). For one thing, developments in the last few years have been so rapid. Half a decade ago, though his name was pretty well known, to judge him the greatest poet of the Victorian age was a perverse and laughable eccentricity. It is not, perhaps, orthodoxy today but even in the academic world it is a debatable proposition; and an undergraduate, on the most solemn and critical occasion, might risk it without being defiantly foolhardy. At any rate, here are Hopkins's letters[1] edited by a Professor of English Language and Literature and placed implicitly alongside those of Keats.

And once again, yet once again – this it is that so especially enforces the irony – Hopkins has an editor who betrays radical hostility to what Hopkins stood and stands for. To have said this without notable provocation would have been ungracious; one is grateful for the services that scholarship can perform. Professor Abbott goes out of his way to challenge plain speaking. Hopkins, he says (both the air and the graces are characteristic) 'is accepted by the young as one of their contemporaries, and – a more doubtful privilege – he has even been affiliated to the Martin Tuppers of our day whose scrannel pipes have infected the field of poetry with mildew and blight.' Professor Abbott nowhere risks anything more specific than this, but the content and tone of the whole Introduction[2] make it quite impossible to hope that, in

1. *The Letters of Gerard Manley Hopkins to Robert Bridges; The Correspondence of Gerard Manley Hopkins and Richard Watson Dixon;* edited by Claude Colleer Abbott.

2. See for instance the 'petty and superfluous', the completely gratuitous, footnote on p. xxxviii: 'Petty and superfluous beside it is that clever and rootless verse of our own day which apes the discovery of kindred desolation.' Another footnote (p. xxvii), it may perhaps be in place to record here, runs (*The*

spite of the tropes in this unfortunate passage, he intends a critical discrimination – a discrimination against the derivative and insignificant. He leaves us no room for doubting that what he intends to discredit is the influence (the source of infection); that what he dislikes is the living force. It would be foolish to make a fuss whenever the academic mind behaves characteristically, but there is a classical quality about this instance – about Professor Abbott's use of Hopkins (whom as a contemporary he would so clearly have scorned) to bolster a self-importance that feels itself threatened by all that Hopkins represents: the disturbing new life, the stir of spirit that manifests itself in unfamiliar forms and does not permit, yet, the easy recognition – the flattering sense – of the placed and known.

The volume of letters to Bridges itself, apart from the Introduction, presents what should be a classical instance, and even without the editor's insisting as he does, there would have been no way of avoiding the unhappy theme. It is central to a consideration of the letters, and to deal with it honestly is a critical duty: history, 'teaching by examples', will go on teaching and repeating itself, but it is certainly the business of criticism to get what general recognition it can for an example so obvious and impressive. And then there is justice to be done to the heroic quality of Hopkins's genius.

Hopkins had, we are told, to be kept waiting for publication till so long after his death because the time was not yet ripe. But in due course it ripened: 'In 1915, in his *Spirit of Man*, Bridges printed seven of his friend's pieces,[1] and it was the wide success and sale of this anthology both in England and America, and the knowledge that the time was now ripe, that led him to agree to Mr Humphrey Milford's wish for an edition of Hopkins's poems.' The world would appear to owe a very considerable debt to Mr Milford. But that is not Professor Abbott's point. After telling us

1. Those who check footnote 5 on p. xix will establish that four of these were pieces of pieces.

Wreck of the Deutschland being in question): 'Is it fanciful to hear behind his rhythm something of Campbell's *Battle of the Baltic* and Cowper's *Loss of the Royal George*?' – And indeed we know for a fact that he had read Campbell's poem, and cannot doubt that he knew Cowper's.

that the poems in the edition of 1918 were 'read with eagerness by the "little clan" that knows "great verse",' he goes on: 'How small this clan was can be seen from the publisher's figures for the edition, which was not exhausted for ten years.[1] They are figures that effectively kill the legend, invented in our own day, of a public panting to read poetry arbitrarily withheld. The taste of the "public" in such matters is always negligible.'

The legend, if it existed, was negligible too. What may be smothered, but cannot be killed, is the fact that the little clan was, until 1918 (Hopkins having died in 1889), given no chance to show its eagerness; if time, during those thirty years, ripened, it did so without the help of the obvious procedure.

What are works of art for? to educate, to be standards. Education is meant for the many, standards are for public use. To produce is of little use unless what we produce is known, if known widely known, the wider known the better, for it is by being known it works, it does its duty, it does good. We must then try to be known, aim at it, take means to it.

Hopkins wrote this to Bridges in 1886 (Letter cxxxvi), exhorting 'you and Canon Dixon and all true poets'. In the spirit of this, where Hopkins's own work was concerned, Canon Dixon had, on his first introduction to specimens, acted with generous and embarrassing impetuosity (see vIa, vIb, vIIb, vIII, Ix and x in the *Correspondence*), convinced that publication, even in the unlikely places open to him, would affect others as he had been himself affected, and begin the process of getting Hopkins known. If Bridges had believed in Hopkins, had seen what the poetry was, he would somehow have contrived to get it published, even if – or, rather because – 'In tone and spirit this work was at a last remove from the characteristic verse and prose of the period.' But – 'Bridges did not wish the book to drop unheeded, nor did he want his friend's name to be environed by the barbarous noise

Of owls and cuckoos, asses, apes and dogs'

(a thoughtlessly unkind way of referring to one's kind – to one's

1. 750 copies were printed; 50 were given away; 180 sold in the first year; 240 in the second year; then an average of 30 a year for six years, rising to 90 in 1927. The last four copies were sold in 1928. The price was twelve shillings and sixpence.

predecessors in the cult of a 'continuous literary decorum')[1]
'Rightly he walked warily. In 1893 he persuaded A. H. Miles
to give Hopkins a place in the well-known anothology, *Poets
of the XIXth Century:* he himself wrote the introductory memoir
to the eleven poems printed, a selection that gives a fair idea of
the poet's range and worth.' The 'eleven poems' were, a footnote tells us: 'part of 50, part of 73, part of 44, selected lines
from 77, 3, 8, 9, 26, 31, 33, 51.' The reader who looks up these
references in the Poems will find that 50 and 44, of which
'parts' were printed, and 77, 8, 9, 26 and 51, from which 'selected
lines' were printed, are sonnets. This, then, was wary walking;
there could be no more final exposure.

Bridges' attitude to Hopkins's poetry is, of course, made plain
enough in the 'Preface to Notes' in the *Poems*. And Bridges' case
no one could diagnose as one of uneasy self-importance. What he
exhibits is a complete security; a complete incapacity to doubt his
competence or to suspect that the criteria by which he condemns,
condones, corrects and improves may not be appropriate. Thus
he can, sincerely intent upon doing his best for his friend and for
English poetry, pick out from Hopkins's sonnets the best parts and
lines for publication; leave out, when printing *Margaret* in *The
Spirit of Man*, the second couplet; and even in the *Poems* print a
completely unauthorized improvement of his own, having (see
note to 51 – the improved version of which sonnet has been per-
petuated 'no doubt that G.M.H. would have made some such)
alteration'. He was, although he had behind him a history of
sustained relevant controversy with Hopkins, truly incapable of
the doubt. As Hopkins wrote to Canon Dixon (*Correspondence*,
IX): 'people cannot, or they will not, take in anything however
plain that departs from what they have been taught and brought
up to expect: I know it from experience.' And Bridges is a superb
example of what education will do for one; his expectations – his
taste, his sense of Form and his love of a 'continuous literary
decorum' – were uncompromising, incorruptible and completely
self-confident. His incapacity was of the same kind as that ex-

1. 'For these blemishes in the poet's style are of such quality and magnitude
as to deny him even a hearing from those who love a continuous literary
decorum, and are grown to be intolerant of its absence.' – Robert Bridges,
Poems of Gerard Manley Hopkins.

hibited by Johnson with respect to *Lycidas* (or *Macbeth*); though the positives behind the taste in which Johnson was trained had so much more body and vitality, and a classical education in his time was so much more solidly and intimately related to English tradition and contemporary life than in Bridges'. Decorum for Bridges had nothing like the Augustan correlations; it was a prim donnish conventionality. What, in fact, Bridges represents is essentially the academic mind, though with such confidence, completeness and conviction of authority as to constitute a truly memorable distinction.

All this is not said wantonly. To put it at the most obvious, we have, in following the letters, to divine what kind of thing Hopkins is answering and what kind of correspondent he is addressing (Bridges' letters are not given us; he is presumed to have destroyed them). There is plenty of evidence to put certain important matters beyond question. That the friend to whom Hopkins cherished a life-long attachment had admirable qualities we cannot doubt; but we have at the same time to note, in appreciating its strength, that the attachment persisted in spite of a constant incomprehension and discouragement, on the friend's part, of Hopkins's genius. This is not guesswork; the evidence is pervasive and conclusive – much more abundant than would suffice for certitude. Bridges' critical attitude, it is plain, remained all the way through essentially that which, at the outset in 1877, drew from Hopkins this (xxxvii):

> You say you would not for any money read my poem again. Nevertheless I beg you will. Besides money, you know, there is love. If it is obscure do not bother yourself with the meaning but pay attention to the best and most intelligible stanzas, as the two last of each part and the narrative of the wreck. If you had done this you wd. have liked it better and sent me some serviceable criticisms, but now your criticism is of no use, being only a protest memoralising me against my whole policy and proceedings.

Hopkins was over-sanguine in supposing that familiarity would make the strange more acceptable to Bridges; that he would, guided by tips as to the approach, come to understand and sympathize sufficiently to be an intelligent critic. A year later Hopkins has to write (xli): 'As for affectation, I do not believe I am guilty of it: you should point out instances but as long as mere novelty and boldness strikes you as affectation your criticism strikes me as – as water of the Lower Isis.' Criticism of that water was what Hopkins continued to get. For instance, we find him in 1882 (XG) explaining that *The Leaden Echo and the Golden Echo* does not derive from Whitman: 'I believe that you are quite mistaken about this piece and that on second thoughts you will find the fancied resemblance diminish and the imitation disappear.' . . . 'The long lines are not rhythm run to seed: everything is weighed and timed in them. Wait till they have taken hold of your ear and you will find it so.' Nevertheless Bridges, apparently, went on tracing affinities. Three years later (CLII) Hopkins writes: 'when you read it (*Harry Ploughman*) let me know if there is anything like it in Walt Whitman, as perhaps there may be, and I should be sorry for that.' Clearly the account of Bridges' attitude given in an earlier letter (LXXVII) is not less than fair: 'I always think however that your mind towards my verse is like mine towards Browning's: I greatly admire the touches and the details, but the general effect, the whole, offends me, I think it repulsive.' Six months before the end Hopkins can throw out (CLXVIII), as a matter of accepted fact: 'now that you disapprove of my γένος as vicious . . .'

No guilt, it should hardly be necessary to insist, is being imputed to Bridges. Try as for friendship's sake he might, he could not make himself understand or like what he was incapable of understanding or liking; and his incapacity sets in a tragic light the heroic strength of Hopkins's genius. 'There is a point with me in matters of any size', he writes (CXXIX), 'when I must absolutely have encouragement as much as crops rain; afterwards I am independent.' We find nowhere much hint of encouragement besides Canon Dixon's, and everywhere the spirit expressed here (CXXVII): 'it is a test too: if you do not like it it is because there is something you have not seen and I see. That at least is my mind, and if the whole world agreed to condemn it or see nothing in it I should only tell them to take a generation and come to me again.' It is, as a matter of fact, a musical composition that is in question here, and in music Hopkins was ordinarily conscious (though the expert, when consulted, thought him opinionated and stubborn) that he had everything to learn; but in poetry he knew – he knew with this certitude what he had done and what he was doing, and was not affected in his knowledge by finding himself alone in it. That he nevertheless suffered (as a poet, that is, as well as in the obvious sense) from isolation, from lack of appreciation, he was well aware: 'To return to composition for a moment: what I want there, to be more intelligible, smoother, and less singular, is an audience.' (CLXVI.)

There is nothing of complacency about his sureness; it goes with the rarest integrity and clairvoyance – that is, with the rarest humility. The complacency is not Hopkins's; when he writes to Bridges (XXX), 'The sonnets are truly beautiful, breathing a grave and feeling genius, and make me proud of you (which by the by is not the same as for you to be proud of yourself: I say it because you always were and I see you still are given to conceit) . . .', we feel that he is in a position to say it. Mere playful intimacy, perhaps? This at any rate is beyond question serious (LXXXV): 'It is long since such things [religious rites] had any significance for you. But what is strange and unpleasant is that you sometimes speak as if they had in reality none for me and you were only waiting with a certain disgust till I too should be disgusted with myself enough to throw off the mask. You said something of the sort walking on the Cowley Road when we were last at Oxford together – in '79 it must have been.' 'However,' he writes five months later (XCIII), having referred to the matter again, 'a man who is deeply in earnest is not very eager to assert his earnestness, as they say when a man is really certain he no longer disputes but is indifferent. And that is all I say now, that to think a man in my position is not in earnest is unreasonable and is to make difficulties. But if you have made them and can solve them, by a solution which must be wrong, no matter.'

Hopkins's earnestness could be doubted by no one capable of reading the poetry. Indeed, the question has been raised whether admirers of the poetry have not some grounds for lamenting that the earnestness was so complete. The letters provide excuse for raising some question; but the better one knows both the letters and the poetry the less ready is one likely to be to say anything, one way or the other. It becomes, in fact, difficult to know just what the question is. 'I cannot in conscience spend time on poetry,' he writes to Bridges in 1879 (LIII), 'neither have I the inducements and inspirations that make others compose. Feeling, love in particular, is the great moving power and spring of verse and the only person that I am in love with seldom, especially now, stirs my heart sensibly and when he does I cannot always "make capital" of it, it would be a sacrilege to do so. Then again I have of myself made verse so laborious.'

The delicacy of the issues is fairly suggested here. The critic inclining to venture that a Hopkins who had escaped being converted at Oxford in the eighteen-sixties might have devoted his life to cultivating more profitably than he actually did a poetic gift essentially the same in its strength, but less hampered and thwarted, would do well before pronouncing to reflect upon the case of Yeats. Yeats, the one major poet of his own generation, was 'free', in a sense, to devote his life to 'poetry'; but was he content to be free – did he, indeed, feel himself to be essentially free? and if he had done, would he have been a major poet? Yeats's best work too, one may note, is full of a bitter sense of thwarting, of sterile, issueless inner tension. And –

> The fascination of what's difficult
> Has dried the sap out of my veins, and rent
> Spontaneous joy and natural content
> Out of my heart.

'Then again I have of myself made verse so laborious.' The laboriousness of the art was in neither poet a wantonly strenuous indulgence, a kind of cross-word addiction – something apart from the general quality and deeper concerns of their lives. Neither could at any time have sung with Bridges (whose interest in technique goes with his interest in spelling):

> For a happier lot
> Than God giveth me,
> It never hath been
> Nor ever shall be.

That Hopkins was far from happy stands out as plainly in the letters as in the poetry. His characteristic dejection and fatigue, it is plain too, were associated with a sense of frustration. (See for example the extracts quoted from Letters CXXX and CLVII on

p. 56.) About the nature of the conflict behind, or beneath, this state he is explicit enough to Canon Dixon (for whom, from reading the volume containing his letters, we come away with affection and esteem and, for Hopkins's sake, gratitude):

The question for me then is not whether I am willing (if I may guess what is in your mind) to make a sacrifice of hopes of fame (let us suppose), but whether I am not to undergo a severe judgement from God for the lothness I have shown in making it, for the reserves I may have in my heart made, for the backward glances I have given with my hand upon the plough, for the waste of time the very compositions you admire may have caused and their preoccupation of the mind which belonged to sacred or more binding duties, for the disquiet and the thoughts of vain glory they may have given rise to. A purpose may look smooth from without but be frayed and faltering from within. I have never wavered in my vocation, but I have not lived up to it. (*Correspondence*, XXI.)

This says all that need be said. At least, I do not think that any attempt to go behind, or explain further or deeper, would bring any essential enlightenment to admirers of *The Windhover*, *Spelt from Sybil's Leaves* and the 'terrible sonnets'. It does not, however, by itself suggest the play of energy, the force and distinction of personality, the genius, apparent in the letters written from 'that coffin of weakness and dejection in which I live, without even the hope of change' (CXXVII). The heroic strength and distinction come out in descriptions of the dejected state itself.

Tomorrow morning I shall have been three years in Ireland, three hard wearying wasting wasted years. (I met the blooming Miss Tynan again this afternoon. She told me that when she first saw me she took me for 20 and some friends of hers for 15; but it won't do: they should see my heart and vitals, all shaggy with the whitest hair.) In those I have done God's will (in the main) and many examination papers.

The astringent vivacity of this is in keeping with Hopkins's characteristic humour – the humour in which his quality manifests itself as much as anywhere. It is plain that this humour was un-congenial to Bridges and often offended his sense of fitness and decorum: 'But alas! you will have been sickened by the vulgarity of my comic poems, I am afraid; especially of "the Church of

England" . . . But I have in me a great vein of blackguardry and have long known I am no gentleman; though I would rather say this than have it said' (LXXIV). This episode reverberates a good deal[1]:

Dearest Bridges, – Let us talk sense. (A) There is no need to 'beg my pardon' for giving me the best advice you have to give, but (B) if you must beg my pardon it takes all the sweet out of it to say 'consistent with', etc. – which nevertheless you had to say: the upshot is that you should not beg pardon. Now about these blessed verses . . . my brother Lionel once wrote that somebody's joke was 'strictly funny' . . . Now staggered as I am and ought to be by your judgement, still the feeling of innocence, the sense of integrity, the consciousness of rectitude have returned and I cannot help thinking, though with hesitation and diffidence, that those verses or some of them are strictly funny . . . I have a little medical anecdote that might amuse you. But I am afraid we are not in agreement about the strictly funny. (LXXVI.)

The distinctly ungentlemanly quality of Hopkins's humour asserts itself in the letters more than once at Bridges' expense.[2] That, on the other hand, Bridges should, in his turn, suffer the following rebuke is all in keeping:

There is a good deal of nonsense about that set, often it sickens one (though Rossetti himself I think had little of it); but still I disapprove of damfooling people. I think it is wrong, narrows the mind, and like a

1. Cf. 'I have it now down in my tablets that a man may joke and joke and be offensive.' (CLXXI.)
2. Cf. this commentary on the first line of *Prometheus the Firegiver* ('From high Olympus and the domeless courts'): 'Courts can never be domed in any case, so that it is needless to tell us that those on Olympus are domeless. No: better to say the Kamptuliconless courts or Minton's–encaustic–tileless courts or vulcanisèd–india–rubberless courts. This would strike a keynote at once and bespeak attention. And if the critics said those things did not belong to the period you would have (as you have now with *domeless*) the overwhelming answer that you never said they did but on the contrary, and that Prometheus, who was at once a prophet and as a mechanician more than equal to Edison and the Jablochoff candle and Moc-main Patent Lever Truss with self-adjusting duplex gear and attachments, meant to say that emphatically they had not got these improvements on Olympus and he did not intend they should. But if you cannot see your way to this "frank" treatment and are inclined to think that fault might be found with *domeless*, then remember that the fault is found in *your first line*.' (XCVI.)

'parvifying glass' makes us see things smaller than the natural size. And I do not like your calling Matthew Arnold Mr Kidglove Cocksure. I have more reason than you for disagreeing with him and thinking him very wrong, but nevertheless I am sure he is a rare genius and a great critic. (XCVIII.)

Hopkins's humour is the humour of a disinterested, mature, perfectly poised and completely serious mind, and has in it nothing of defensiveness, superiority or donnishness.[1] It appears often as clarity of critical perception and direct force of expression, as here (CXXIII): 'Swinburne, perhaps you know, has also tried his hand – without success. Either in fact he does not see nature at all or else he overlays the landscape with such phantasmata, secondary images, and what not of a delirium-tremendous imagination that the result is a kind of bloody broth: you know what I mean. At any rate, there is no picture.' It would be possible to multiply illustrations of this kind, showing the critic; but if anything further is to be given it had better be chosen to show the artist, the born creator writer, who is so apparent in the letters:

There was a lovely and passionate scene (for about the space of the last trump) between me and a tallish gentleman (I daresay he was a cardsharper) in your carriage who was by way of being you; I smiled, I murmured with my lips at him, I waved farewell, but he would not give in, till with burning shame (though the whole thing was, as I say, like the duels of archangels) I saw suddenly what I was doing. (LXXXV.)

That 'cardsharper', perhaps, expresses in its innocent way an

1. 'It was too bad of you to think I was writing to you to tell you you were no gentleman; that you should be saying, like Mrs Malaprop, whom I saw amusingly played lately, "Me, that means me, Captain Absolute." It is true, remarks of universal application must apply even to present company and one cannot well help remarking that they do; I cannot say "all must die" and politely except my hearers and myself; but beyond this I did not aim at you. No, if I had wanted a conspicuous instance of a blackguard I should have taken myself, as I was going to do and to tell a good story too thereanent, but refrained because I thought it might look as if I wanted to draw a faint protest from you and because humility is such a very sensitive thing the least touch smutches it and well meant attempts to keep it from jolting, like the Ark when the cattle shook it, do more harm than good; but all the same I shd. have been sadly sincere and sadly truthful.' (C.)

ironical element habitual in Hopkins's contemplation of the correct, the secure, the English gentleman – the critical element that becomes more than a velleity when Bridges says that the monks in Italy were dirty. 'Next your countrymen at Cambridge keep their rooms, you told me, "dirty, yea filthy", and they are not poor . . . And our whole civilization is dirty, yea filthy, and especially in the north; for is it not dirty, yea filthy, to pollute the air as Blackburn and Widnes and St Helen's are polluted and the water as the Thames and the Clyde and the Irwell are polluted?' (CLXIX.) Hopkins, as Professor Abbott tells us, was a patriot. His patriotic idealism expresses itself more than once in denunciation of Gladstone. But, as appears in the passage just quoted, it was not a complacent or blinkered idealism. And in noting Hopkins's patriotism it is well to note also that he professes himself, 'in a manner', a Communist, though 'it was the red Commune that murdered five of our Fathers lately.' (XXVII – Jan. 1874.)

. . . but then I remember that you never relished 'the intelligent artisan' . . . Horrible to say, in a manner I am a Communist. Their ideal bating some things is nobler than that professed by any secular statesman I know of (I must own I live in bat-light and shoot at a venture). Besides it is just, – I do not mean the means of getting it are. But it is a dreadful thing for the greatest and most necessary part of a very rich nation to live a hard life without dignity, knowledge, comforts, delights, or hopes in the midst of plenty – which plenty they make. They profess that they do not care what they wreck and burn, the old civilisation and order must be destroyed. This is a dreadful look out but what has the old civilisation done for them? As it at present stands in England it is itself in great measure founded on wrecking. But they got none of the spoils, they came in for nothing but harm from it then and thereafter. England has grown hugely wealthy but this wealth has not reached the working classes; I expect it has made their condition worse. (XXVI.)

(Bridges, we gather, didn't like this.) – We recall *Tom's Garland* (42 in Poems), a piece commented on, relevantly to the above, in Letters CLIX.

And this brings us finally to what is, though here reserved for so late a place, a main interest of the letters: the immediate bearing they have on the poetry. There are direct discussions of practice and principle, general remarks, particular elucidations (notably one of *Henry Purcell* – xcvii)[1] and so on. It is pleasant to be confirmed so explicitly in one's observations regarding the relation between poetry as Hopkins conceived of it and wrote it and the spoken language:

So also I cut myself off from the use of *ere, o'er, wellnigh, what time, say not* (for *do not say*), because, though dignified, they neither belong to nor could arise from, or be the elevation of, ordinary modern speech. For it seems to me that the poetical language of the age should be the current language heightened, to any degree heightened and unlike it, but not (I mean normally: passing freaks and graces are another thing) an obsolete one. (LXII.)

Again and again he deplores archaism, in prose as well as in verse. Concerning Doughty he replies (CLXIII): 'You say it is free from the taint of Victorian English. H'm. Is it free from the taint of Elizabethan English? Does it not stink of that? for the sweetest flesh turns to corruption. Is not Elizabethan English a corpse these centuries?' He remarks characteristically (LXXXV) on the 'weakness in idiom of all mediaeval Latin verse (except say the Dies Irae: I do not mean the weakness in classical idiom – that does not matter – but want of feeling for or command of any idiom)'.[2] He says (XXXVII) that he uses 'sprung rhythm' because it is nearest to 'the native and natural rhythm of speech . . . combining, as it seems to me, opposite and, one would have thought, incompatible excellences, markedness of rhythm – that is rhythm's self – and naturalness of expression – for why, if it is forcible in prose to say "lashed rod", am I obliged to weaken this in

---

1. He says elsewhere (LXI): 'My sonnet means "Purcell's music is none of your d—d subjective rot" (so to speak). Read it again.'

2. It seems relevant to introduce here another illustration of the anti-academic spirit: 'Some learned lady having shown by the flora that the season of the action in *Hamlet* is March to May, a difficulty is raised about the glowworm's ineffectual fire in the first act, since glowworms glow chiefly from May to September. Mr Furnival having consulted an authority learns that the grub, though not so easily found, shines nearly as bright as the full-grown worm, that is beetle, and begins in March, and so all is saved. Does not all this strike you as great trifling? Shakespeare had the finest faculty of observation of all men that ever breathed, but it is ordinary untechnical observation, neither scientific nor even, like a farmer's, professional, and he might overlook that point of season. But if he knew it he would likely enough neglect it.' (*Correspondence*, XXXV.)

verse, which ought to be stronger, not weaker, into "láshed birch-ród" or something?' Of Dryden, upholding him against Bridges who did not think him a poet (see CLXII), he says (CLV): 'he is the most masculine of our poets; his style and rhythms lay the strongest stress of all our literature on the naked thew and sinew of the English language.' His own verse, he reiterates, is for the ear rather than for the eye, for performance rather than mere reading. 'Sprung rhythm', and his views on rhythm and metre generally, he explains in a letter (XII) to Canon Dixon far more satisfactorily than in the essay that stands as Preface to the *Poems*.

If this survey has seemed to comprise an inordinate amount of quoting, that has not been through any ambition of making an exhaustive anthology, but rather to suggest what remains unquoted. In spite of the letter-writer's repeated complaints of weakness and dejection the effect is of rich and varied vitality. Hopkins's energy was certainly very remarkable. Not content with being as completely original a poet and as extraordinary a technical innovator as the language has to show, he aspired to compose music and devoted himself to the study of musical technicalities; we even find him drawing; he was for the last years of his life a Professor of Greek; he sent communications to *Nature* and he lets out in a letter to Canon Dixon (XXXV) that he is writing a 'popular account of Light and Ether' ('Popular is not quite the word; it is not meant to be easy reading.')[1]

The letters do not produce the constant overwhelming impression of genius that Lawrence's do, but greatness is unmistakably there. A classic is added to the language; and it is indeed matter for rejoicing, especially in times like these, to be admitted to intimacy with a spirit so pure, courageous and humane.

---

1. 'The study of physical science,' he writes in the same letter, 'has, unless corrected in some way, an effect the very opposite of what one would suppose. One would think it might materalise people (no doubt it does make them or, rather I should say, they become materialists; but that is not the same thing: they do not believe in the matter more but in God less); but in fact they seem to end in conceiving only of a world of formulas, with its being properly speaking in thought, towards which the outer world acts as a sort of feeder, supplying examples for literary purposes. And they go so far as to think the rest of mankind are in the same state of mind as themselves.'

THE IRONY OF SWIFT

SWIFT is a great English writer. For opening with this truism I have a reason: I wish to discuss Swift's writings – to examine what they are; and they are (as the extant commentary bears witness) of such a kind that it is peculiarly difficult to discuss them without shifting the focus of discussion to the kind of man that Swift was. What is most interesting in them does not so clearly belong to the realm of things made and detached that literary criticism, which has certainly not the less its duties towards Swift, can easily avoid turning – unawares, and that is, degenerating – into something else. In the attempt to say what makes these writings so remarkable, reference to the man who wrote is indeed necessary; but there are distinctions. For instance, one may (it appears), having offered to discuss the nature and import of Swift's satire, find oneself countering imputations of misanthropy with the argument that Swift earned the love of Pope, Arbuthnot, Gay, several other men and two women: this should not be found necessary by the literary critic. But the irrelevancies of Thackeray and of his castigator, the late Charles Whibley – irrelevancies not merely from the point of view of literary criticism – are too gross to need placarding; more insidious deviations are possible.

The reason for the opening truism is also the reason for the choice of title. To direct the attention upon Swift's irony gives, I think, the best chance of dealing adequately, without deviation or confusion, with what is essential in his work. But it involves also (to anticipate an objection) a slight to the classical status of *Gulliver's Travels*, a book which, though it may represent Swift's most impressive achievement in the way of complete creation – the thing achieved and detached – does not give the best opportunities for examining his irony. And *Gulliver's Travels*, one readily agrees, hasn't its classical status for nothing. But neither is it for nothing that, suitably abbreviated, it has become a classic for children. What for the adult reader constitutes its peculiar force – what puts it in so different a class from *Robinson Crusoe* – resides for the most part in the fourth book (to a less extent in the third).

The adult may re-read the first two parts, as he may *Robinson Crusoe*, with great interest, but his interest, apart from being more critically conscious, will not be of a different order from the child's. He will, of course, be aware of an ingenuity of political satire in *Lilliput*, but the political satire is, unless for historians, not very much alive today. And even the more general satire characteristic of the second book will not strike him as very subtle. His main satisfaction, a great deal enhanced, no doubt, by the ironic seasoning, will be that which Swift, the student of the *Mariner's Magazine* and of travellers' relations, aimed to supply in the bare precision and the matter-of-fact realness of his narrative.

But what in Swift is most important, the disturbing characteristic of his genius, is a peculiar emotional intensity; that which, in *Gulliver*, confronts us in the Struldbrugs and the Yahoos. It is what we find ourselves contemplating when elsewhere we examine his irony. To lay the stress upon an emotional intensity should be matter of commonplace: actually, in routine usage, the accepted word for Swift is 'intellectual'. We are told, for instance, that his is pre-eminently 'intellectual satire' (though we are not told what satire is). For this formula the best reason some commentators can allege is the elaboration of analogies – their 'exact and elaborate propriety'[1] – in *Gulliver*. But a muddled perception can hardly be expected to give a clear account of itself; the stress on Swift's 'intellect' (Mr Herbert Read alludes to his 'mighty intelligence')[2] registers, it would appear, a confused sense, not only of the mental exercise involved in his irony, but of the habitually critical attitude he maintains towards the world, and of the negative emotions he specializes in.

From 'critical' to 'negative' in this last sentence is, it will be observed, a shift of stress. There are writings of Swift where 'critical' is the more obvious word (and where 'intellectual' may seem correspondingly apt) – notably, the pamphlets or pamphleteering essays in which the irony is instrumental, directed and limited to a given end. The *Argument Against Abolishing Christianity* and the *Modest Proposal*, for instance, are discussible in the terms in which satire is commonly discussed: as the criticism of vice, folly, or other aberration, by some kind of reference to positive standards. But even here, even in the *Argument*, where

1. Churton Collins.   2. *English Prose Style*.

Swift's ironic intensity undeniably directs itself to the defence of something that he is intensely concerned to defend, the effect is essentially negative. The positive itself appears only negatively – a kind of skeletal presence, rigid enough, but without life or body; a necessary pre-condition, as it were, of directed negation. The intensity is purely destructive.

The point may be enforced by the obvious contrast with Gibbon – except that between Swift's irony and Gibbon's the contrast is so complete that any one point is difficult to isolate. Gibbon's irony, in the fifteenth chapter, may be aimed against, instead of for, Christianity, but contrasted with Swift's it is an assertion of faith. The decorously insistent pattern of Gibbonian prose insinuates a solidarity with the reader (the implied solidarity in Swift is itself ironical – a means to betrayal), establishes an understanding and habituates to certain assumptions. The reader, it is implied, is an eighteenth-century gentleman ('rational', 'candid', 'polite', 'elegant', 'humane'); eighteen hundred years ago he would have been a pagan gentlemen, living by these same standards (those of absolute civilization); by these standards (present everywhere in the stylized prose and adroitly emphasized at key points in such phrases as 'the polite Augustus', 'the elegant mythology of the Greeks') the Jews and early Christians are seen to have been ignorant fanatics, uncouth and probably dirty. Gibbon as a historian of Christianity had, we know, limitations; but the positive standards by reference to which his irony works represent something impressively realized in eighteenth-century civilization; impressively 'there' too in the grandiose, assured and ordered elegance of his history. (When, on the other hand, Lytton Strachey, with a Gibbonian period or phrase or word, a 'remarkable', 'oddly', or 'curious', assures us that he feels an amused superiority to these Victorian puppets, he succeeds only in conveying his personal conviction that he feels amused and superior.)

Gibbon's irony, then, habituates and reassures, ministering to a kind of judicial certitude or complacency. Swift's is essentially a matter of surprise and negation; its function is to defeat habit, to intimidate and to demoralize. What he assumes in the *Argument* is not so much a common acceptance of Christianity as that the reader will be ashamed to have to recognize how fundamentally unchristian his actual assumptions, motives, and attitudes are. And in general the implication is that it would shame people if they were made to recognize themselves unequivocally. If one had to justify this irony according to the conventional notion of satire, then its satiric efficacy would be to make comfortable non-recognition, the unconsciousness of habit, impossible.

A method of surprise does not admit of description in any easy formula. Surprise is a perpetually varied accompaniment of the grave, dispassionate, matter-of-fact tone in which Swift delivers his intensities. The dissociation of emotional intensity from its usual accompaniments inhibits the automatic defence-reaction:

> He is a Presbyterian in politics, and an atheist in religion; but he chooses at present to whore with a Papist.

> What bailiff would venture to arrest Mr Steele, now he has the honour to be your representative? and what bailiff ever scrupled it before?

Or inhibits, let us say, the normal response; since 'defence' suggests that it is the 'victim' whose surprise we should be contemplating, whereas it is our own, whether Swift's butt is Wharton or the atheist or mankind in general. 'But satire, being levelled at all, is never resented for an offence by any, since every individual makes bold to understand it of others, and very wisely removes his particular part of the burden upon the shoulders of the World, which are broad enough and able to bear it'.[1] There is, of course, no contradiction here; a complete statement would be complex. But, actually, the discussion of satire in terms of offence and castigation, victim and castigator, is unprofitable, though the idea of these has to be taken into account. What we are concerned with (the reminder is especially opportune) is an arrangement of words on the page and their effects – the emotions, attitudes and ideas that they organize.

Our reaction, as Swift says, is not that of the butt or victim; nevertheless, it necessarily entails some measure of sympathetic self-projection. We more often, probably, feel the effect of the words as an intensity in the castigator than as an effect upon a victim: the dissociation of animus from the usual signs defines for

1. *A Tale of a Tub*: the Preface.

our contemplation a peculiarly intense contempt or disgust. When, as sometimes we have to do, we talk in terms of effect on the victim, then 'surprise' becomes an obviously apt word; he is to be betrayed, again and again, into an incipient acquiescence:

Sixthly. This would be a great Inducement to Marriage, which all wise Nations have either encouraged by Rewards, or enforced by Laws and Penalties. It would increase the Care and Tenderness of Mothers towards their Children, when they were sure of a Settlement for Life, to the poor Babes, provided in some Sort by the Publick, to their annual Profit instead of Expence; we should soon see an honest Emulation among the married Women, *which of them could bring the fattest Child to the Market*. Men would become as *fond* of their Wives, during the Time of their Pregnancy, as they are now of their *Mares* in Foal, their *Cows* in Calf, or *Sows* when they are ready to farrow, nor offer to beat or kick them (as is too *frequent* a Practice) for fear of a Miscarriage.

The implication is: 'This, as you so obligingly demonstrate, is the only kind of argument that appeals to you; here are your actual faith and morals. How, on consideration, do you like the smell of them?'

But when in reading the *Modest Proposal* we are most engaged, it is an effect directly upon ourselves that we are most disturbingly aware of. The dispassionate, matter-of-fact tone induces a feeling and a motion of assent, while the burden, at the same time, compels the feelings appropriate to rejection, and in the contrast – the tension – a remarkably disturbing energy is generated. A sense of an extraordinary energy is the general effect of Swift's irony. The intensive means just indicated are reinforced extensively in the continuous and unpredictable movement of the attack, which turns this way and that, comes now from one quarter and now from another, inexhaustibly surprising – making again an odd contrast with the sustained and level gravity of the tone. If Swift does for a moment appear to settle down to a formula it is only in order to betray; to induce a trust in the solid ground before opening the pitfall.

'His *Tale of a Tub* has little resemblance to his other pieces. It exhibits a vehemence and rapidity of mind, a copiousness of images, a vivacity of diction, such as he afterwards never possessed, or never exerted. It is of a mode so distinct and peculiar, that it must be considered by itself; what is true of that, is not true of anything else he has written'. What Johnson is really testifying to here is the degree in which the *Tale of a Tub* is characteristic and presents the qualities of Swift's genius in concentrated form. 'That he has in his works no metaphors, as has been said, is not true,' says Johnson a sentence or two later, 'but his few metaphors seem to be received rather by necessity than choice'. This last judgement may at any rate serve to enforce Johnson's earlier observation that in the *Tale of a Tub* Swift's powers function with unusual freedom. For the 'copiousness of images' that Johnson constates is, as the phrase indicates, not a matter of choice but of essential genius. And, as a matter of fact, in this 'copiousness of images' the characteristics that we noted in discussing Swift's pamphleteering irony have their supreme expression.

It is as if the gift applied in *Gulliver* to a very limiting task – directed and confined by a scheme uniting a certain consistency in analogical elaboration with versimilitude – were here enjoying free play. For the bent expressing itself in this 'copiousness' is clearly fundamental. It shows itself in the spontaneous metaphorical energy of Swift's prose – in the image, action or blow that, leaping out of the prosaic manner, continually surprises and disconcerts the reader: 'such a man, truly wise, creams off Nature, leaving the sour and the dregs for philosophy and reason to lap up'. It appears with as convincing a spontaneity in the sardonic vivacity of comic vision that characterizes the narrative, the presentment of action and actor. If, then, the continual elaborate play of analogy is a matter of cultivated habit, it is a matter also of cultivated natural bent, a congenial development. It is a development that would seem to bear a relation to the Metaphysical fashion in verse (Swift was born in 1667). The spirit of it is that of a fierce and insolent game, but a game to which Swift devotes himself with a creative intensity.

And whereas the mind of man, when he gives the spur and bridle to his thoughts, does never stop, but naturally sallies out into both extremes of high and low, of good and evil, his first flight of fancy commonly transports him to ideas of what is most perfect, finished, and exalted, till, having soared out of his own reach and sight, not well perceiving how near the frontiers of height and depth border upon each other, with the same course and wing he falls down plump into the lowest bottom of things, like one who travels the east into the west, or like a straight line drawn by its own length into a circle. Whether a tincture of malice in our natures makes us fond of furnishing every bright idea with its reverse, or whether reason, reflecting upon the sum of things, can, like the sun, serve only to enlighten one half of the globe, leaving the other half by necessity under shade and darkness, or whether fancy, flying up to the imagination of what is highest and best, becomes over-short, and spent, and weary, and suddenly falls, like a dead bird of paradise, to the ground. . . .

One may (without difficulty) resist the temptation to make the point by saying that this is poetry; one is still tempted to say that the use to which so exuberant an energy is put is a poet's. 'Exuberant' seems, no doubt, a paradoxical word to apply to an energy used as Swift uses his; but the case is essentially one for paradoxical descriptions.

In his use of negative materials – negative emotions and attitudes – there is something that it is difficult not to call creative, though the aim always is destructive. Not all the materials, of course, are negative; the 'bird of paradise' in the passage above is alive as well as dead. Effects of this kind, often much more intense, are characteristic of the *Tale of a Tub*, where surprise and contrast operate in modes that there is some point in calling poetic. 'The most heterogeneous ideas are yoked by violence together' – and in the juxtaposition intensity is generated.

'Paracelsus brought a squadron of stink-pot-flingers from the snowy mountains of Rhaetia' – this (which comes actually from the *Battle of the Books*) does not represent what I have in mind; it is at once too simple and too little charged with animus. Swift's intensities are intensities of rejection and negation; his poetic juxtapositions are, characteristically, destructive in intention, and when they most seem creative of energy are most successful in spoiling, reducing, and destroying. Sustained 'copiousness', continually varying, and concentrating surprise in sudden local foci, cannot be represented in short extracts; it must suffice here to say that this kind of thing may be found at a glance on almost any page:

Meantime it is my earnest request that so useful an undertaking may be entered upon (if their Majesties please) with all convenient speed, because I have a strong inclination before I leave the world to taste a blessing which we mysterious writers can seldom reach till we have got into our graves, whether it is that fame, being a fruit grafted on the body, can hardly grow and much less ripen till the stock is in the earth, or whether she be a bird of prey, and is lured among the rest to pursue after the scent of a carcass, or whether she conceives her trumpet sounds best and farthest when she stands on a tomb, by the advantage of a rising ground and the echo of a hollow vault.

It is, of course, possible to adduce Swift's authority for finding that his negations carry with them a complementary positive – an implicit assertion. But (*pace* Charles Whibley) the only thing in the nature of a positive that most readers will find convincingly present is self-assertion – *superbia*. Swift's way of demonstrating his superiority is to destroy, but he takes a positive delight in his power. And that the reader's sense of the negativeness of the *Tale of a Tub* is really qualified comes out when we refer to the Yahoos and the Struldbrugs for a test. The ironic detachment is of such a kind as to reassure us that this savage exhibition is mainly a game, played because it is the insolent pleasure of the author: 'demonstration of superiority' is as good a formula as any for its prevailing spirit. Nevertheless, about a superiority that asserts itself in this way there is something disturbingly odd, and again and again in the *Tale of a Tub* we come on intensities that shift the stress decisively and remind us how different from Voltaire Swift is, even in his most complacent detachment.

I propose to examine in illustration a passage from the *Digression Concerning the Original, the Use, and Improvement of Madness in a Commonwealth* (i.e. Section IX). It will have, in the nature of the case, to be a long one, but since it exemplifies at the same time all Swift's essential characteristics, its length will perhaps be tolerated. I shall break up the passage for convenience of comment, but, except for the omission of nine or ten lines in the second instalment, quotation will be continuous:

For the brain in its natural position and state of serenity disposeth its owner to pass his life in the common forms, without any thought of subduing multitudes to his own power, his reasons, or his visions, and the more he shapes his understanding by the pattern of human learning, the less he is inclined to form parties after his particular notions, because that instructs him in his private infirmities, as well as in the stubborn ignorance of the people. But when a man's fancy gets astride on his reason, when imagination is at cuffs with the senses, and common understanding as well as common sense is kicked out of doors, the first proselyte he makes is himself; and when that is once compassed, the difficulty is not so great in bringing over others, a strong delusion always operating from without as vigorously as from within. For cant and vision are to the ear and the eye the same that tickling is to the touch. Those entertainments and pleasures we most value in life are such as dupe and play the wag with the senses. For if we take an examination of what is generally understood by happiness, as it has respect either to the understanding or to the senses, we shall find all its properties and adjuncts will herd under this short definition, that it is a perpetual possession of being well deceived.

Swift's ant-like energy – the business-like air, obsessed intentness and unpredictable movement – have already had an effect. We are not, at the end of this instalment, as sure that we know just what his irony is doing as we were at the opening. Satiric criticism of sectarian 'enthusiasm' by reference to the 'common forms' – the Augustan standards – is something that, in Swift, we can take as very seriously meant. But in the incessant patter of the argument we have (helped by such things as, at the end, the suggestion of animus in that oddly concrete 'herd') a sense that direction and tone are changing. Nevertheless, the change of tone for which the next passage is most remarkable comes as a disconcerting surprise:

And first, with relation to the mind or understanding, it is manifest what mighty advantages fiction has over truth, and the reason is just at our elbow; because imagination can build nobler scenes and produce more wonderful revolutions than fortune or Nature will be at the expense to furnish. . . . Again, if we take this definition of happiness and examine it with reference to the senses, it will be acknowledged wonderfully adapt. How sad and insipid do all objects accost us that are not conveyed in the vehicle of delusion! How shrunk is everything as it appears in the glass of Nature, so that if it were not for the assistance of artificial mediums, false lights, refracted angles, varnish, and tinsel, there would be a mighty level in the felicity and enjoyments of mortal men. If this were seriously considered by the world, as I have a certain reason to suspect it hardly will, men would no longer reckon among their high points of wisdom the art of exposing weak sides and publishing infirmities – an employment, in my opinion, neither better nor worse than that of unmasking, which, I think, has never been allowed fair usage, either in the world or the playhouse.

The suggestion of changing direction does not, in the first part of this passage, bring with it anything unsettling: from ridicule of 'enthusiasm' to ridicule of human capacity for self-deception is an easy transition. The reader, as a matter of fact, begins to settle down to the habit, the steady drift of this irony, and is completely unprepared for the sudden change of tone and reversal of attitude in the two sentences beginning 'How sad and insipid do all objects', etc. Exactly what the change means or is, it is difficult to be certain (and that is of the essence of the effect). But the tone has certainly a personal intensity and the ironic detachment seems suddenly to disappear. It is as if one found Swift in the place – at the point of view – where one expected to find his butt. But the ambiguously mocking sentence with which the paragraph ends reinforces the uncertainty.

The next paragraph keeps the reader for some time in uneasy doubt. The irony has clearly shifted its plane, but in which direction is the attack going to develop? Which, to be safe, must one dissociate oneself from, 'credulity' or 'curiosity'.

In the proportion that credulity is a more peaceful possession of the mind than curiosity, so far preferable is that wisdom which converses about the surface to that pretended philosophy which enters into the depths of things and then comes gravely back with informations and discoveries, that in the inside they are good for nothing. The two senses to which all objects first address themselves are the sight and the touch; these never examine further than the colour, the shape, the size, and whatever other qualities dwell or are drawn by art upon the outward of bodies; and then comes reason officiously, with tools for cutting, and opening, and mangling, and piercing, offering to demonstrate that they are not of the same consistence quite through. Now I take all this to be the last degree of perverting Nature, one of whose eternal laws is to put her best furniture forward. And therefore, in order to save the charges of all such expensive anatomy for the time to come, I do here think fit to inform the reader that in such conclusions as these reason is certainly in the right; and that in most corporeal beings which have fallen under my cognisance the outside hath been infinitely preferable to the in, whereof I have been further convinced from some late experiments. Last week I saw a woman flayed, and you will hardly believe how much it altered her person for the worse.

The peculiar intensity of that last sentence is, in its own way, so decisive that it has for the reader the effect of resolving uncertainty in general. The disturbing force of the sentence is a notable instance of a kind already touched on: repulsion is intensified by the momentary co-presence, induced by the tone, of incipient and incompatible feelings (or motions) of acceptance. And that Swift feels the strongest animus against 'curiosity' is now beyond all doubt. The natural corollary would seem to be that 'credulity', standing ironically for the 'common forms' – the sane, socially sustained, common-sense illusions – is the positive that the reader must associate himself with and rest on for safety. The next half-page steadily and (to all appearances) unequivocally confirms this assumption:

Yesterday I ordered the carcass of a beau to be stripped in my presence, when we were all amazed to find so many unsuspected faults under one suit of clothes. Then I laid open his brain, his heart, and his spleen, but I plainly perceived at every operation that the farther we proceeded, we found the defects increase upon us in number and bulk; from all of which I justly formed this conclusion to myself, that whatever philosopher or projector can find out an art to sodden and patch up the flaws and imperfections of Nature, will deserve much better of mankind and teach us a much more useful science than that, so much in present esteem, of widening and exposing them (like him who held anatomy to be the ultimate end of physic). And he whose fortunes and dispositions have placed him in a convenient station to enjoy the fruits of this noble art, he that can with Epicurus content his ideas with the films and images that fly off upon his senses from the superficies of things, such a man, truly wise, creams off Nature, leaving the sour and the dregs for philosophy and reason to lap up.

Assumption has become habit, and has been so nourished that few readers note anything equivocal to trouble them in that last sentence: the concrete force of 'creams off', 'sour', 'dregs' and 'lap up' seems unmistakably to identify Swift with an intense animus against 'philosophy and reason' (understood implicitly to stand for 'curiosity' the anatomist). The reader's place, of course, is with Swift.

The trap is sprung in the last sentence of the paragraph:

This is the sublime and refined point of felicity called the possession of being well-deceived, the serene peaceful state of being a fool among knaves.

What is left? The next paragraph begins significantly: 'But to return to madness'. This irony may be critical, but 'critical' turns out, in no very long run, to be indistinguishable from 'negative'. The positives disappear. Even when, as in the Houyhnhnms, they seem to be more substantially present, they disappear under our 'curiosity'. The Houyhnhnms, of course, stand for Reason, Truth and Nature, the Augustan positives, and it was in deadly earnest that Swift appealed to these; but how little at best they were anything solidly realized, comparison with Pope brings out. Swift did his best for the Houyhnhnms, and they may have all the reason, but the Yahoos have all the life. Gulliver's master 'thought Nature and reason were sufficient guides for a reasonable animal', but nature and reason as Gulliver exhibits them are curiously negative, and the reasonable animals appear to have nothing in them to guide. 'They have no fondness for their colts or foals, but the care they take in educating them proceeds entirely from the dictates of reason'. This freedom from irrational feelings and impulses simplifies other matters too: 'their language doth not abound in variety of words, because their wants and passions are fewer than among us'. And so conversation, in this model society, is simplified: 'nothing passed but what was useful, expressed in the fewest and most significant words . . .' 'Courtship, love, presents, jointures, settlements, have no place in their thoughts, or terms whereby to express them in their language. The young couple meet and are joined, merely because it is the determination of their parents and friends: it is what they see done every day, and they look upon it as one of the necessary actions of a reasonable being'. The injunction of 'temperance, industry, exercise, and cleanliness . . . the lessons enjoined to the young ones of both sexes', seems unnecessary; except possibly for exercise, the usefulness of which would not, perhaps, be immediately apparent to the reasonable young.

The clean skin of the Houyhnhnms, in short, is stretched over a void; instincts, emotions and life, which complicate the problem of cleanliness and decency, are left for the Yahoos with the dirt and the indecorum. Reason, Truth and Nature serve instead; the Houyhnhnms (who scorn metaphysics) find them adequate. Swift too scorned metaphysics, and never found anything better to contend for than a skin, a surface, an outward show. An outward show is, explicitly, all he contends for in the quite unironical *Project for the Advancement of Religion*, and the difference between the reality of religion and the show is, for the author of the *Tale of a Tub*, hardly substantial. Of Jack we are told, 'nor could all the world persuade him, as the common phrase is, to eat his victuals like a Christian'. It is characteristic of Swift that he should put in these terms, showing a complete incapacity even to guess what religious feeling might be, a genuine conviction that Jack should be made to kneel when receiving the Sacrament.

Of the intensity of this conviction there can be no doubt. The Church of England was the established 'common form', and, moreover, was Swift's church: his insane egotism reinforced the savagery with which he fought to maintain this cover over the void, this decent surface. But what the savagery of the passage from the *Digression* shows mainly is Swift's sense of insecurity and of the undisguisable flimsiness of any surface that offered.

The case, of course, is more complex. In the passage examined the 'surface' becomes, at the most savage moment, a human skin. Swift's negative horror, at its most disturbing, becomes one with his disgust-obsession: he cannot bear to be reminded that under the skin there is blood, mess and entrails; and the skin itself, as we know from *Gulliver*, must not be seen from too close. Hypertrophy of the sense of uncleanness, of the instinct of repulsion, is not uncommon; nor is its association with what accompanies it in Swift. What is uncommon is Swift's genius and the paradoxical vitality with which this self-defeat of life – life turned against itself – is manifested. In the *Tale of a Tub* the defeat is also a triumph; the genius delights in its mastery, in its power to destroy, and negation is felt as self-assertion. It is only when time has confirmed Swift in disappointment and brought him to more intimate contemplation of physical decay that we get the Yahoos and the Struldbrugs.

Here, well on this side of pathology, literary criticism stops. To attempt encroachments would be absurd, and, even if one were qualified, unprofitable. No doubt psychopathology and medicine have an interesting commentary to offer, but their help is not necessary. Swift's genius belongs to literature, and its appreciation to literary criticism.

We have, then, in his writings probably the most remarkable expression of negative feelings and attitudes that literature can offer – the spectacle of creative powers (the paradoxical description seems right exhibited consistently in negation and rejection. His verse demands an essay to itself, but fits in readily with what has been said. 'In poetry', he reports of the Houyhnhnms, 'they must be allowed to excel all other mortals; wherein the justness of their similes and the minuteness as well as exactness of their descriptions are, indeed, inimitable. Their verses abound very much in both of these . . .' The actuality of presentment for which Swift is notable, in prose as well as verse, seems always to owe its convincing 'justness' to, at his least actively malicious, a coldly intense scrutiny, a potentially hostile attention. 'To his domesticks', says Johnson, 'he was naturally rough; and a man of rigorous temper, with that vigilance of minute attention which his works discover, must have been a master that few could bear'. *Instructions to Servants* and the *Polite Conversation* enforce obviously the critical bearing and felicity of Johnson's remark.

A great writer – yes; that account still imposes itself as fitting, though his greatness is no matter of moral grandeur or human centrality; our sense of it is merely a sense of great force. And this force, as we feel it, is conditioned by frustration and constriction; the channels of life have been blocked and perverted. That we should be so often invited to regard him as a moralist and an idealist would seem to be mainly a witness to the power of vanity, and the part that vanity can play in literary appreciation: *saeva indignatio* is an indulgence that solicits us all, and the use of literature by readers and critics for the projection of nobly suffering selves is familiar. No doubt, too, it is pleasant to believe that unusual capacity for egotistic animus means unusual distinction of intellect; but, as we have seen, there is no reason to lay stress on intellect in Swift. His work does indeed exhibit an extraordinary play of mind; but it is not great intellectual force that is exhibited in his indifference to the problems raised – in, for instance, the *Voyage to the Houyhnhnms* – by his use of the concept, or the word

'Nature'. It is not merely that he had an Augustan contempt for metaphysics; he shared the shallowest complacencies of Augustan common sense: his irony might destroy these, but there is no conscious criticism.

He was, in various ways, curiously unaware – the reverse of clairvoyant. He is distinguished by the intensity of his feelings, not by insight into them, and he certainly does not impress us as a mind in possession of its experience.

We shall not find Swift remarkable for intelligence if we think of Blake.

'THE DUNCIAD'

YES, one concedes grudgingly, overcoming the inevitable re-vulsion, as one turns the pages of this new edition (The 'Twickenham'), in which the poem trickles thinly through a desert of apparatus, to disappear time and again from sight – yes, there has to be a *Dunciad* annotated, garnished and be-prosed in this way. A very large proportion of the apparatus, after all, comes down from the eighteenth century with the poem, and the whole, though to read it all though will be worth no one's while, is enlightening documentation of the age that produced Pope and of which Pope made poetry. Yet, as the editor in his Introduction insists – 'It has never sufficiently been recognized that in the *Dunciad* one of the greatest artists in English poetry found the perfect material for his art', he did make poetry, and it is the poetry that matters; so that one has to follow up one's con-cession with the remark that, though this new monument of scholarship will have to go into all the libraries for reference, it is not the edition in which the *Dunciad* should be read. The material is one thing, the poetry another. In fact, the sufficient recognition won't come except in company with the recognition that notes are not necessary: the poetry doesn't depend upon them in any essential respect.

'The art', says Professor Sutherland, 'which Pope lavished upon this poem has too often been obscured by an unnecessary concern for his victims'. Yes; and more generally, by an unnecessary concern *with* his victims – a concern of a kind that notes, especially obtrusive ones, inevitably encourage. The 'fading of its per-sonalities', remarked by Professor Sutherland as something that appreciated of the *Dunciad* suffers from, is really an advantage, and one we ought not to refuse. For eighteenth-century readers it must have been hard not to start away continually from the poetry to thinking about the particular historical victim and the grounds of Pope's animus against him; for modern readers it should be much easier to appreciate the poetry as poetry – to realize that Pope has created something the essential interest of which lies within itself, in what it is. Yet where satire is concerned there appear to be peculiar difficulties in the way of recognizing the nature of art and of the approach to it, as Professor Sutherland bears inadvertent witness in the last sentence of his Introduction:

the criticism of the nineteenth and twentieth centuries has been far too much concerned with the moral issues raised by Pope's satire, and too little interested in its purely aesthetic values.

'Aesthetic' is a term the literary critic would do well to deny himself. Opposed to 'moral', as it is in this sentence, it certainly doesn't generate light. Moral values enter inevitably into the appreciation of the *Dunciad*, if it is judged to be a considerable work; the problem is to bring them in with due relevance, and the bringing of them in is the appreciation of Pope's art. How are malice, resentment, spite, contempt, and the other negative attitudes and feelings that we can't doubt to have played a large part in the genesis of his poetry, turned in that poetry into something that affects us as being so very different?

We don't feel the personalities as personal. More than that, we don't, for the most part, even in places where animus is very apparent, feel the total effect to be negative, expressing a hostile and destructive will. The force of this judgement comes out when we look by way of comparison at Swift. The final impression that Swift, in any representative place, leaves us with is one of having been exposed to an intense, unremitting and endlessly resourceful play of contempt, disgust, hatred and the will to spoil and destroy. The contrast brings home to us the sense in which Pope, in practising his art of verse, is engaged, whatever his materials, in positive creation. It is Swift's prose I am thinking of in the first place, but the contrast is no less striking and significant when made between verse and verse. In verse, in fact, Swift is more barely and aridly negative (the air is 'thoroughly small and dry'), and more summarily destructive, than in prose; he never achieves anything approaching the complexity characteristic of the *Digression Concerning the Use of Madness in a Commonwealth*. In the following we have the richest, in the way of organization, that his verse yields:

> When Celia in her glory shews,
> If Strephon would but stop his nose,
> (Who now so impiously blasphemes
> Her ointments, daubs, and paints, and creams,
> Her washes, slops, and every clout,
> With which he makes so foul a rout;)
> He soon would learn to think like me,
> And bless his ravish'd sight to see
> Such order from confusion sprung,
> Such gaudy tulips raised from dung.

Effects like that of the closing couplets are not common in Swift's verse, but the sourly nagging meanness, the sawing meagreness, of the movement in general is representative. No one, of course, would carry out a solemn comparison of Swift and Pope as poets. My point is simply, by the contrast with Swift, who is not positively an Augustan – though he is nothing else positive – to bring out what is meant by saying that Pope, in practising his art of verse, is being an Augustan of a most positive kind. Against any of Swift's verse (if you want decasyllabics take the close of *A City Shower*) set this:

> This labour past, by Bridewell all descend,
> (As morning-pray'r and flagellation end)
> To where Fleet-ditch with disemboguing streams
> Rolls the large tribute of dead dogs to Thames,
> The King of Dykes! than whom, no sluice of mud
> With deeper sable blots the silver flood.

It is not enough to talk in the usual way (I have just seen a Sunday review that quotes the passage, which I had already marked) about the beauty of that last couplet. That beauty is inseparable from the whole habit of the versification. And in saying this one recognizes that 'versification' here involves more than the term is generally felt to convey. When Pope is preoccupied with the metrical structure, the weight, and the pattern of his couplets, he is bringing to bear on his 'materials' habits of thought and feeling, and habits of ordering thought and feeling. The habits are those of a great and ardent representative of Augustan civilization. The result is that even when he is closest to Swift he remains very un-Swiftian in effect: what we note at once as the characteristic movement (no simple etrical matter, of course) makes a radical difference:

> Like the vile straw that's blown about the streets
> The needy Poet sticks to all he meets,
> Coach'd, carted, trod upon, now loose, now fast,
> In the Dog's tail his progress ends at last.

The part of Augustan civilization in Pope's creative triumph is peculiarly apparent in the Fourth Book of the *Dunciad*. The pre-eminence of this book doesn't seem to be at all generally recognized. There is no sign, for instance, that the present editor recognizes it any more than Leslie Stephen did, writing his 'English Men of Letters' *Pope* before 1880. There can, then, be no harm in reiterating that the Fourth Book stands, not only (so much later in date as it is) apart from the other books, but much above them: it is a self-sufficient poem. The opening has an obvious relevance to my immediate argument:

> Yet, yet a moment one dim Ray of Light
> Indulge, dread Chaos, and eternal Night!
> Of darkness visible so much be lent,
> As half to shew, half veil the deep Intent.
> Ye Pow'rs! whose Mysteries restor'd I sing,
> To whom Time bears me on his rapid wing,
> Suspend a while your Force inertly strong,
> Then take at once the Poet and the Song.

This astonishing poetry ought to be famous and current for the unique thing it is. Consider how triumphantly it enlists Milton into an Augustan sublime. Faced with this passage as a detached fragment, and forgetting (if that can be granted as credible) where one had read it, what would one make of it? It could have been written, one would have to conclude, only by Pope, but one would hardly guess that it belonged to a satire. Yet within ten lines the poem breaks out into a most lively play of imaginative wit, overtly satirical, and the transition is irresistibly sure:

> Now flam'd the Dog-star's unpropitious ray,
> Smote ev'ry Brain, and wither'd ev'ry Bay;
> Sick was the Sun, the Owl forsook his bow'r,
> The moon-struck Prophet felt the madding hour:

Then rose the Seed of Chaos, and of Night,
To blot out Order, and extinguish Light,
Of dull and venal a new World to mold,
And bring Saturnian days of Lead and Gold.
    She mounts the Throne: her head a Cloud conceal'd,
In broad Effulgence all below reveal'd,
('Tis thus aspiring Dullness ever shines)
Soft on her lap her Laureat son reclines.
    Beneath her foot-stool, Science groans in Chains,
And *Wit* dreads Exile, Penalties and Pains.
There foam'd rebellious *Logic*, gagg'd and bound,
There, stript, fair *Rhet'ric* languish'd on the ground;
His blunted Arms by *Sophistry* are born,
And shameless Billingsgate her Robes adorn.
Morality, by her false Guardians drawn,
Chicane in Furs, and *Casuistry* in Lawn,
Gasps as they straiten at each end the cord,
And dies, when Dullness gives her Page the word.
Mad *Mathesis* alone was unconfin'd,
Too mad for mere material chains to bind,
Now to pure Space lifts her extatic stare,
Now running round the Circle, finds it square.

The key to Pope's command of the sublime, and to his mastery
of transition, presents itself in the couplet:

Then rose the Seed of Chaos, and of Night,
To blot out Order, and extinguish Light. . . .

Order' for Pope is no mere word, but a rich concept imaginatively realized: ideal Augustan civilization. It is his greatness as a
poet that he can relate the polite Augustan social culture always
present in Augustan idiom and movement with something
more profound than a code of manners: a code adequate to being
thought of as the basis and structure of a great civilization. We
have him doing it in this book of the *Dunciad*. 'Order' (associated
with 'Light') imparts its grandeur to the opening, and it is the
comprehensive positive from which the satire works (in ways I
discuss in *Revaluation*, c. III). It is everywhere implicitly there, or
within easy recall, and it explains the mastery of transition that
goes with Pope's astonishing variety. As the antithesis of triumph-

ant Chaos it informs the prophetic vision of the close with that
tremendously imaginative and moving grandeur.[1]

That close, of course, with its reminders of the century of
Marvell and Donne, gives us a Pope who is more than Augustan.
And in so doing it serves as an admonition against leaving an over-
simplifying account of him uncorrected. Though it is his creativeness – for all his satiric bent, he is an essentially creative spirit – that
puts Pope in so different a relation to Augustan culture from
Swift's, his creativeness is not merely a matter of his being able to
realize an ideal Augustan order. The contrast with Swift comes
out in another way. The respect in which the two writers (who
were closely associated in the brewing of the *Dunciad*) have most
affinity is represented by the characteristic piece of Swift's prose
which I quote at the foot of p. 79. Nowhere does the habit of
mind and expression illustrated here come nearer, in Swift, to
producing an effect in which the satisfaction of the creative impulse plainly predominates. Very often the negative and destructive functions of the play of images and analogies are much
more insistent: the strangeness – 'the most heterogeneous ideas
are yoked by violence together' – is intensely malevolent, and the
surprise is brutally shocking. How essentially negative, in this
sense, the passage just quoted is comes out when we set it by any
of Pope's in which his kindred habit asserts itself. Take this, for
instance:

> And now had Fame's posterior Trumpet blown,
> And all the Nations summon'd to the Throne.
> The young, the old, who feel her inward sway,
> One instinct seizes, and transports away.
> None need a guide, by sure Attraction led,
> And strong impulsive gravity of Head:

1. Cf. Leslie Stephen (*Pope*, p. 123): 'There are some passages marked by
Pope's usual dexterity, but the whole is awkwardly constructed, and has no
very intelligible connexion with the first part. It was highly admired at the
time, and, amongst others, by Gray. He specially praises a passage which
has often been quoted as representing Pope's highest achievement in his art.
At the conclusion the goddess Dulness yawns, and a blight falls upon art,
science and philosophy. I quote the lines, which Pope himself could not
repeat without emotion, and which have received the highest eulogies from
Johnson and Thackeray.'

> None want a place, for all their Centre found,
> Hung to the Goddess, and coher'd around.
> Not closer, orb in orb, conglob'd are seen
> The buzzing Bees about their dusky Queen.

The formal attitude here is one of satiric antipathy, but plainly
the positive satisfaction taken by the poet in creating this marvellously organized complexity of surprising tropes, felicitously odd
images, and profoundly imaginative puns, determines the pre-
dominant feeling, which, in fact, might fairly be called genial. So
again here in a simpler instance (the first that presents itself at a
turn of the page):

> Ah, think not, Mistress! more true Dulness lies
> In Folly's Cap, than Wisdom's grave disguise.
> Like buoys, that never sink into the flood,
> On Learning's surface we but lie and nod.
> Thine is the genuine head of many a house.
> And much Divinity without a *Nous*.
> Nor could a BARROW work on ev'ry block,
> Nor has one ATTERBURY spoil'd the flock.
> See! still thy own, the heavy Canon roll,
> And Metaphysic smokes involve the Pole.

And in general, the same predominance of creativeness, de-
lighting in the rich strangeness of what it contemplates, is to be
found whenever Pope devotes himself to 'expressing' or 'ridicul-
ing' (as we are expected to say, considering him as a satirist) the
varied absurdities of the human scene.

> A Nest, a Toad, a Fungus, or a Flow'r

– here we have, typified in brief, the kind of effect he so obviously
loves; and the line serves as a reminder that 'human scene' is too
limiting in suggestion.

> The common Soul, of Heav'n's more frugal make,
> Serves but to keep fools pert, and knaves awake:
> A drowsy Watchman, that just gives a knock,
> And breaks our rest, to tell us what's a clock.
> Yet by some object ev'ry brain is stirr'd;
> The dull may waken to a Humming-bird;

> The most recluse, discreetly open'd, find
> Congenial matter in the Cockle-kind;
> The mind, in Metaphysics at a loss,
> May wander in a wilderness of Moss;
> The head that turns at super-lunar things,
> Pois'd with a tail, may steer on Wilkins' wings.

Pope's interest in the objects of absorbing contemplation which he ascribes to the 'virtuosi' he is satirizing may not be precisely theirs, but it is unmistakably a positive interest. What fascinates him are effects of fantastic incongruity; effects that at the same time seem to evoke a more exciting reality than that of common sense. And in creating these effects he is undoubtedly registering certain insistent qualities of experience as it came, good Augustan though he was, to him.

The relation between his interest in these qualities and his concern for Augustan order constitutes one of the most striking aspects of his genius. There is no hostility between them; they associate together harmoniously in a perfect creative alliance. What we find in the part, in the relation between vivid nightmare absurdity and the decorous Augustanism of the verse, we find in large in the totality of the poem. Worked pregnantly in between the Augustan sublimities of the opening and the close, we have, not an ordered development of a corresponding theme, argument or action, but a packed heterogeneity that corresponds in the large to

> A Nest, a Toad, a Fungus, or a Flow'r.

Into this can go with perfectly congruous incongruity a satirically straightforward piece of Augustan 'Sense':

> Then thus. 'Since Man from beast by Words is known,
> Words are Man's province, Words we teach alone.
> When Reason doubtful, like the Samian letter,
> Points him two ways, the narrower is the better.
> Plac'd at the door of Learning, youth to guide,
> We never suffer it to stand too wide.
> To ask, to guess, to know, as they commence,
> As Fancy opens the quick springs of Sense,
> We ply the Memory, we load the brain,
> Bind rebel Wit, and double chain on chain.

> Confine the thought, to exercise the breath;
> And keep them in the pale of Words till death.
> Whate'er the talents, or howe'er designed,
> We hang one jingling padlock on the mind.

Such a passage comes in so naturally and easily because of the pervasive rationality of the Augustan versification and idiom. And that Pope can use these as he does in evoking his fantastic incongruities shows that there is nothing repressive about the Order that commands his imagination. His sense of wonder has been richly and happily nourished, and can invest what offers itself as satiric fantasy with the enchantment of fairy-tale:

> Wide, and more wide, it spread o'er all the realm;
> Ev'n Palinurus nodded at the Helm. . . .

His ability to unite Augustan with seventeenth-century Wit has profound concomitants.

JOHNSON AND AUGUSTANISM

MR KRUTCH'S book,[1] I must confess, surprised me very agreeably. It is not only inoffensive; it is positively good. I had better add at once that I write in England and as an Englishman. In this country, to those seriously interested in literature, the cult of Johnson is an exasperation and a challenge. It is a branch of good-mixing, and its essential *raison-d'être* is anti-highbrow; it is to further the middlebrow's game of insinuating the values of good-mixing into realms where they have no place – except as a fifth-column, doing their hostile work from within. Johnson, one finds oneself having again and again to insist, was not only the Great Clubman[2]; he was a great writer and a great highbrow – or would have been, if the word, and the conditions that have produced it, had existed; that is, he assumed a serious interest in things of the mind, and, for all his appeal to 'the common reader', was constantly engaged in the business of bringing home to his public and his associates, whose cult of him was a tribute to the force with which he did it, that there were standards in these things above the ordinary level of the ordinary man. But when the University of Oxford conferred a doctorate *honoris causa* on P. G. Wodehouse, it was exemplifying the ethos of our modern Johnson club. And there is too good reason for expecting that a new book on Johnson by one of the academic custodians of the 'humanities' will exhibit the kind of literary accomplishment that goes with an admiration for the prose of (say) Miss Dorothy Sayers, the brilliance of Mr C. S. Lewis, and the art of Lytton Strachey.

Mr Krutch, however, shows no interest in that kind of accomplishment. And while he doesn't sport the style that adorns vacuity or anti-highbrow animus, neither has he written one of

---

1. *Samuel Johnson*. By Joseph Wood Krutch.
2. 'It may well be that like Johnson he [Charles Whibley] will live rather through the influence which he exerted on those who were privileged to know him than through the written word.' – From the blurb in *The Radio Times*, January 22, 1950, for a talk in the Third Programme on Whibley.

those depressing 'contributions to knowledge' which are so patently uninformed by any firsthand perception of why the subject should be worth study. In fact, an Englishman must see in him something very much to the credit of American academic letters. At any rate, it is difficult to imagine a don or a literary person on this side of the Atlantic producing a book with the virtues of Mr Krutch's. It is a new general book on Johnson that justifies itself. Mr Krutch has brought together, with unobtrusive but admirable skill, all the sources. He has related them so as to form the most coherent and complete exhibition of Johnson possible (and as part of the process has given us penetrating studies of Boswell and Mrs Thrale). His commentaries, which are never forced and always seem to issue naturally from the presented data, exemplify in a quietly acute way the peculiarly appropriate virtue of good sense; there is no obtrusion of 'psychology' and no psychoanalytic knowingness. It is as if the facts were so arranged as to expose their significance, so that when Mr Krutch renders this in statement, what he says is obviously just. It is a kind of obviousness that an expositor should aim at, but its achievement implies uncommon devotion and disinterestedness.

Inevitably, most of what he says about Johnson doesn't strike the reader as particularly new. But, said in that way – emerging as it does from the relevant facts in their significant order – it brings an increase in real knowledge. And, without going in for paradoxes, Mr Krutch does firm and sensitive justice to the complexity of the facts. There is, at the centre of the subject, the peculiar nature of Johnson's Toryism and his piety. Their relation to his scepticism is well brought out. It is 'clear beyond any question', says Mr Krutch (having shown it to be so), 'that his orthodoxy was not the result of any bigoted conviction concerning the unique rightness of the Anglican Church, but quite simply a part of his general tendency to favour social unity and social conformity'. And the strength of this tendency was correlated with the strength of his scepticism: he was, in this respect, not unlike Swift.

Johnson accepted the miracles of the Bible because he could not refuse to do so without plunging himself into an abyss of intolerable doubt on the brink of which he always shuddered back; but even in works of pure imagination the supernatural was likely to trouble him, and what he said of the vein of 'stubborn rationality' that kept him from the Roman Catholic Church may give warrant for the guess that he would have been more comfortable if even Anglicanism had put less strain upon it.

'Mr Johnson's incredulity,' says Mrs Thrale, 'amounted almost to disease' – she is reporting Hogarth to the effect: 'that man is not contented with believing the Bible, but he fairly resolves, I think, to believe nothing *but* the Bible.' Where ghosts are in question, it is an admirably critical mind that Mr Krutch shows us: 'Johnson was genuinely skeptical – which is to say, neither credulous, on the one hand nor, on the other, unwilling to consider the possibility that anything not disproved might be true.' And it is wholly characteristic of Johnson to have written: 'Prodigies are always seen in proportion as they are expected.'

As for his Toryism, how far it was from being the mere 'sturdy' John Bullishness, endearingly prejudiced, overbearing and robust, which it tends to become in the current legend, Mr Krutch's book makes it impossible not to recognize. The theme involves so much of Johnson that to sketch Mr Krutch's treatment of it would be to summarize a large part of the book. But one point may be made that engages a great deal: Johnson had no bent towards hard authoritarianism or cynical 'realism'. It is in his polemic against the Americans that he appears most repugnantly as the Tory, but it should be noted that the gusto with which he indulges his worst side here is significantly correlated with his indignant hatred of slavery:

But perhaps the best proof that when Johnson derided the idea of liberty he was thinking only of that sort of which the deprivation produces merely 'metaphysical distresses' is to be found in his attitude towards Negro slavery. Boswell was the 'friend of Paoli' and hence a champion of liberty – but chiefly, it appears, of the sort whose effects are exclusively 'metaphysical'. To *him* Negro slavery was an institution so marvellously humane and just that it should be contemplated with delighted wonder. To the Tory Johnson, on the other hand, it was an abomination concerning which he could not speak without rage. Near the very beginning of his career and at a time when the Quakers were still slave dealers, he spoke of 'the natural right of the Negroes to liberty and independence'. A little later he described Jamaica as 'a place of great wealth and dreadful wickedness, a den of tyrants and a dungeon of slaves'; and still later he could write: 'I do not much wish well to discoveries, for I am always afraid they will end in conquest and robbery'. In 1777 he dictated for Boswell a brief in favour of a Negro suing in Scotland to regain his freedom, and at Oxford, once, this defender of 'subordination' and scorner of liberty gave as his toast 'Here's to the next insurrection of the negroes in the West Indies'.

This is the Johnson who could say: 'Let the authority of the English government perish, rather than be maintained by iniquity.'

One of the good things Mr Krutch does is to bring out Johnson's extravagant and disqualifying abnormality, and his deep sense of it, and the part played by this sense in some of his most notorious characteristics. There is, for instance, his so-called 'dogmatism', which colours the general notion of his Toryism. I myself, when I hear this dogmatism spoken of, recall his own distinction: 'what I have here not dogmatically but deliberately written . . .' (*Preface to Shakespeare*). But it is plain that the weight of utterance that is of the essence of his style, and the inescapable mark of his genius, tends to be confused – for the most part admiringly, no doubt – with the crushing powers he commanded when 'talking for victory', and that people are partly thinking of this trait when they call him 'dogmatic'. Here is a relevant observation from Mr Krutch:

Perhaps it has never been sufficiently remarked that one reason for his domineering manner, for his insistence on winning almost every argument by fair means or foul, is his realization that he must dominate any group of which he did not expect to become quickly the butt. In many respects he was made to be laughed at.

Concerning another notorious trait Mr Krutch remarks: 'He was almost desperately sociable because he could never become part of any society.' The same considerations are brought to bear on that extraordinary household he collected and made himself responsible for.

For Johnson, of course, the supreme social activity was the art of conversation; he couldn't do without the social milieu that enabled him to extend himself in talk. Mr Krutch is good on Johnson as a talker; the chapter, 'Folding his Legs', is one of the best in the book. Yet when we come to this subject we come in sight of Mr Krutch's limitations, and qualifying criticism begins. For the consideration of Johnson's strength as a talker cannot properly be separated from that of his strength as a writer, and to Johnson's greatness as a writer Mr Krutch is not adequate. His inadequacy is most unquestionable as it appears in his treatment of the poems. I think he is right in suggesting that Mr T. S. Eliot, at any rate in effect, overrates *London* when he fails to stress its inferiority to *The Vanity of Human Wishes*. But that is surely a venial lapse (a matter of presentment rather than of judgement, I imagine) compared with a failure to see that *The Vanity of Human Wishes* is great poetry. And Mr Krutch does unmistakably fail; the superiority he sees amounts to little. He is not impressed; he is not (it would seem) even interested.

If you can't appreciate Johnson's verse you will fail in appreciation of his prose; and you will not be able to follow-through the considerations involved in the appreciation of his talk. 'I could not help remarking', notes Fanny Burney, 'how very like Dr Johnson is to his writing; and how much the same thing it was to hear him or to read him; but that nobody could tell that without coming to Streatham, for his language was generally imagined to be laboured and studied, instead of the mere common flow of his thoughts.' About the extraordinary vigour and discipline exhibited by this 'mere common flow' Mr Krutch says a great deal that is to the point. He quotes Boswell:

What the deepest source of these powers was is well described by Boswell in his final summing up: 'As he was general and unconfined in his studies, he cannot be considered as master of any one particular science; but he had accumulated a vast and various collection of learning and knowledge, which was so arranged in his mind, as to be ever in readiness to be brought forth. But his superiority over other learned men consisted chiefly in what may be called the art of thinking, the art of using the mind; a certain continual power of seizing the useful substance of all that he knew, and exhibiting it in a clear and forceful manner; so that knowledge, which we often see to be no better than lumber in men of dull understanding, was, in him, true, evident and actual wisdom.'

And yet, endorsing this, Mr Krutch can say on another page that 'Johnson did not merely write abstractly; he thought abstractly'. To call Johnson's style 'abstract' is misleading if you don't go on at once to explain that abstractness here doesn't exclude concreteness, or (since these words, at any rate as used by literary critics, are not very determinate in force) to insist that the style is remarkable for body. It is a generalizing style; its extraordinary weight is a generalizing weight; and the literary critic should be occupied with analysing this, and with explaining how Johnson's generalities come to be so different in effect from ordinary abstractness.

> Yet should thy Soul indulge the gen'rous heat,
> Till captive Science yields her last retreat;
> Should Reason guide thee with her brightest ray,
> And pour on misty Doubt resistless day;
> Should no false kindness lure to loose delight,
> Nor Praise relax, nor Difficulty fright;
> Should tempting Novelty thy cell refrain,
> And Sloth effuse her opiate fumes in vain;
> Should Beauty blunt on fops her fatal dart,
> Nor claim the triumph of a letter'd heart;
> Should no Disease thy torpid veins invade,
> Nor Melancholy's phantoms haunt thy shade;
> Yet hope not life from grief or danger free,
> Nor think the doom of man revers'd for thee.

There is an achieved substance answering to the suggestion of that phrase, 'the doom of man'. Johnson's abstractions and generalities are not mere empty explicitnesses substituting for the concrete; they focus a wide range of profoundly representative experience – experience felt by the reader as movingly present. I won't offer an analysis of the passage and its working; some of the main points are fairly obvious. What need to be discussed here are certain conditions of that remarkable power Johnson commands of using so abstract and conventional an idiom with such vitality.

Mr Krutch deals pretty well with them as they come up in the consideration of Johnson's talk. If he was a great virtuoso, it was in a recognized art, one much cultivated and highly esteemed. 'Johnson and his friends sat down for a talk as deliberately as another group would sit down to play chamber music or cards.' They went in for 'conscious virtuosity without the triviality which so often accompanies conversation deliberately practised as an art'. 'Certain traditions were pretty scrupulously observed, and they determined a form of conversation' that was 'always *about* something, and though nowhere has the epigram been more appreciated, the kind of epigram most admired was the kind that owes its distinction to the fact that it says something more quickly, more adroitly, and more conclusively than it has even been said before, not the kind that is sheer empty virtuosity . . .' Discussion proceeded on the 'assumption that, in so far as a subject was discussible at all, it was best discussed in terms of what is generally called (without further definition) "common sense" and that any intelligent and well-educated gentleman, no matter what his special aptitudes might be, was as competent as any other to settle questions philosophical, theological or even scientific'. The assumption could be so effective for an art of conversation because what it involved was remarkably positive and determinate as well as comprehensive: 'we may define "commonsense" as the acceptance of certain current assumptions, traditions and standards of value which are never called in question because to question any of them might be to necessitate a revision of government, society and private conduct more throughgoing than anyone liked to contemplate.'

That is, Johnson's art had behind it something far more determinate than 'common sense' suggests to us. And these 'assumptions, traditions and standards of value' had an operative currency as idiom – the period idiom to which they gave its strongly positive character; they informed the linguistic conventions and habits of expression that seemed to the age natural and inevitable. Further – what Mr Krutch doesn't note, or doesn't sufficiently note – they were current as *literary* convention. Their nature, significance and control of thought and judgement are most apparent in the verse of the age. For most eighteenth-century verse, and all verse of the Augustan tradition, has a social movement – a movement that suggests company deportment, social gesture and a code of manners: it is polite. Literary form is intimately associated with Good Form.

To put it in this way is to recall the worst potentialities of Polite Letters – the superficialities and complacencies conjured up by that significant phrase. The positive, concentrated, and confident civilization we see registered in *The Tatler* and *The Spectator* is impressive, but no profound analysis is necessary to elicit from those bland pages the weaknesses of a culture that makes the Gentleman *qua* Gentleman its criterion, as Queen Anne Augustanism does ('the Man writes much like a Gentleman, and goes to Heaven with a very good Mien'). Yet Pope's name is enough to bring home to us that to write in Augustan idiom and convention is not necessarily to be superficial, and that a code of manners can engage something profound. If Pope wrote *The Rape of the Lock* and the *Essay on Man*, he also wrote the fourth book of the *Dunciad*. And if Johnson could find the Augustan tradition so inevitable and right, that is triumphant proof that a writer could embrace it without condemning himself to remain on the social surface. For Johnson did, of course, embrace it. He found it so congenial that he was able, quite naturally, to adapt its idiom and convention to the needs of his own sensibility and time. As a literary tradition of convention and technique it became for him something in the nature of a morality of literary practice. And on tone, movement and diction his seriousness imposed its weight. The politeness became a kind of high public decorum, and Good Form deepened into that conception of a profound unquestionable order in human things which is represented by the characteristic phrase: 'he that thinks reasonably must think morally'.

But Johnson's conception of form and order is not narrowly moral. 'He found it brick, and he left it marble'. In praising Dryden he endorses the essential Augustan pretension; that referred to by Mr Krutch when he says that 'Johnson's *Dictionary* was thus a contribution to a much more inclusive task which the eighteenth century had set itself – the task, namely, of discovering and establishing in all human affairs (including language) the most reasonable, most durable, most efficient, and most elegant procedure.'

This, then, is surely central to the interest Johnson should have for us: a genius of robust and racy individuality, notably direct and strong in his appeal to firsthand experience, he nevertheless finds himself very much at home in a cultural tradition that lays a peculiarly heavy stress on the conventional and social conditioning of individual achievement, and is peculiarly insistent in its belief that individual thought and expression must exemplify a social discipline, and enlist tradition as a collaborator, or be worthless. Johnson is not, like the Romantic poet, the enemy of society, but consciously its representative and its voice, and it is his strength – something inseparable from his greatness – to be so. This aspect of Johnson's interest Mr Krutch is unable to develop to the full because he is insufficiently a literary critic.

It is in his treatment of Johnson the poet that the insufficiency is most apparent. It is in the verse that we can see most clearly the extremely positive civilization to which Johnson belonged expressing itself as literary convention. The poet to whom such a convention and such an idiom are so congenial exemplifies a relation of artist to contemporary civilization of a kind that we are not familiar with – we should find it the more significant. The unfamiliarity is too much for Mr Krutch. He cannot see that the Augustan tradition as we have it in Johnson's verse represents the strength of the eighteenth century in poetry. So when he comes to the poem on the death of Robert Levet, which he rightly finds a 'singularly touching poem' ('readers who have little taste for formal satire in couplets may well find it the best of Johnson's verse'), he thinks it worth suggesting that the 'rhythm and diction are perhaps influenced by Gray's Elegy.' Here for once (the implication appears to be) we have Johnson responding to the 'novel elements' in the poetry of the time. In any case, the reference to Gray reveals a disabling ignorance of eighteenth-century verse (I mean ignorance not by academic, but by critical standards). There is indeed an element in the *Elegy* that constitutes an affinity with Johnson; but no one who saw it would see it as a reason for suggesting that Johnson was influenced by Gray. It is the element that enables Johnson to 'rejoice to concur with the common reader', and exalt the *Elegy* as a classic of the profound commonplace:

The Churchyard abounds with images which find a mirror in every mind, and with sentiments to which every bosom returns an echo. The four stanzas beginning, 'Yet even these bones' are to me original; I have never seen the notions in any other place; yet he that reads them here persuades himself that he has always felt them. Had Gray written often thus, it had been vain to blame and useless to praise.

Gray succeeded in blending in the *Elegy* the two lines of eighteenth century verse-tradition: the meditative-Miltonic, specializing in 'mouldered' ruins, ivy-mantled towers and guaranteed poetical sentiment, with the Augustan. His stanzas have the Augustan social gait and gesture (they have a movement as of the couplet extended) and the Augustan prose-strength – that strength which seeks the virtues of statement: the *mot juste*, the final phrase, and the neatness and precision that run to wit.

How naturally and radically Augustan Gray's sensibility was, comes out in the *Impromptu* he left behind in a dressing-table drawer in the country. It seems to me the best poem he did (which is not to say that it can aspire to the classical status of the *Elegy*; but the *Elegy* pays for its substance and size with unevenness and instability). Since it is virtually unknown (though it is to be found in the Oxford *Gray and Collins*, where my attention was called to it by Dom Hilary Steuert), and since its coming from Gray enforces my point, I will give the poem here (the *Impromptu* was 'suggested by a view, in 1766, of the seat and ruins of a deceased nobleman, at Kingsgate, in Kent'):

> Old, and abandon'd by each venal friend,
>   Here Holland form'd the pious resolution
> To smuggle a few years, and strive to mend
>   A broken character and constitution.
>
> On this congenial spot he fix'd his choice;
>   Earl Goodwin trembled for his neighbouring sand;
> Here sea-gulls scream, and cormorants rejoice.
>   And mariners, though shipwreck'd, dread to land.
>
> Here reigns the blustering North and blighting East,
>   No tree is heard to whisper, bird to sing;
> Yet Nature could not furnish out the feast,
>   Art he invokes new horrors still to bring.
>
> Here mouldering fanes and battlements arise,
>   Turrets and arches nodding to their fall,
> Unpeopled monasteries delude our eyes,
>   And mimic desolation covers all.
>
> 'Ah!' said the sighing Peer, 'had Bute been true,
>   Nor Mungo's, Rigby's, Bradshaw's friendship vain,
> Far better scenes than these had blest our view,
>   And realiz'd the beauties which we feign.
>
> 'Purg'd by the sword, and purified by fire,
>   Then had we seen proud London's hated walls;
> Owls would have hooted in St Peter's choir,
>   And foxes stunk and litter'd in St Paul's'.

This is an unalloyed Augustan; the 'mouldering fanes and battlements', significantly, are present only for ironical attention. But this is the strength that raises the *Elegy* above all the verse in the meditative-Miltonizing line to which the elegiac Gray also belongs. And this is the strength that relates Gray to Johnson, the strength of the central Augustan tradition. Failure to realize that centrality, and the mistaken ideas about the decay of the Augustan tradition that go with illusions about the vitality of the 'novel elements' (which, for the most part, are incurably minor-poetical, and wholly dependent on the Augustan), means a failure to realize to the full the nature and significance of Johnson's genius.

Closely correlated with Mr Krutch's inability to appreciate Johnson's verse is his inability to see clearly Johnson's limitations as a critic of Shakespeare. He states quite well where the stress falls in Johnson's appreciation. It falls, one might say, on Shakespeare the novelist, and is in keeping with his approval of Richardson and of the new art of fiction:

This therefore is the praise of Shakespeare, that his drama is the mirrour of life; that he who has mazed his imagination, in following the phantoms which other writers raise up before him, may here be cured of his delirious extasies, by reading human sentiments in human language, by scenes from which a hermit may estimate the transactions of the world, and a confessor predict the progress of the passions.

On the positive aspects of this critical attitude Mr Krutch is good. But when he comes to the question of what there may be in Shakespeare that Johnson fails to appreciate, or to appreciate adequately, Mr Krutch can only suppose that we must be thinking of Johnson's lack of interest in ' "imagination" as a source of transcendental knowledge'.

What of the highest flight of fancy and imagination? What of all the things which seem to be outside anyone's possible experience? What of the world sometimes described as the world of sheer beauty and transcendental truth?

Mr Krutch fumbles a good deal with these (as they seem to me) not very profitable questions, and concludes with satisfaction that 'Johnson's Shakespeare is, first of all, the people's Shakespeare rather than either the Shakespeare of learned critics or the Shakespeare of the aesthete'. But he doesn't mention the major limitation that stares him in the face.

It is overt and unequivocal. Here are two passages from the *Preface to Shakespeare*:

He therefore indulged his natural disposition, and his disposition, as Rhymer has remarked, led him to comedy. In tragedy he often writes, with great appearance of toil and study, what is written at last with little felicity; but in his comick scenes, he seems to produce without labour, what no labour can' improve. In tragedy he is always struggling after some occasion to be comick; but in comedy he seems to repose, or to luxuriate, as in a mode of thinking congenial to his nature. In his tragick scenes there is always something wanting, but his comedy often surpasses expectation or desire. His comedy pleases by the thoughts and the language, and his tragedy for the greater part by incident and action. His tragedy seems to be skill, his comedy to be instinct.

In tragedy his performance seems constantly to be worse, as his labour is more. The effusions of passion which exigence forces out are for the most part striking and energetick; but whenever he solicits his invention, or strains his faculties, the offspring of his throes is tumour, meanness, tediousness, and obscurity.

The critic who can in this way exalt the comedy above the tragedy exhibits a failure in the appreciation of Shakespeare that no one today, surely, would hold to be anything but major.

There is plenty in the *Preface*, as well as plenty elsewhere in Johnson, to make the force of the last-quoted passage quite plain. His limitation in the face of Shakespearean tragedy goes with a limitation in the face of Shakespearean poetry. He cannot appreciate the Shakespearean handling of language. Mr Krutch argues that, in the notorious commentary on the 'Come, thick night' speech from *Macbeth*, Johnson is merely discussing a convention-engendered disability that he doesn't share. But the evidence, and there is abundance of it, is all the other way. If Johnson can scarcely contain his 'risibility' when he hears of the 'avengers of guilt *peeping through a blanket*', that is because he doesn't respond fully to Shakespeare's poetry. He cannot, because his training opposes; a state of affairs made plain by the paradoxical way in which he shows appreciation while giving the irresistible reasons for 'disgust':

In this passage is exerted all the force of poetry, that force which calls new powers into being, which embodies sentiment, and animates matter; yet, perhaps, scarce any man now peruses it without some disturbance of his attention from the counteraction of the words to the ideas. . . .

This training was in the very positive tradition described above – a tradition focussed in a literary code. Mr Krutch, discussing Johnson's talk, says well: 'he seems seldom to have uttered a word to which his intellect had not assigned a purpose.' This might very well be applied to the Augustan use of language in general. Every word in a piece of Augustan verse has an air of being able to give the reasons why it has been chosen, and placed just there. The thoughts that the Augustan poet, like any other Augustan writer, sets himself to express are amply provided for by the ready-minted concepts of the common currency. What he has to do is to put them together with elegance and point according to the rules of grammar, syntax and versification. The exploratory-creative use of words upon experience, involving the creation of concepts in a free play for which the lines and configurations of the conventionally charted have no finality, is something he has no use for; it is completely alien to his habit. So that even when he is Johnson, whose perception so transcends his training, he cannot securely appreciate the Shakespearean creativeness. He will concede almost unwillingly that here we have 'all the force of poetry, that force which calls new powers into being, which embodies sentiment and animates matter', but as conscious and responsible critic he knows what has to be said of the Shakespearean complexity:

It is incident to him to be now and then entangled with an unwieldy sentiment, which he cannot well express, and will not reject; he struggles with it a while, and if it continues stubborn, comprises it in words such as occur, and leaves it to be disentangled and evolved by those who have more leisure to bestow on it. (*Preface to Shakespeare*.)

Johnson, the supreme Augustan writer, is never entangled with an unwieldy sentiment, which he cannot well express; the mode of creation suggested by 'comprising' anything in 'words such as occur' is one that the Augustan tradition cannot recognize. That so robustly individual a talent could find himself so at home in such a tradition, that it should so have fostered his extraordinary powers, tells us something about the civilization that produced it. Over a considerable period the distinguished minds of the age could accept as a final achievement the very positive conventional ordering of experience offered by that civilization in the name of Reason, Truth and Nature. The literary intellectual could feel that in his own grapplings with experience he had society, not merely as ideal tradition, but as a going concern, with him – could feel it in such a way that he didn't need to be conscious of it. Clearly, there was real achievement to justify the Augustan pretensions.

But it is the limitation that has to be insisted on at the moment. Johnson was representative in his inability to appreciate the more profoundly creative uses of language – for that was his case. There is more significance in his exaltation of the passage from *The Mourning Bride* than Mr Krutch recognizes. True, it is as 'description' (Mr Krutch's point) that Johnson exalts it above anything of Shakespeare's; but Mr Krutch (with Shakespeare to help him) ought to be able to see that 'description' *can* be done by poetic-creative methods, and that Congreve can only offer us the usual post-Dryden rhetoric, with neat illustrative parallels – thought-image, point-by-point – instead of concreteness and metaphorical life. The method is that of prose-statement, the only use of language Johnson understands. That is, he cannot appreciate the life-principle of drama as we have it in the poetic-creative use of language – the use by which the stuff of experience is presented to speak and act for itself.

This disability has its obvious correlative in Johnson's bondage (again representative) to moralistic fallacy and confusion. He complains of Shakespeare (in the *Preface*):

He sacrifices virtue to convenience, and is so much more careful to please than to instruct, that he seems to write without any moral purpose. From his writings indeed a system of moral duty may be selected, for he that thinks reasonably must think morally; but his precepts drop casually from him; he makes no just distribution of good or evil, nor is always careful to show in the virtuous a disapprobation of the wicked; he carries his persons indifferently through right and wrong, and at the close dismisses them without further care, and leaves their example to operate by chance.

Johnson cannot understand that works of art *enact* their moral valuations. It is not enough that Shakespeare, on the evidence of his works, 'thinks' (and feels), morally; for Johnson a moral judgement that isn't *stated* isn't there. Further, he demands that the whole play shall be conceived and composed as statement. The dramatist must start with a conscious and abstractly formulated moral and proceed to manipulate his puppets so as to demonstrate and enforce it.

Here we have a clear view of the essential tendency of the Augustan tradition. Such a use of language, so unchallenged and unqualified in its assumption of omnicompetence (how it came to prevail with this completeness would be a large and compli-cated inquiry, taking in more than the English scene) must tend to turn forms and conventions from agents of life into debilitating conventionalities, such as forbid the development of the in-dividual sensibility and set up an insulation against any vitalizing recourse to the concrete. But the perception of this should not prevent us from giving the strength of *The Vanity of Human Wishes* (or of the poem on Levet) its due. Nor should it lead us to overrate the poetic strength of Shelley's use of language. I bring it down to Shelley in order to keep the discussion within bounds. He is a poet of undoubted genius, and he may fairly be taken as representing the tendency of the reaction against the Augustan. His use of language might seem to be as far removed from the *stating* use as possible; it is often hard to find a para-phrasable content in his verse. Yet he is not, as a poet, the anti-thesis of Johnson in the sense that he practises what I have called the dramatic use of language. His use is at least as far removed from that as Johnson's is – if removed on the other side. His handling of emotion may not be 'statement'; but in order to describe it we need a parallel term. It is a matter of *telling* us; telling us, 'I feel like this,' and telling us how we, the audience, are to feel. Intended intensities are indicated by explicit insistence and emphasis. While Johnson starts with an intellectual and moral purpose Shelley starts with an emotional purpose, a dead set at an emotional effect, and pursues it in an explicit mode that might very reasonably be called 'statement' in contrast with the Shake-spearean mode, which is one of presenting something from which the emotional effect (or whatever else) derives. What Shelley does in *The Cenci* (Act V, Sc. iv) with that speech of Claudio's which he unconsciously remembers from *Measure for Measure* (Act III, Sc. i) is characteristic:

> *Beatrice* (wildly):   O
> My God! Can it be possible I have
> To die so suddenly? So young to go
> Under the obscure, cold, rotting wormy ground!
> To be nailed down into a narrow place;
> To see no more sweet sunshine; hear no more. . . .

In spite of the reminiscence, this is as remote as possible from the Shakespearean original:

> Ay, but to die, and go we know not where;
> To lie in cold obstruction, and to rot;
> This sensible warm motion to become
> A kneaded clod; and the delighted spirit
> To bathe in fiery floods, or to reside
> In thrilling region of thick-ribbed ice. . . .

I leave the reader to look up, if he likes, the two speeches, and I won't develop the comparison (there are some relevant notes in the chapter on Shelley in my *Revaluation*). In the juxtaposition as I give it here it will be seen that there is nothing in Claudio's lines corresponding to the direct explicit emotionality of the O (so significantly placed) *My God*, though the Shakespearean passage has so much the stronger effect. If the whole Shelleyan speech is turned up (or the whole play) it will be found to be, in essence, wholly a matter of 'O'. It might, in fact, be said that the criticism of the tradition adorned by Johnson is that it led to the conditions in which Shelley did this with his genius.

Johnson, of course, was not inclined to be indulgent to the 'romantic' consequences of Augustanism. As Mr Krutch says: 'No one of his contemporaries seemed more completely outside the energizing romantic movement, or more insensitive to the novel elements that were beginning to be evident in the work of Gray or even in that of his friend Goldsmith.' What Mr Krutch doesn't see is that in Johnson's lack of sympathy for the 'novel elements' (which aren't on the whole so very novel) we have his strength rather than his limitation. The formula for Johnson as critic is this: he is strong where an Augustan training is in place, and his limitations appear when the training begins to manifest itself as unjustifiable resistance. That 'unjustified', of course, will involve an appeal to one's own judgement. I myself judge that Johnson discriminates with something approaching infallibility between what is strong and what is weak in the eighteenth century. Where Milton is concerned he shows an interesting resistance, which *Paradise Lost* has no difficulty in overcoming. Milton has a subject and his use of language offers none of the difficulty of the Shakespearean; it is concerned with direct declamatory statement and observes a high decorum. (All the same, Johnson can say of the diction, unanswerably: 'The truth is, that, both in prose and verse, he had formed his style by a perverse and pedantic principle. He was desirous to use English words with a foreign idiom. This in all his prose is discovered and condemned; for there the judgement operates freely. . . .')

It is in his treatment of Pope that we come on a really striking and significant limitation in the critic. Mr Krutch quotes some acute comparative observations on Pope and Dryden that, for all their acuteness, leave us feeling that Johnson doesn't appreciate the full difference between the two – doesn't, that is, appreciate Pope's greatness. Mr Krutch himself, while he can jibe (not unjustifiably) at the modish in our time 'who sometimes seem to pay lip service to Dryden less because they generally admire him than in order to emphasize the fact that they do not consider themselves romantics', cannot see that Pope is a poet of another and greater kind. Faced with the *Verses to the Memory of an Unfortunate Lady* he can say that Pope 'succeeds as well as Pope could be expected to succeed with such a subject', and makes it plain that in his view Johnson's failure of sympathy is a minor matter (measured by the loss involved) compared with his failure in respect of *Lycidas*. But the *Unfortunate Lady* is one of the most remarkable poems in the *Oxford Book* ('Yes, there's some true and tender sentiment there,' 'Q' replied when, not without mischievous intention, I had congratulated him on having included *that* piece of Pope). In it appears unmistakably the genius that finds its fullest expression in that great poem, the fourth book of the *Dunciad*. That Johnson shouldn't be able to appreciate the genius that could transmute into Augustan poetry elements that so strikingly transcend the Augustanism of the *Essay on Man*, the *Epistle to Arbuthnot* or *The Rape of the Lock* throws a significant light on the decline of the Augustan tradition. Johnson was representative, and the Pope whom he saw stood as a 'Chinese Wall' between the eighteenth century and the seventeenth – though for Pope (see the opening of the *Dunciad IV*) Milton was no Chinese Wall.

At the end of the chapter on the *Lives*, Mr Krutch discusses the kind of critic that Johnson was. Of the criticism he says: 'Its manner is objective, and its aim is not to present "the truth as I (and probably no one else) sees it," but to make statements which the reader will accept as true for himself and all normal men.' That is (I myself should say), it is essentially critical. But is it – Mr Krutch anticipates the question – pure? In giving the answer, though his attitude seems to me sound, he fumbles. As so often, the term 'aesthetic' signals a lack of grip. Mr Krutch says quite rightly that Johnson 'did not think of his criticism as something that ought to be essentially different from that general criticism of life which he had made it his business to offer since he first began to write.' But take this account of Johnson's attitude (p. 449):

There are no unique literary values. No specialist conceptions, no special sensibilities, no special terms, even, are necessary. Anyone who has the equipment to judge men and manners and morals has the equipment to judge literature, for literature is merely a reflection of men and manners and morals. To say this is, of course, to say that for Johnson there is no realm of the exclusively aesthetic.

I don't think that for any critic who understands his job there are any 'unique literary values' or any 'realm of the exclusively aesthetic'. But there *is*, for a critic, a problem of relevance: it is, in fact, his ability to be relevant in his judgements and commentaries that makes him a critic, if he deserves the name. And the ability to be relevant, where works of literary art are concerned, is not a mere matter of good sense; it implies an understanding of the resources of language, the nature of conventions and the possibilities of organization such as can come only from much intensive literary experience accompanied by the habit of analysis. In this sense it certainly implies a specially developed sensibility. I know of nothing said by Johnson that leads me to suppose he would (unless in 'talking for victory') have disputed this.

It is because Mr Krutch is not sufficiently a critic in the sense defined that his book gives lodgement for the criticisms I have passed on it. I feel it is a little ungrateful and ungracious in me to have insisted on them so. For, I repeat, it is a good book. Indeed, I think it will become (as it deserves to do) something of a classic – which is a reason for taking it seriously. I have found it an admirable challenge to stating my own sense of the living interest and importance of the subject.

And it will be proper, as well as pleasant, to end on a note of agreement with Mr Krutch. He thinks highly of *Rasselas*. 'To Johnson's contemporaries', he tells us, indicating its more obvious relation to Johnson's Augustanism, 'the book was a dazzling specimen of that "true wit" which consists in the perfect statement of something which "oft was thought but ne'er so well expressed".' But, he rightly insists,

Johnson did something more than merely rephrase the commonplaces which have long served to demonstrate that all is vanity. . . . His pessimism, in other words, was not merely of that vulgar sort which is no more than a lament over the failure of worldly prosperity. It was, instead, the pessimism which is more properly called the tragic sense of life. . . .

It was a tragic sense of life that was, at the same time, both moral centrality and a profound commonsense: '*Vivite laeti* is one of the great rules of health', he wrote to Mrs Thrale – Mrs Thrale who knew the tragic Johnson as Boswell did not. We can see why Jane Austen, whose 'civilization' is so different a thing from what the modish cult makes it, admired *Rasselas* to such effect that its influence is to be found, not only on the surface (where it is obvious enough), but in the very ethos of her work; so that *Rasselas* has more right to a place in the history of the English novel than Defoe and Sterne together. Further, in *Rasselas* we have something deeply English that relates Johnson and Jane Austen to Crabbe.

JOHNSON AS POET

THE addition of Johnson's poems to the *Oxford English Texts* is a matter for quiet satisfaction. Everyone, of course, knows that Johnson was a great Man of Letters, but it doesn't follow that the proposition, 'Johnson, after all, was a great English writer', is not one to which those who see its truth as evident are often provoked. In fact, it cannot even be said that the Johnson of general currency is Boswell's Johnson; he is Boswell's Johnson edited in the interests of middlebrow complacency; revised downwards to the level of a good-mixing that, unlike the sociality of the eighteenth-century Club, is hostile to serious intellectual standards. For though poor Boswell was quite unintelligent about literature, as he betrays whenever he expresses for our benefit those respectful disagreements with Johnson's judgements, he exhibits in his concern to stress Johnson's intellectual distinction (see, for instance, the recurrent transcriptions of opinions, argued at length, about points of law) a seriousness that has no place in the modern cult of the Great Clubman.

These are the days, indeed, in which you can stock up on Johnson – traits, points, anecdotage, all the legend with its picturesque and humorous properties – without being bothered to read even Boswell He and Mrs Thrale might seem to be readable enough, but those little works of mediation which come out from time to time are apparently offered as being more so. Johnson, like his prose, is paid the tribute of appreciative parody. The limitations of such appreciation are, of course, radical: just as those witty prose-parodies cultivate an obtuseness to the unique Johnsonian strength, so the exploitations of Johnson the personality provoke one to the comment that, after all, for Boswell Johnson represented challenging and exacting standards, intellectual and moral – standards far above the level of *l'homme sensuel moyen*.

Johnson was a great prose-writer, and it has been well said that his poetry has the virtues of his prose. This last proposition can count on a general unenthusiastic concurrence. It is worth noting that in the *Oxford Book of Eighteenth Century Verse*, which has

over seven hundred pages and the anthologist of which is one of
the editors of the Oxford Johnson, *The Vanity of Human Wishes*
(which forms a considerable proportion of the good poetry produced in the century by poets other than Pope, and, though a
great poem, is not very long) is represented by four short extracts,
occupying four pages in all. But we may take it that to include a
poet in the Oxford Standard Texts is to recognize his substantial
classical standing.

However, while to see Johnson the poetic classic paid all the
honours of exhaustive scholarship must give satisfaction, the satisfaction, as noted above, is quiet. For a perusal of the four hundred
pages of this handsome and scrupulously edited volume (a
necessary acquisition for all the libraries) yields nothing to add to
the familiar small body of his verse that deserves currency. *The
Vanity of Human Wishes*, the inferior *London*, the Drury Lane *Pro-
logue*, *A Short Song of Congratulation* ('Long-expected one and
twenty'), and the stanzas on the death of Levet – what other
poem (though no doubt a whole list of odds and ends could be
collected) is there to add to this list?

A large proportion of the volume consists of Latin verse, the
presence of which serves to provoke reflections on the difference
between Johnson's Latinizing and Milton's. For though (to speak
with Johnsonian largeness) no one ever again will read Johnson's
Latin, yet that his English would not have been what it is but for
his cultivation of Latin is indisputable. He, like Ben Jonson, aims
at Latin qualities and effects, yet contrives to be in his own way, as
Ben Jonson is in his, natively and robustly English. They have in
common this general difference from Milton, and the particular
nature and conditions of this difference in each case might, by a
university director of literary studies, be proposed to a student as
a profitable matter of inquiry.

Over a hundred pages of the volume are occupied by *Irene*. As
one re-reads it one's mind goes back to the characteristic definition: 'A dramatick exhibition is a book recited with concomitants that increase or diminish the effect'. Partly, of course,
this is to be taken as expressing (what one sympathizes with) a
literary bias – a bias, wholly respectable in an age when elevated
drama, by Shakespeare or by Home, was an opportunity for
Garrick, and declamatory histrionic virtuosity was the highest the

theatre had to offer. The assumption that a work of art in words is to be judged as literature seems in any case reasonable, and in not being, where dramatic literature was in question, alive to the complications attendant on the qualifying adjective Johnson, in that age, was not alone. Yet, as one re-reads *Irene* – so patently conceived as a book to be recited, and so patently leaving to the 'concomitants' the impossible task of making it a theatre-piece – one realizes that 'literary bias' misses what is most interesting in Johnson's case. That he has no sense of the theatre, and worse, cannot present or conceive his themes dramatically – these points are obvious. The point one finds oneself making is a matter of noting afresh certain familiar characteristics of his literary habit: his essential bent is undramatic in a sense of the adjective that goes deeper than the interest of the 'dramatic critic'. His good poetry is as radically undramatic as good poetry can be, and the failure in dramatic conception so patent in *Irene* is intimately related to the essential qualities of *The Vanity of Human Wishes*. This is great poetry, though unlike anything that this description readily suggests to modern taste; it is a poetry of statement, exposition and reflection: nothing could be remoter from the Shakespearean use of language – 'In this passage is exerted all the force of poetry, that force which calls new powers into being, which embodies sentiment, and animates matter' – than the Johnsonian. Johnson – and in this he is representative of his age – has neither the gift nor the aim of capturing in words, and presenting to speak for themselves, significant particularities of sensation, perception and feeling, the significance coming out in complex total effects, which are also left to speak for themselves; he starts with general ideas and general propositions, and enforces them by discussion, comment and illustration. It is by reason of these characteristics that his verse, like that which he found most congenial, may fairly be said to have the virtues of good prose. And it seems reasonable to associate with his radically undramatic habit ('dramatic incapacity' it might be called, if we remember that the positive result of a positive training will have its negative aspect) Johnson's concern for poetic justice, and his inability to appreciate the ways in which works of art *act* their moral judgements. 'He sacrifices virtue to convenience, and is so much more careful to please than to instruct, that he seems to write without any moral purpose'.

The conditions that enable Johnson to give his moral declamation the weight of lived experience and transform his eighteenth-century generalities into that extraordinary kind of concreteness[1] –

> Delusive Fortune hears th' incessant call
> They mount, they shine, evaporate, and fall.
>
> When first the college rolls receive his name
> The young enthusiast quits his ease for fame,
> Through all his veins the fever of renown
> Burns from the strong contagion of the gown;
> O'er Bodley's dome his future labours spread,
> And Bacon's mansion trembles o'er his head.
>
> Such bribes the rapid Greek o'er Asia whirl'd,
> For such the steady Romans shook the world

– these conditions fail him when he attempts drama. His characters declaim eloquent commonplaces – he cannot make them do anything else, but the dramatic ambition has robbed them of the familiar strength and substance; the great moralist, reduced to making a show of speaking through his *personæ*, is less than himself:

> Submissive and prepar'd for each event,
> Now let us wait the last award of Heaven,
> Secure of Happiness from Flight or Conquest,
> Nor fear the Fair and Learn'd can want Protection.
> The mighty Tuscan courts the banish'd Arts
> To kind Italia's hospitable Shades;
> There shall soft Leisure wing th' excursive Soul,
> And Peace propitious smile on fond Desire;
> There shall despotic Eloquence resume
> Her ancient Empire o'er the yielding Heart;
> There Poetry shall tune her sacred Voice,
> And wake from Ignorance the Western World.

Irene is all like that. And there too we have the measure of Johnson's blank verse. He is clearly determined that *his* verse shall not be changed into the 'periods of a declaimer', and that it shall not be said that the audience cannot easily perceive 'where the

1. I have discussed it in some detail in *Revaluation*

lines end or begin' (see his remarks on blank-verse in the *Life* of Milton). In couplets, of course, he couldn't have written so dismally. With the absence of rhyme and of the movement of the couplet goes the absence of wit. And without the wit he is without the Johnsonian weight.

TRAGEDY AND THE 'MEDIUM'

A Note on Mr Santayana's 'Tragic Philosophy'

THERE appeared in *Scrutiny* some years ago (March 1936) an essay by Mr Santayana, *Tragic Philosophy*, in which I have always found valuable stimulus to disagreement. To say 'always' is to suggest that I have re-read it a good deal, and I have. In fact, I am indebted to the essay for its use as a stock resort in the discussion of Tragedy with undergraduates reading for the English Tripos. I don't want to suggest that the debt incurred has been purely a matter of opportunities for disagreement. *Tragic Philosophy* exhibits Mr Santayana's characteristic brilliance and wit – that rare wit (not rare in Mr Santayana, of course) which is the focussed sharpness of illuminating intelligence. But it has striking weaknesses (or so I see them), and it is the considerations raised by one of them in particular that I am concerned with here. They are considerations that take me back to a point I made in discussing Johnson's criticism.

Many admirers of Mr Santayana besides myself must have been surprised at the way in which he plays off Macbeth's speech beginning *Tomorrow and tomorrow and tomorrow* against the passage attributed by Dante to Piccarda de Donati in which occurs the line

E'n la sua volontade è nostra pace.

True, earlier in the essay he has said that Shakespeare 'like an honest miscellaneous dramatist . . . was putting into the mouths of his different characters the sentiments that, for the moment, were suggested to him by their predicaments'. But he unmistakably slips into arguing as if Macbeth's comment on the plight to which the action has brought him may be taken as Shakespeare's, just as Piccarda may be taken as speaking for Dante. Mr Santayana's point, I recognize, is that Shakespeare hasn't a settled and coherent philosophy to set against Dante's – though 'possibly if he had been pressed by some troublesome friend to propound a personal philosophy, he might have found in his irration nothing

else to fall back upon than the animal despair of Macbeth. Fortunately we may presume that burgherly comfort and official
orthodoxy saved him from being unreasonably pressed'. But we
are at the same time invited, unambiguously, to take Macbeth's
speech as representing such substitute for a philosophy as Shakespeare, in this play, has to offer:

I questioned at the beginning whether the poetic value of unlike
things could be pronounced equal: and if now I compare this whole
passage with the passage from *Macbeth* I find that to my sense they are
incommensurable. Both are notable passages, if that is all that was
meant; but they belong to different poetic worlds, appealing to and
developing different sides of the mind. And there is more than disparity
between these two worlds; there is contrariety and hostility between
them, in as much as each professes to include and to subordinate the
other, and in so doing to annul its tragic dignity and moral finality. For
the mood of Macbeth, religion and philosophy are insane vapours; for
the mood of Dante, Macbeth is possessed by the devil. There is no
possible common ground, no common criterion even of taste or beauty.

For the mood of Shakespeare too, we are moved to retort,
Macbeth is possessed by the devil: the tragic dignity and moral
finality of Shakespeare's world are focussed in Macbeth's cry of
'animal despair' only in so far as this refers us, inevitably (one
would have thought), to the quite other effect of the total action
– the total action in relation to which the speech has its significance. By his plunge into crime, taken in fatal ignorance of his
nature –

> If it were done, when 'tis done, then 'twere well
> It were done quickly

– he has confounded 'this little state of man' and the impersonal
order from which it is inseparable. It is not on his extinction after
a tale of sound and fury, signifying nothing, that the play ends,
and his valedictory nihilism is the vindication of the moral and
spiritual order he has outraged, and which is re-established in the
close.

How, one asks, can Mr Santayana have failed to see things so
obvious? The answer follows immediately on the sentence of his
last quoted:

We might at best say that both poets succeed in conveying what they wish to convey, and that in that sense their skill is equal: but I hardly think this is true in fact, because in Shakespeare the medium is rich and thick and more important than the idea; whereas in Dante the medium is as unvarying and simple as possible, and meant to be transparent. Even in this choice passage, there are stretches of pure scholastic reasoning, not poetical at all to our sensuous and romantic apprehension; yet the studious and rapt poet feels himself carried on those wings of logic into a paradise of truth, where choir answers choir, and everything is beautiful. A clear and transparent medium is admirable, when we love what we have to say; but when what we have to say is nothing previously definite, expressiveness depends on stirring the waters deeply, suggesting a thousand half-thoughts and letting the very unutterableness of our passion become manifest in our disjointed words. The medium then becomes dominant: but can this be called success in expression? It is rather success in making an impression, if the reader is impressed . . .

The critic who falls so complete a victim to the word 'medium' as Mr Santayana here shows himself, doesn't, it is plain, understand the poetic – and the essentially dramatic – use of language that Shakespeare's verse supremely exemplifies. He cannot, then, understand the nature of the organization that goes with that use of language: he cannot appreciate the ways in which the themes and significances of the play are dramatically presented. Take, for instance, this betraying sentence:

So at this point in *Macbeth*, where Seneca would have unrolled the high maxims of orthodox Stoicism, Shakespeare gives us the humours of his distracted hero; a hero nonplussed, confounded, stultified in his own eyes, a dying gladiator, a blinded lion at bay.

We don't, when we are responding properly, say that 'Shakespeare gives us Macbeth's speech': it comes to us, not from the author, but from the play, emerging dramatically from a dramatic context. It offers no parallel to Seneca's 'high maxims'. And the 'philosophy', moral significance, or total upshot, of the play isn't stated but enacted. But for Mr Santayana significance is a matter of 'ideas', and 'ideas' have to be stated, and so, looking for an epitomizing statement, he excises that speech from the organism to which it belongs and fixes it directly on Shakespeare, and gives us his surprising commentary.

We have only shifted the question a stage further back, of

course. How can so subtle an intelligence as Mr Santayana's have let itself be so victimized? The answer, I think, is that he is a philosopher. This is not to suggest that a philosopher can, for his own purposes, safely dispense with the ability to comprehend Shakespearean poetry. On the contrary, Mr Santayana's inappreciation seems to me to go with a naïveté about the nature of conceptual thought that is common among philosophers, to their disadvantage as such. In venturing so far I may be merely exposing myself; but this, I am sure, must be said: to demand that poetry should be a 'medium' for 'previously definite' ideas is arbitrary, and betrays a radical incomprehension. What Mr Santayana calls 'Shakespeare's medium' creates what it conveys; 'previously definite' ideas put into a 'clear and transparent' medium wouldn't have been definite enough for Shakespeare's purpose. It is in place to quote again here a passage of D. W. Harding on Isaac Rosenberg:

Usually when we speak of finding words to express a thought we seem to mean that we have the thought rather close to formulation and use it to measure the adequacy of any possible phrasing that occurs to us, treating words as servants of the idea. 'Clothing a thought in language', whatever it means psychologically, seems a fair metaphorical description of most speaking and writing. Of Rosenberg's work it would be misleading. He – like many poets in some degree, one supposes – brought language to bear on the incipient thought at an earlier stage of its development. Instead of the emerging idea being racked slightly so as to fit a more familiar approximation of itself, and words found for *that*, Rosenberg let it manipulate words almost from the beginning, often without insisting on the controls of logic and intelligibility.

The control over Shakespeare's words in *Macbeth* (for what Harding describes is the essentially poetic use of language, a use in which Shakespeare is pre-eminent) is a complex dramatic theme vividly and profoundly realized – not thought of, but possessed imaginatively in its concreteness, so that, as it grows in specificity, it in turn possesses the poet's mind and commands expression. To explain how so marvellous a definiteness of conception and presentment can have been missed by Mr Santayana one has to invoke a training in inappropriate linguistic habits – inappropriate, that is, to the reading of Shakespeare: unable to relinquish irrelevant demands, the critic cannot take what is offered; misinformed and blinded by preconceptions, he cannot see what is there.

The case, readers will have noted, has much in common with Johnson's. Mr Santayana too has a way of paradoxically appreciating, while exhibiting his inability to appreciate, like that I have pointed to in Johnson's dealings with Shakespeare:

But as living poetry, as a mould and stimulus for honest feeling, is Dante for us at all comparable to Shakespeare? Shakespeare, in passages such as this from *Macbeth*, is orchestrated. He trills away into fancy: what was daylight a moment ago, suddenly becomes a candle: we are not thinking or reasoning, we are dreaming. He needs but to say 'all our yesterdays', and presently the tedium of childhood, the tedium of labour and illness, the vacancy of friendships lost, rise like ghosts before us, and fill us with a sense of the unreality of all that once seemed most real. When he mentions 'a poor player' we think at once of the poet himself, because our minds are biographical and our sympathies novelesque; we feel the misery and the lurid contrasts of a comedian's life; and the existence that just now seemed merely vain now seems also tempestuous and bitter.

Can we say that the author of this cannot understand the Shakespearean use of language, and cannot therefore appreciate the nature and force of the Shakespearean 'medium'? What we have here implies, surely, a pretty good analysis of the speech? But Mr Santayana goes on:

And the rhythms help; the verse struts and bangs, holds our attention suspended, obliges our thoughts to become rhetorical, and brings our declamation round handsomely to a grand finale. We should hardly have found courage in ourselves for so much passion and theatricality; but we bless Shakespeare for enabling us still to indulge in such emotions, and to relieve ourselves of a weight that we hardly knew we were carrying.

These sentences are perhaps not so unequivocal as Johnson's pejorative remarks, but it is nevertheless impossible not to take them as cancelling the appreciation. We relate them to these earlier sentences, and their significant failure to distinguish between irresponsible exuberance and that mature Shakespearean mastery of language:

Shakespeare was a professional actor, a professional dramatist; his greatness lay there, and in the gift of the gab: in that exuberance and joy in language which everybody had in that age, but he supremely. The Renaissance needed no mastering living religion, no mastering living philosophy. Life was gayer without thim.

The implications are plain enough. It would clearly be misleading to say that the critic who can express himself thus can properly appreciate Shakespeare's poetry. He clearly cannot appreciate the organization that has its local life in the verse. He has no inkling of the way in which the mastering living theme commands and controls the words.

It will have been noted that in the former of the two passages just quoted Mr Santayana gives us an account of tragic catharsis. It is peculiarly interesting because in it he associates the cathartic effect with a poetic use (as he understands it) of language. We are bound to question his understanding, and in attempting to provide our own account of a poetic use we find ourselves exploring for a profounder and more satisfactory account of Tragedy – of the tragic – than he implies here, or offers elsewhere in his essay. This at any rate is what, in my experience, gives the essay its peculiar value.

The view of the tragic implied in Mr Santayana's account of catharsis seems a very limited one. Does Shakespearean tragedy, does the tragic in *Macbeth*, amount to no more than this? If so, where can we look for anything profounder? For surely the tragic experience is, or can be, a more important and serious matter than Mr Santayana here suggests?

To postulate a 'tragic experience' or 'tragic effect' and then seek to define it is to lay oneself open to the suspicion of proposing a solemn and time-honoured academic game. Yet the critical contemplation of the profoundest things in literature does lead to the idea of such an experience, and we can see to it that the attempt at definition shall not be the kind of futility we associate with the Grand Style or the Sublime and the Beautiful. It need hardly be said, for instance, that what we are concerned with will not be found in all tragedies, or in most. And next, it is well to put aside the term 'catharsis': its promptings don't seem to be at all helpful, and the exercise of refining upon, or interpreting away, Aristotle's medical metaphor may be left to the unfortunate student who knows that he may be required to 'apply' the *Poetics* to Shakespeare, Webster, Racine, Ibsen or Eugene O'Neill in the examination-room. If 'calm' may properly be predicted of the tragic experience, it is certainly not 'calm of mind, all passion spent' in the natural suggestion of that phrase. According to what seems valid in the current notion of the tragic there is rather something in the nature of an exalting effect. We have contemplated a painful action, involving death and the destruction of the good, admirable and sympathetic, and yet instead of being depressed we enjoy a sense of enhanced vitality.

I take this general account as granted – as recognized for sound as far as it goes. The conditions of something ostensibly answering to it are described by Mr Santayana in his account of the Senecan tragic attitude or philosophy:

Mr Eliot says that this philosophy is derived from Seneca; and it is certain that in Seneca's tragedies, if not in his treatises, there is a pomp of diction, a violence of pose, and a suicidal despair not unlike the tone of this passage. But would Seneca ever have said that life signifies nothing? It signified for him the universal reign of law, of reason, of the will of God. Fate was inhuman, it was cruel, it excited and crushed every finite wish; yet there was something in man that shared that disdain for humanity, and triumphed in that ruthless march of order and necessity. Something superior, not inferior, Seneca would have said; something that not only raised the mind into sympathy with the truth of nature and the decrees of heaven, but that taught the blackest tragedy to sing in verse. The passions in foreseeing their defeat became prophets, in remembering it became poets, and they created the noblest beauties by defying and transcending death.

Mr Santayana seems to imply (he says nothing crude, of course, and he shows considerable suppleness in presenting his case) that Seneca has an advantage over Shakespeare in this tragic philosophy, however the total comparison between the two poets may work out. Without granting this, we may at any rate feel that the formula for the tragic it represents, in Mr Santayana's account of it, deserves pondering. It deserves pondering because, though clearly unsatisfactory, it has (we feel) something of the right form.

It is most clearly unsatisfactory because, in the terms in which it stands, it is equivocal. In spite of the 'something superior, not inferior', it reminds us too much of 'the bitter beauty of the universe and the frail human pride that confronts it for a moment undismayed'. It is, in fact, not clearly enough distinguishable from *A Free Man's Worship:*

> Brief and powerless is Man's life; on him and all his race the slow, sure doom falls pitiless and dark. Blind to good and evil, reckless of destruction, omnipotent matter rolls on its relentless way; for Man, condemned today to lose his dearest, tomorrow himself to pass through the gate of darkness, it remains only to cherish, ere yet the blow falls, the lofty thoughts that ennoble his little day; disdaining the coward terrors of the slave of Fate, to worship at the shrine that his own hands have built; undismayed by the empire of chance, to preserve a mind free from the wanton tyranny that rules his outward life; proudly defiant of the irresistible forces that tolerate, for a moment, his know-ledge and his condemnation, to sustain alone, a weary but un-yielding Atlas, the world that his own ideals have fashioned despite the tramp-ling march of unconscious power.[1]

The tragic experience, however it is to be defined, is certainly not anything that encourages, or permits, an indulgence in the dramatization of one's nobly-suffering self. Mr Santayana's Seneca, of course, doesn't propose anything as crude. Neverthe-less, as we ponder the '*disdain* for humanity' and the '*defying* . . . death', it strikes us that the Senecan attitude as described is peri-lously ready to subside into something of a kindred order to the prose of *A Free Mans' Worship*: the differences aren't radical enough. We recall Mr Eliot's observations (in *Shakespeare and the Stoicism of Seneca*) on the Senecan influence in Elizabethan drama, and its relation to the trick of rhetorical self-boosting.

And whether Mr Eliot is right or not in associating Othello's self-dramatizing habit with the Senecan influence, he gives us the cue for saying that the attitude represented by Othello's last speech is radically untragic. This is so obvious as to seem, perhaps, not worth saying: Othello, for those who don't join in the traditional sentimentalization of the play, is a very obvious case. The essential point that has to be made is that his valedictory *coup de théâtre* represents a rhetorical inflation, a headily emotional glorification, of an incapacity for tragic experience that marks the ordinary moments of us all.

1. Bertrand Russell, *Mysticism and Logic*, p. 56.

There is a passage of one of D. H. Lawrence's letters[1] that came into my mind when this point was under discussion:

I am so sick of people: they preserve an evil, bad, separating spirit under the warm cloak of good words. That is intolerable in them. The Conservative talks about the old and glorious national ideal, the Liberal talks about this great struggle for right in which the nation is engaged, the peaceful women talk about disarmament and international peace. Bertie Russell talks about democratic control and the educating of the artisan, and all this, all this goodness, is just a warm and cosy cloak for a bad spirit. They all want the same thing: a continuing in this state of disintegration wherein each separate little ego is an independent little principality by itself. What does Russell really want? He wants to keep his own established ego, his finite and ready-defined self intact, free from contact and connexion. He wants to be ultimately a free agent. That is what they all want, ultimately – that is what is at the back of all international peace-for-ever and democratic control talks: they want an outward system of nullity, which they call peace and goodwill, so that in their own souls they can be independent little gods, referred nowhere and to nothing, little mortal Absolutes, secure from question. That is at the back of all Liberalism, Fabianism and democracy. It stinks. It is the will of the louse. And the Conservative either wants to bully or to be bullied. And the young authoritarian, the young man who turns Roman Catholic in order to put himself under the authority of the Church, in order to enjoy the aesthetic quality of obedience, he is such a swine with cringing hind-quarters . . . etc.

The particular justice or injustice of these animadversions needn't be discussed: one wouldn't go to Lawrence for judicial fairness towards persons or parties, and there are necessary political and kindred activities at levels at which the characteristic Laurentian contribution may well appear the reverse of helpful or encouraging. But it is just his part, as he sees it, to insist – with a passionate insistence exasperating to energizers for movements and policies – that there are profounder levels; levels of experience that, though they tend constantly to be ignored, are always, in respect of any concern for life and health, supremely relevant. The most effective insistence would be tragic art. Lawrence, in fact, might fairly (for my present purpose) be said to be pronouncing of the attitudes he stigmatizes that they are incompatible with tragic experience.

1. *Letters*, p. 247.

At any rate, it is an essential part of the definition of the tragic that it breaks down, or undermines and supersedes, such attitudes. It establishes below them a kind of profound impersonality in which experience matters, not because it is mine – because it is to me it belongs or happens, or because it subserves or issues in purpose or will, but because it is what it is, the 'mine' mattering only in so far as the individual sentience is the indispensable focus of experience.

The attainment in literature of this level, and of organization at this level, would seem to involve the poetic use of language, or of processes that amount to that. By the 'poetic' use of language I mean that which I described as 'dramatic' in discussing Johnson's criticism and the limits to his appreciation of Shakespeare. For Johnson, I said, expression was necessarily statement; critically, he couldn't come to terms with the use of language, not as a medium in which to put 'previously definite' ideas, but for exploratory creation. Poetry as creating what it presents, and as presenting something that stands there to speak for itself, or, rather, that isn't a matter of saying, but of being and enacting, he couldn't properly understand. In this he is representative of the eighteenth century, and (the point was made in discussion) it is significant that that century, which went in so much for formal tragedy, should have shown itself so utterly incapable of attaining the tragic. The use of language for the expression of 'previously definite' ideas needn't, of course, carry with it social and rational conventions as obviously limiting as the Augustan, but in proposing for the poet as his true business the lucid arrangement of ready-minted concepts Mr Santayana proposes (it seems to me) limitations as essentially disabling for tragedy as the Augustan. It may not be altogether true to say that in such a use of language – in the business of expressing 'previously definite' ideas – one is necessarily confined to one's 'established ego', one's 'ready-defined self'. But it does seem as if the 'tragic' transcendence of ordinary experience that can be attained by a mind tied to such a use must inevitably tend towards the rhetorical order represented by Mr Santayana's account of Seneca's tragic philosophy (or – shall I say? – by the Senecan attitude as no doubt fairly conveyed by Mr Santayana).

Such an attitude is really an exaltation of the 'established ego' and, as we have seen, cannot be securely distinguished from the kind of attitude one strikes. The attainment of the level of experience at which emancipation from the 'ready-defined self' is compelled involves an essentially different order of expression; one in which heightening is deeping, exaltation has nothing alcoholic about it, and rhetoric (as in *Othello* – for those who take what Shakespeare offers) is 'placed'.

It is interesting to see Yeats, in his own way and by his own characteristic approach, making the point in question. He rebels, in his Aesthetically-given youth, against the flatness of the dialogue in post-Ibsenian drama (see *Essays*). Modern naturalistic speech, he feels, precludes beauty and significance. We can never, of course, feel quite safe, reading these protests in Yeatsian prose, against a suggestion of 'Rosa Alchemica' and the 'trembling of the veil'. Nevertheless he makes the necessary points and makes them firmly. You cannot, he notes (see, *e.g.*, p. 339), be passionate in educated modern speech: Ibsen in the attempt to overcome this difficulty invented a conventional rhetoric. Poetry, with attendant non-naturalistic conventions (see the essay on *Certain Noble Plays of Japan*), is necessary in order to provide the distance and the frame without which there can be no intensity of the right kind. And then we come to this (*The Tragic Theatre*): 'I saw plainly what should have been plain from the first line I had written, that tragedy must always be a drowning, a breaking of the dykes that separate man from man . . .' Yeats's intention in this, which is immediately related to his preoccupations with convention and the 'medium', has unmistakably the directest relation to what I have been trying to say above.

We might further invoke as obviously relevant Nietzsche's insistence on the Dionysiac. But perhaps after all the Nietzschean witness had better be dispensed with; at the best it introduces a disturbing vibration. The Nietzschean context is uncongenial to the present purpose, and a glance at it prompts the remark that the tragic calm (if 'calm' is the word), while not the product of any laxative catharsis, is not in the least the calm of the tensed and self-approving will.

The sense of heightened life that goes with the tragic experience is conditioned by a transcending of the ego – an escape from all attitudes of self-assertion. 'Escape', perhaps, is not altogether a

good word, since it might suggest something negative and irresponsible (just as 'Dionysiac' carries unacceptable suggestions of
the Dark Gods). Actually the experience is constructive or
creative, and involves a recognizing positive value as in some way
defined and vindicated by death. It is as if we were challenged at
the profoundest level with the question, 'In what does the significance of life reside?', and found ourselves contemplating, for
answer, a view of life, and of the things giving it value, that
makes the valued appear unquestionably more important than
the valuer, so that significance lies, clearly and inescapably, in the
willing adhesion of the individual self to something other than
itself. Here, for instance, is D. A. Traversi writing[1] on *Antony and
Cleopatra* (with his relative valuation of which, I had better add
by the way, I don't agree):

> For death, which had seemed in the Sonnets and early tragedies to be
> incontrovertible evidence of the subjection of love and human values to
> Time, now becomes by virtue of Shakespeare's poetic achievement an
> instrument of release, the necessary condition of an experience which,
> though dependent upon Time and circumstance, is by virtue of its
> *value* and intensity incommensurate with them – that is 'immortal'.
> The emotions of Antony and Cleopatra are built upon 'dungy earth',
> upon 'Nilus' slime', and so upon Time which these elements by their
> nature imply; but, just as earth and slime are quickened into fire and
> air, whilst retaining their sensible qualities as constituent parts of the
> final experience, so Time itself becomes a necessary element in the
> creation of 'immortality'.

I quote this for its relevant suggestiveness. It seems to me to
compare very interestingly with the following passage from
D. W. Harding (whose distinctive strength in criticism – I add,
in case I should have appeared to be betraying metaphysical
ambitions – goes with a psychologist's approach):

> Death in itself was not his concern, but only death at the moment
> when life was simplified and intensified; this he felt had a significance
> which he represents by immortality. For him it was no more than the
> immortality of the possibilities of life. This immortality and the value
> he glimpses in the living effort of war in no way mitigate his suffering
> at the human pain and waste. The value of what was destroyed seemed
> to him to have been brought into sight only by the destruction, and he

1. *Approach to Shakespeare*, pp. 126–7.

had to respond to both facts without allowing either to neutralize the other. It is this which is most impressive in Rosenberg – the complexity of experience which he was strong enough to permit himself and which his technique was fine enough to reveal.[1]

I will not attempt to develop the kind of discussion of Tragedy that the juxtaposition of these passages might seem to promise – or threaten. It suits my purpose rather to note the stress laid by Harding on 'complexity' and 'technique' (compare Traversi's 'poetic achievement' – a phrase that sums up much preceding analysis of Shakespeare's verse), and to note further that he passes on to 'impersonality':

> To say that Rosenberg tried to understand all that the war stood for means probably that he tried to expose the whole of himself to it. In one letter he describes as an intention what he obviously achieved: 'I will not leave a corner of my consciousness covered up, but saturate myself with the strange and extraordinary new conditions of this life . . .' This willingness – and ability – to let himself be new-born into the new situation, not subduing his experience to his established personality, is a large part, if not the whole secret of the robustness which characterizes his best work . . . Here as in all the war poems his suffering and discomfort are unusually *direct*; there is no secondary distress arising from the sense that these things *ought not* to be. He was given up to realizing fully what *was*. He expressed his attitude in *The Unicorn*:

> Lilith: I think there is more sorrow in the world
>   Than man can bear.

> Nubian: None can exceed their limit, lady:
>   You either bear or break.

> It was Rosenberg's exposure of his whole personality that gave his work its quality of impersonality.[2]

What Harding says about Rosenberg in these passages has clearly the closest relevance to Tragedy. And it is especially significant, for my theme, that they belong to the essay containing that discussion of the poetic use of language which I have found so useful in defining the limitations, in respect of the tragic, of Johnson and (I suggest) Mr Santayana.

This significance, my main concern in this note, will get a

1. *Scrutiny*, Vol. III, pp. 362–3 (*The Poetry of Isaac Rosenberg*).
2. *Ibid.*

suitable parting stress, if we consider I. A. Richard's treatment of 'impersonality', which has, on the surface, resemblances to Harding's. Dr Richards deals with 'impersonality' and Tragedy together in the same chapter (xxxii) of *The Principles of Literary Criticism*. These pages (245–253) contain some of the most valuably suggestive things in the book, and if, for my convenience, I dwell on the weakness, I have at any rate the justification that they are entailed by Richards's essential Neo-Benthamite ambition, which is irreconcilable with his best insight. (And I am urging that these pages should be read, or re-read.)

The ambition asserts itself characteristically when Richards, having told us that, in the full tragic experience, the 'mind does not shy away from anything, it does not protect itself with any illusion, it stands uncomforted, unintimidated, alone and self-reliant', goes on to pronounce toughly (p. 246):

The joy which is so strangely at the heart of the experience is not an indication that 'all's right with the world' or that 'somewhere, somehow, there is Justice'; it is an indication that all is right here and now in the nervous system.

For him, of course, Tragedy is the supreme instance of the inclusive organization of impulses; it is 'perhaps the most general all-accepting, all-ordering experience known' (p. 247). Experience, for the purposes of the new science, must be reducible to unit impulses, so that evaluation may be quantitative. We are not, then, surprised when we read (p. 248):

This balanced poise, stable through its power of inclusion, not through the force of its exclusions, is not peculiar to Tragedy. It is a general characteristic of all the most valuable experiences of the arts. It can be given by a carpet or a pot or by a gesture as unmistakably as by the Parthenon, it may come about through an epigram as clearly as through a Sonata.

I must confess myself to have found, with surprise, that I had carried away a wrong impression from this passage – an impression that Richards actually pronounces the tragic experience to be obtained from a carpet or a pot. But it is easy to see how I came to form it, the argument moving as it does, with so easy and uninhibited a transition. And it is not at all easy to see how Richards can satisfactorily explain the differences between any experience

fitly to be called 'tragic' and the most inclusively-poised experience a carpet or a pot can be supposed to give. The scientifico-
psychological ambition entails his taking his diagrams of poised
and organized 'impulses' or 'appetencies' too seriously: he
couldn't go on supposing he took his science seriously if he even
began to recognize the remoteness of their relevance to concrete
experiences.

This may seem, so late in the day, too obvious a kind of
criticism to be worth reiterating; but I want to give it a special
point in relation to my main argument. No theory of Tragedy
can amount to more than a blackboard diagram, a mere schematic
substitute for understanding, unless it is associated with an
adequate appreciation of the subtleties of poetic (or creative)
language – the subtleties that are supremely illustrated in the
poetry of Shakespeare. Such an appreciation, if operative, would
have inhibited Dr Richard's reliance on his 'impulses' and his
'nervous system'. This point is not the less worth making because
he has always, in his Neo-Benthamite way, been interested in
language and the meaning of meaning. He has, since the phase represented by *The Principles of Literary Criticism*, specialized in
Semasiology. But no interest in language that is Benthamite in
spirit, or controlled by a Neo-Benthamite ambition, can afford to
recognize the profoundest aspects of linguistic 'communication'
– those we find ourselves contemplating when we contemplate in
the concrete the nature of tragic impersonality. Such an interest
can no more be adequate to them than the Utilitarian calculus –
with its water-tight unit self, confined, for all self-transcendence,
to external transactions with other selves – could engage on the
kind of interest in moral issues taken by George Eliot.

DIABOLIC INTELLECT AND THE NOBLE HERO:

or *The Sentimentalist's Othello*

*O*THELLO, it will be very generally granted, is of all Shakespeare's great tragedies the simplest: the theme is limited and sharply defined, and the play, everyone agrees, is a brilliantly successful piece of workmanship. The effect is one of a noble, 'classical' clarity – of firm, clear outlines, unblurred and undistracted by cloudy recessions, metaphysical aura, or richly symbolical ambiguities.[1] There would, it seems, be something like a consensus in this sense. And yet it is of *Othello* that one can say bluntly, as of no other of the great tragedies, that it suffers in current appreciation an essential and denaturing falsification.

The generally recognized peculiarity of *Othello* among the tragedies may be indicated by saying that it lends itself as no other of them does to the approach classically associated with Bradley's name: even *Othello* (it will be necessary to insist) is poetic drama, a dramatic poem, and not a psychological novel written in dramatic form and draped in poetry, but relevant discussion of its tragic significance will nevertheless be mainly a matter of character-analysis. It would, that is, have lent itself uniquely well to Bradley's approach if Bradley had made his approach consistently and with moderate intelligence. Actually, however, the section on *Othello* in *Shakespearean Tragedy* is more extravagant in misdirected scrupulosity than any of the others; it is, with a concentration of Bradley's comical solemnity, completely wrongheaded – grossly and palpably false to the evidence it offers to weigh. Grossly and palpably? – yet Bradley's *Othello* is substan-

1. Cf. 'We seem to be aware in it of a certain limitation, a partial suppression of that element in Shakespeare's mind which unites him with the mystical poets and with the great musicians and philosophers.' – A. C. Bradley, *Shakespearean Tragedy*, p. 185.

'*Othello* is a story of intrigue rather than a visionary statement.' – G. Wilson Knight, *The Wheel of Fire*, p. 107.

tially that of common acceptance. And here is the reason for dealing with it, even though not only Bradley but, in its turn, disrespect for Bradley (one gathers) has gone out of fashion (as a matter of fact he is still a very potent and mischievous influence).

According to the version of *Othello* elaborated by Bradley the tragedy is the undoing of the noble Moor by the devilish cunning of Iago. Othello we are to see as a nearly faultless hero whose strength and virtue are turned against him. Othello and Desdemona, so far as their fate depended on their characters and untampered-with mutual relations, had every ground for expecting the happiness that romantic courtship had promised. It was external evil, the malice of the demi-devil, that turned a happy story of romantic love – of romantic lovers who were qualified to live happily ever after, so to speak – into a tragedy. This – it is the traditional version of *Othello* and has, moreover, the·support of Coleridge – is to sentimentalize Shakespeare's tragedy and to displace its centre.

Here is Bradley:

> Turning from the hero and the heroine to the third principal character we observe (what has often been pointed out) that the action and catastrophe of *Othello* depend largely on intrigue. We must not say more than this. We must not call the play a tragedy of intrigue as distinguished from a tragedy of character. (p. 179.)

And we must not suppose that Bradley sees what is in front of him. The character he is thinking of isn't Othello's. 'Iago's plot', he goes on,

> Iago's plot is Iago's character in action.

In fact the play (we need hardly stop short of saying) is Iago's character in action. Bradley adds, it is true, that Iago's plot 'is built on his knowledge of Othello's character, and could not otherwise have succeeded'. But Iago's knowledge of Othello's character amounts pretty much to Bradley's knowledge of it (except, of course, that Iago cannot realize Othello's nobility quite to the full): Othello is purely noble, strong, generous, and trusting, and as tragic hero is, however formidable and destructive in his agonies, merely a victim – the victim of Iago's devilish 'intellectual superiority' (which is 'so great that we watch its advance fascinated and appalled'). It is all in order, then, that Iago

should get one of the two lectures that Bradley gives to the play,
Othello sharing the other with Desdemona. And it is all in the
tradition; from Coleridge down, Iago – his motivation or his
motivelessness – has commonly been, in commentaries on the
play, the main focus of attention.

The plain fact that has to be asserted in the face of this sustained
and sanctioned perversity is that in Shakespeare's tragedy of
Othello Othello is the chief personage – the chief personage in
such a sense that the tragedy may fairly be said to be Othello's
character in action. Iago is subordinate and merely ancillary. He
is not much more than a necessary piece of dramatic mechanism –
that at any rate is a fit reply to the view of Othello as necessary
material and provocation for a display of Iago's fiendish intellectual superiority. Iago, of course, is sufficiently convincing as a
person; he could not perform his dramatic function otherwise.
But something has gone wrong when we make him interesting in
this kind of way:

> His fate – which is himself – has completely mastered him: so that,
> in the later scenes, where the improbability of the entire success of a
> design built on so many different falsehoods forces itself on the reader,
> Iago appears for moments not as a consummate schemer, but as a man
> absolutely infatuated and delivered over to certain destruction.

We ought not, in reading those scenes, to be paying so much
attention to the intrinsic personal qualities of Iago as to attribute
to him tragic interest of that kind.

This last proposition, though its justice is perhaps not self-
evident, must remain for the time being a matter of assertion.
Other things come first. Othello has in any case the prior claim on
our attention, and it seems tactically best to start with something
as easy to deal with as the view – Bradley's and Coleridge's[1] –
and of course, Othello's before them – that Othello was 'not
easily jealous'. Easy to deal with because there, to point to, is the
text, plain and unequivocal. And yet the text was there for

1. 'Finally, let me repeat that Othello does not kill Desdemona in jealousy,
but in a conviction forced upon him by the almost superhuman art of Iago,
such a conviction as any man would and must have entertained who had
believed Iago's honesty as Othello did.' – Coleridge, *Essays and Lectures on
Shakespeare*.

Coleridge, and Bradley accompanies his argument with constant particular reference to it. It is as extraordinary a history of triumphant sentimental perversity as literary history can show. Bradley himself saves us the need of insisting on this diagnosis by carrying indulgence of his preconception, his determined sentimental preconception, to such heroic lengths:

Now I repeat that *any* man situated as Othello was would have been disturbed by Iago's communications, and I add that many men would have been made wildly jealous. But up to this point, where Iago is dismissed [III, iii, 238] Othello, I must maintain, does not show jealousy. His confidence is shaken, he is confused and deeply troubled, he feels even horror; but he is not yet jealous in the proper sense of that word.

The 'proper sense of that word' is perhaps illustrated by these lines (not quoted by Bradley) in which, Bradley grants, 'the beginning of that passion may be traced':

> Haply, for I am black
> And have not those soft parts of conversation
> That chamberers have, or for I am declined
> Into the vale of years – yet that's not much –
> She's gone; I am abused, and my relief
> Must be to loathe her. O curse of marriage,
> That we can call these delicate creatures ours,
> And not their appetites! I had rather be a toad,
> And live upon the vapour of a dungeon,
> Than keep a corner in the thing I love
> For others' uses.

Any reader not protected by a very obstinate preconception would take this, not for a new development of feeling, but for the fully explicit expression of something he had already, pages back, registered as an essential element in Othello's behaviour – something the evoking of which was essential to Iago's success. In any case, jealous or not jealous 'in the proper sense of that word', Othello has from the beginning responded to Iago's 'communications' in the way Iago desired and with a promptness that couldn't be improved upon, and has dismissed Iago with these words:

> Farewell, farewell:
> If more thou dost perceive, let me know more;
> Set on thy wife to observe

– to observe Desdemona, concerning whom Iago has just said:

> Ay, there's the point: as – to be bold with you –
> Not to affect many proposed matches
> Of her own clime, complexion and degree,
> Whereto we see in all things nature tends –
> Foh! one may smell in such a will most rank,
> Foul disproportion, thoughts unnatural.
> But pardon me: I do not in position
> Distinctly speak of her, though I may fear
> Her will, recoiling to her better judgement,
> May fall to match you with her country forms,
> And happily repent.

To say that it's not jealousy here is hardly (one would have thought) to bring Othello off clean; but Bradley's conclusion is not (as might have seemed inevitable) that there may be other faults than jealousy that are at least as damaging to a man in the character of husband and married lover. He is quite explicit:

Up to this point, it seems to me, there is not a syllable to be said against Othello. (p. 194.)

With such resolute fidelity does Bradley wear these blinkers that he can say,

> His trust, where he trusts, is absolute,

without realizing the force of the corollary: Othello's trust, then, can never have been in Desdemona. It is the vindication of Othello's perfect nobility that Bradley is preoccupied with, and we are to see the immediate surrender to Iago as part of that nobility. But to make absolute trust in Iago – trust at Desdemona's expense – a manifestation of perfect nobility is (even if we ignore what it makes of Desdemona) to make Iago a very remarkable person indeed. And that, Bradley, tradition aiding and abetting, proceeds to do.

However, to anyone not wearing these blinkers it is plain that no subtilization and exaltation of the Iago-devil (with consequent subordination of Othello) can save the noble hero of Bradley's devotion. And it is plain that what we should see in Iago's prompt success is not so much Iago's diabolic intellect as Othello's readiness to respond. Iago's power, in fact, in the temptation-scene is that he represents something that is in Othello – in Othello the husband of Desdemona: the essential traitor is within the gates. For if Shakespeare's Othello too is simple-minded, he is nevertheless more complex than Bradley's. Bradley's Othello is, rather, Othello's; it being an essential datum regarding the Shakespearean Othello that he has an ideal conception of himself.

The tragedy is inherent in the Othello–Desdemona relation, and Iago is a mechanism necessary for precipitating tragedy in a dramatic action. Explaining how it should be that Othello, who is so noble and trustful ('Othello, we have seen, was trustful, and thorough in his trust'), can so immediately doubt his wife, Bradley says:

> But he was newly married; in the circumstances he cannot have known much of Desdemona before his marriage. (p. 192.)

Again we read:

> But it is not surprising that his utter powerlessness to repel it [Iago's insinuation] on the ground of knowledge of his wife . . . should complete his misery . . . (p. 193.)

Bradley, that is, in his comically innocent way, takes it as part of the datum that Othello really knows nothing about his wife. Ah, but he was in love with her. And so poetically. 'For', says Bradley, 'there is no love, not that of Romeo in his youth, more steeped in imagination than Othello's'. Othello, however, we are obliged to remark (Bradley doesn't make the point in this connexion) is not in his youth; he is represented as middle-aged – as having attained at any rate to maturity in that sense. There might seem to be dangers in such a situation, quite apart from any intervention by an Iago. But then, we are told Othello is 'of a great openness and trustfulness of nature'. – It would be putting it more to the point to say that he has great consciousness of worth and confidence of respect.

The worth is really and solidly there; he is truly impressive, a noble product of the life of action – of

> The big wars
> That make ambition virtue.

'That make ambition virtue' – this phrase of his is a key one: his virtues are, in general, of that kind; they have, characteristically,

something of the quality suggested. Othello, in his magnanimous
way, is egotistic. He really is, beyond any question, the nobly
massive man of action, the captain of men, he sees himself as
being, but he does very much see himself:

> Keep up your bright swords, for the dew will rust them.

In short, a habit of self-approving self-dramatization is an
essential element in Othello's make-up, and remains so at the
very end.

It is, at the best, the impressive manifestation of a noble egotism.
But, in the new marital situation, this egotism isn't going to be the
less dangerous for its nobility. This self-centredness doesn't mean
self-knowledge: that is a virtue which Othello, as soldier of
fortune, hasn't had much need of. He has been well provided by
nature to meet all the trials a life of action has exposed him to. The
trials facing him now that he has married this Venetian girl with
whom he's 'in love' so imaginatively (we're told) as to outdo
Romeo and who is so many years younger than himself (his
colour, whether or not 'colour-feeling' existed among the
Elizabethans, we are certainly to take as emphasizing the disparity
of the match) – the trials facing him now are of a different order.

And here we have the significance of the storm, which puts so
great a distance between Venice and Cyprus, between the old life
and the new, and makes the change seem so complete and so
momentous. The storm is rendered in that characteristic heroic
mode of the play which Professor Wilson Knight[1] calls the
'Othello music':

> For do but stand upon the foaming shore,
> The chidden billows seem to chide the clouds;
> The wind-shaked surge, with high and monstrous mane,
> Seems to cast water on the burning bear,
> And quench the guards of the ever-fixed pole:
> I never did like molestation view
> On the enchafed flood.   [II, i]

This mode (Professor Wilson Knight, in his own way, describes
it well) gives the effect of a comparatively simple magnificence;
the characteristic verse of *Othello* is firm, regular in outline,

1. See that valuable book, *The Wheel of Fire*.

buoyant and sonorous. It is in an important sense Othello's own verse, the 'large-mouthed utterance' of the noble man of action. Bradley's way of putting it is that Othello, though he 'has not, indeed, the meditative or speculative imagination of Hamlet,' is 'in the strictest sense of the word' 'more poetic than Hamlet' (p. 188). We need not ask Bradley what the 'strictest sense of the word' is, or stop to dispute with him whether or not Othello is 'the greatest poet' of all Shakespeare's heroes. If characters in poetic drama speak poetry we ought to be able to notice the fact without concluding that they are poets. In *Othello*, which is poetic drama, Shakespeare works by poetic means: it is through the characteristic noble verse described above that, very largely, we get our sense of the noble Othello. If the impression made by Othello's own utterance is often poetical as well as poetic, that is Shakespeare's way, not of representing him as a poet, but of conveying the romantic glamour that, for Othello himself and others, invests Othello and what he stands for.

'For Othello himself' – it might be said that to express Othello's sense of himself and make us share it is the essential function of this verse, the 'Othello music'. But, of course, there are distinctions to be noted. The description of the storm quoted above, though it belongs to the general heroic mode of the play, cannot be said to exhibit the element of self-dramatization that is characteristic of Othello's own utterances. On the other hand, the self-dramatizing trick commands subtle modulations and various stops. It is not always as assertive as in

> Behold, I have a weapon. [V, ii, 257]

or the closing speech. In these speeches, not only is it explicit, it clearly involves, we may note, an attitude *towards* the emotion expressed – an attitude of a kind we are familiar with in the analysis of sentimentality.

The storm, within the idealizing mode, is at the other extreme from sentimentality; it serves to bring out the reality of the heroic Othello and what he represents. For his heroic quality, realized in this verse (here the utterance of others) is a real thing, though it is not, as Othello takes it to be, the whole of the reality. Another way of making the point would be to say that the distinctive style under discussion, the style that lends itself to Othello's self-dramatization and conveys in general the tone and ideal import of this, goes, in its confident and magnificent buoyancy, essentially with the outer storm that both the lovers, in their voyage to Cyprus, triumphantly outride.

With that kind of external stress the noble Othello is well qualified to deal (if he went down – and we know he won't – he would go down magnificently). But it is not that kind of stress he has to fear in the new life beginning at Cyprus. The stresses of the spiritual climate are concentrated by Iago (with his deflating, unbeglamouring, brutally realistic mode of speech) into something immediately apprehensible in drama and comparable with the storm. In this testing, Othello's inner timbers begin to part at once, the stuff of which he is made begins at once to deteriorate and show itself unfit. There is even a symbolic foundering when, breaking into incoherent ejaculations, he 'falls in a trance'. [IV, i, 35.]

As for the justice of this view that Othello yields with extraordinary promptness to suggestion, with such promptness as to make it plain that the mind that undoes him is not Iago's but his own, it does not seem to need arguing. If it has to be argued, the only difficulty is the difficulty, for written criticism, of going in detailed commentary through an extended text. The text is plain enough. Iago's sustained attack begins at about line 90 in Act III, Sc. iii, immediately upon Desdemona's exit and Othello's exclamation:

> Excellent wretch! Perdition catch my soul,
> But I do love thee! and when I love thee not,
> Chaos is come again.

In seventy lines Othello is brought to such a state that Iago can, without getting any reply but

> O misery,

say

> O, beware, my lord, of jealousy,

and use the word 'cuckold'. In ninety lines Othello is saying

> Why did I marry?

The explanation of this quick work is given plainly enough here:

Iago: I would not have your free and noble nature
            Out of self-bounty be abused; look to't:
            I know our country disposition well;
            In Venice they do let heaven see the pranks
            They dare nor show their husbands; their best conscience
            Is not to leave't undone, but keep't unknown.

Othello: Dost thou say so?

Iago: She did deceive her father, marrying you;
            And when she seem'd to shake and fear your looks,
            She loved them most.

Othello: And so she did.

There in the first two lines is, explicitly appealed to by Iago,[1] Othello's ideal conception of himself: it would be a pity if he let it be his undoing (as it actually was – the full irony Iago can hardly be credited with intending). And there, in the last line we have the noble and magnanimous Othello, romantic hero and married lover, accepting as evidence against his wife the fact that, at the willing sacrifice of everything else, she had made with him a marriage of romantic love. Iago, like Bradley, points out that Othello didn't really know Desdemona, and Othello acquiesces in considering her as a type – a type outside his experience – the Venetian wife. It is plain, then, that his love is composed very largely of ignorance of self as well as ignorance of her: however nobly he may feel about it, it isn't altogether what he, and Bradley with him, thinks it is. It may be love, but it can be only in an oddly qualified sense love of her: it must be much more a matter of self-centred and self-regarding satisfactions – pride, sensual possessiveness, appetite, love of loving – than he suspects.

This comes out unmistakably when he begins to let himself go; for instance, in the soliloquy that follows Iago's exit:

> She's gone; I am abused, and my relief
> Must be to loathe her. O curse of marriage,
> That we can call these delicate creatures ours,
> And not their appetites! I had rather be a toad,
> And live upon the vapour of a dungeon,
> Than keep a corner in the thing I love
> For others' uses.

1. Who has described Othello [I, i, 12] as 'loving his own pride and purposes.'

Even the actual presence of Desdemona, who enters immediately upon the close of this soliloquy, can avail nothing against the misgivings of angry egotism. Pointing to his forehead he makes an allusion to the cuckold's horns, and when she in her innocence misunderstands him and offers to soothe the pain he rebuffs her. The element of angry sensuality is insistent:

> What sense had I of her stol'n hours of lust?
> . . . .
> I had been happy if the general camp,
> Pioners and all, had tasted her sweet body.

It is significant that, at the climax of the play, when Othello, having exclaimed

> O blood, blood, blood,

kneels to take a formal vow of revenge, he does so in the heroic strain of the 'Othello music'. To Iago's

> Patience, I say; your mind perhaps may change,

he replies:

> Never, Iago. Like to the Pontic sea,
> Whose icy current and compulsive course
> Ne'er feels retiring ebb, but keeps due on
> To the Propontic and the Hellespont;
> Even so my bloody thoughts, with violent pace,
> Shall ne'er look back, ne'er ebb to humble love,
> Till that a wide and capable revenge
> Swallow them up. Now, by yond marble heaven,
> In the due reverence of a sacred vow
> I here engage my words.

At this climax of the play, as he sets himself irrevocably in his vindictive resolution, he reassumes formally his heroic self-dramatization – reassumes the Othello of 'the big wars that make ambition virtue'. The part of this conscious nobility, this noble egotism, this self-pride that was justified by experience irrelevant to the present trials and stresses, is thus underlined. Othello's self-idealization, his promptness to jealousy and his blindness are shown in their essential relation. The self-idealization is shown as blindness and the nobility as here no longer something real, but the disguise of an obtuse and brutal egotism. Self-pride becomes stupidity, ferocious stupidity, an insane and self-deceiving passion. The habitual 'nobility' is seen to make self-deception invincible, the egotism it expresses being the drive to catastrophe. Othello's noble lack of self-knowledge is shown as humiliating and disastrous.

Bradley, however, his knowledge of Othello coinciding virtually with Othello's, sees nothing but the nobility. At the cost of denaturing Shakespeare's tragedy, he insistently idealizes. The 'feelings of jealousy proper', he says (p. 194), 'are not the chief or deepest source of Othello's suffering. It is the feeling, "If she be false, oh then Heaven mocks itself;" the feeling, "O Iago, the pity of it, Iago!"' It is Shakespeare's tragedy of Othello that the man who exclaims this can exclaim three lines later, when he next speaks [IV, i, 204]:

> I will chop her into messes. Cuckold me!

Again, three lines further on he says:

> Get me some poison, Iago; this night. I'll not expostulate with her, lest her body and beauty unprovide my mind again: this night, Iago.

This surely has some bearing on the nature of 'the pity of it': to equate Bradley's knowledge of Othello with Othello's own was perhaps unfair to Othello.

In any case, this association of strong sensuality with ugly vindictive jealousy is insistent in Shakespeare's play:

> Now he tells how she plucked him to my chamber. O, I see that nose of yours, but not that dog I shall throw it to.   [IV, i, 140]

> I would have him nine years a-killing. A fine woman! a fair woman! a sweet woman!   [IV, i, 181]

'O Iago, the pity of it, Iago!': it is plain here that 'fine', 'fair' and 'sweet' apply, not to Desdemona as a complete person (the immediate provocation is Iago's remark, 'she gave it him and he hath given it [the handkerchief] his whore'), but to her person in abstraction from the character of the owner, whom Othello hardly, at this point, respects. And the nature of this regret, this tragically expressed regret, bears an essential relation to the nature of the love with which Othello, however imaginatively and Romeo-like, loved Desdemona. That romantic idealizing love could be as dubiously grounded in reality as this is an essential condition of the tragedy. But Bradley's own idealizing is invincible. He can even say (p. 197):

> An ineradicable instinct of justice, rather than any last quiver of hope, leads him to question Emilia.

That's no doubt how Othello would have put it; but for the reader – the unidealizing reader – what the questioning of Emilia [IV, ii] shows in brutal, resolute, unrestricted predominance is the antithesis of any instinct of justice.

With obtuseness to the tragic significance of Shakespeare's play goes insensibility to his poetry – to his supreme art as exhibited locally in the verse (it is still not superfluous to insist that the poetic skill is one with the dramatic). This is Bradley's commentary on Act V, Sc. ii:

> The supposed death of Cassio [v, i] satiates the thirst for vengeance. The Othello who enters the bed-chamber with the words,
>
> > It is the cause, it is the cause, my soul,
>
> is not the man of the Fourth Act. The deed he is bound to do is no murder, but a sacrifice. He is to save Desdemona from herself, not in hate but in honour; in honour, and also in love. His anger has passed; a boundless sorrow has taken its place; and
>
> > this sorrow's heavenly:
> > It strikes where it doth love.
>
> Even when, at the sight of her apparent obduracy, and at the hearing of words which by a crowning fatality can only reconvince him of her guilt, these feelings give way to others, it is to righteous indignation they give way, not to rage: and, terribly painful as this scene is, there is almost nothing here to diminish the admiration and love which heighten pity. (p. 197.)

That again, no doubt, is how Othello (though as for satiated thirst, he says at line 74,

> Had all his hairs been lives, my great revenge
> Had stomach for them all)

would like to see it. But Bradley, in the speech he quotes from, misses all the shifts of tone by which Shakespeare renders the shifting confusion of Othello's mind. For it is a speech one might have chosen with the express view of illustrating that subtle command of tone which marks Shakespeare's mature art, and which makes the poetry of *Othello* so different in kind from that of *Romeo and Juliet*, and the two dramas consequently incomparable.

It opens with the accent of a contained holy revulsion, the containing power appearing as inexorable, impersonal justice:

> It is the cause, it is the cause, my soul!
> Let me not name it to you, you chaste stars!
> It is the cause.

Now comes a shrinking back from the deed:

> Yet I'll not shed her blood,
> Nor scar that whiter skin of hers than snow
> And smooth as monumental alabaster.

Tenderness here quite clearly is that characteristic voluptuousness of Othello's which, since it is unassociated with any real interest in Desdemona as a person, slips so readily into possessive jealousy. Now the accent of impersonal justice is heard again –

> Yet she must die, else she'll betray more men

– but the accent is so clearly unrelated to any effectual motive in Othello that the concern for justice, the self-bracing to noble sacrifice, appears as self-deception. Next come misgivings over the finality of the deed:

> Put out the light, and then put out the light:
> If I quench thee, thou flaming minister,
> I can again thy former light restore,
> Should I repent me: but once put out thy light,
> Thou cunning'st pattern of excelling nature,
> I know not where is that Promethean heat
> That can thy light relume. When I have pluck'd the rose
> I cannot give it vital growth again,
> It must needs wither: I'll smell it on the tree.

Tenderness here is less specifically voluptuous sensuality than it
was earlier, but we nevertheless remember:

> Get me some poison, Iago; this night. I'll not expostulate with her,
> lest her body and beauty unprovide my mind again: this night, Iago.
>
> [IV, i, 208]

And there is in Othello a curious and characteristic effect of self-
preoccupation, of preoccupation with his emotions rather than
with Desdemona in her own right:

> O balmy breath, that almost dost persuade
> Justice to break her sword! One more, one more:
> Be thus when thou art dead, and I will kill thee,
> And love thee after: one more, and this the last.
> So sweet was ne'er so fatal. I must weep,
> But they are cruel tears: this sorrow's heavenly;
> It strikes where it doth love. She wakes.

When she is awake and so is no longer a mere body, but a person,
it is not sorrowful love or noble self-bracing to a sacrifice that she
becomes aware of in Othello:

> Alas, why gnaw you so your nether lip?
> Some bloody passion shakes your very frame:
> These are portents.

Moreover, though Othello says

> I would not kill thy unprepared spirit,

actually he refuses her the time to say one prayer.

When he discovers his mistake, his reaction is an intolerably
intensified form of the common 'I could kick myself':

> Whip me, ye devils
> From the possession of this heavenly sight!
> Blow me about in winds! roast me in sulphr!
> Wash me in steep-down gulfs of liquid fire!
> O Desdemona! Desdemona! dead!
> Oh! Oh! Oh!

But he remains the same Othello; he has discovered his mistake,
but there is no tragic self-discovery. The speech closing with the
lines just quoted is that beginning

> Behold, I have a weapon,

one of the finest examples in the play of the self-dramatizing trick. The noble Othello is now seen as tragically pathetic, and he sees himself as pathetic too:

> Man but a rush against Othello's breast,
> And he retires. Where shall Othello go?

He is ruined, but he is the same Othello in whose essential make-up the tragedy lay: the tragedy doesn't involve the idea of the hero's learning through suffering. The fact that Othello tends to sentimentalize should be the reverse of a reason for our sentimentalizing too.

For even, or rather especially, in that magnificent last speech of his Othello does tend to sentimentalize,[1] though to say that and no more would convey a false impression, for the speech conveys something like the full complexity of Othello's simple nature, and in the total effect the simplicity is tragic and grand. The quiet beginning gives us the man of action with his habit of effortless authority:

> Soft you; a word or two before you go.
> I have done the State some service, and they know't.
> No more of that. I pray you in your letters,
> When you shall these unlucky deeds relate,
> Speak of me as I am; nothing extenuate,
> Nor set down aught in malice . . .

Othello really is, we cannot doubt, the stoic-captain whose few words know their full sufficiency: up to this point we cannot say he dramatizes himself, he simply *is*. But then, in a marvellous way (if we consider Shakespeare's art), the emotion works itself up until in less than half-a-dozen lines the stoic of few words is eloquently weeping. With

> Then must you speak
> Of one that loved not wisely but too well,

the epigrammatic terseness of the dispatch, the dictated dispatch, begins to quiver. Then, with a rising emotional swell, description

1. There is, I find, an admirable note on this speech in Mr T. S. Eliot's essay, *Shakespeare and the Stoicism of Seneca.*

becomes unmistakably self-dramatization – self-dramatization as un-self-comprehending as before:

> Of one not easily jealous, but being wrought,
> Perplex'd in the extreme; of one whose hand,
> Like the base Indian, threw a pearl away
> Richer than all his tribe; of one whose subdued eyes,
> Albeit unused to the melting mood,
> Drop tears as fast as the Arabian trees
> Their medicinal gum.

Contemplating the spectacle of himself, Othello is overcome with the pathos of it. But this is not the part to die in: drawing himself proudly up, he speaks his last words as the stern soldier who recalls, and re-enacts, his supreme moment of deliberate courage:

> Set you down this;
> And say besides, that in Aleppo once,
> Where a malignant and a turban'd Turk
> Beat a Venetian and traduced the state,
> I took by the throat the circumcised dog
> And smote him, thus.   [Stabs himself.]

It is a superb *coup de théâtre*.

As, with that double force, a *coup de théâtre*, it is peculiarly right ending to the tragedy of Othello. The theme of the tragedy is concentrated in it – concentrated in the final speech and action as it could not have been had Othello 'learnt through suffering'. That he should die acting his ideal part is all in the part: the part is manifested here in its rightness and solidity, and the actor as inseparably the man of action. The final blow is as real as the blow it re-enacts, and the histrionic intent symbolically affirms the reality: Othello dies belonging to the world of action in which his true part lay.

That so many readers – Coleridge, Swinburne, Bradley, for instance – not belonging to that world should have found Othello's part irresistibly attractive, in the sense that they have preferred to see the play through Othello's eyes rather than Shakespeare's, is perhaps not after all surprising. It may be suggested that the cult of T. E. Lawrence has some relevance here. And Othello is not merely a glamorous man of action who dominates all companies, he is (as we have all been) cruelly and tragically wronged – a victim of relentless intrigue, and, while remaining noble and heroic, is allowed to appreciate the pathos of his own fate. He has, in fact, all the advantages of that last speech, where the invitation to identify oneself with him is indeed hardly resistible. Who does not (in some moments) readily see himself as the hero of such a *coup de théâtre*?

The exaltation of Iago, it has already been suggested, is a corollary of this response to Othello. What but supremely subtle villainy could have brought to this kind of ruin the hero whose perfect nobility we admire and love? Bradley concludes that

to compare Iago with the Satan of *Paradise Lost* seems almost absurd, so immensely does Shakespeare's man exceed Milton's fiend in evil. (p. 206.)

However, to be fair to Bradley, we must add that he also finds Iago decidedly less great than Napoleon.[1] Nevertheless, even if Iago hasn't 'intellectual supremacy', we are to credit him with vast 'intellectual superiority': 'in intellect . . . and in will . . . Iago *is* great' (p. 219). If we ask the believers in Iago's intellect where they find it, they can hardly point to anything immediately present in the text, though it is true that he makes some acute and cynical observations at times. The evidence of his intellect is the success of his plot: if he hadn't had an extraordinary intellect, how could he have succeeded? That is the essential argument. It is an odd kind of literary criticism. 'The skill of Iago was extraordinary,' says Bradley, 'but', he adds, with characteristic scrupulousness, 'so was his good fortune'.

Yes, so was his good fortune – until Shakespeare gave him bad. That it should be possible to argue so solemnly and pertinaciously on the assumption that Iago, his intellect and his good fortune belong, like Napoleon and his, to history, may be taken as showing that Shakespeare succeeded in making him plausible enough for the purposes of the drama. And yet even Bradley betrays

1. 'But compare him with one who may perhaps be roughly called a bad man of supreme intellectual power, Napoleon, and you see how mean and negative Iago's mind is, incapable of his military achievements, much more incapable of his political constructions.' (p. 236.)

certain misgivings. Noting the astonishing (when one thinks of it) contrast between the devilish reality of Iago and the impression he makes on everyone (including his wife)[1] except Roderigo, Bradley comments (p. 217):

> What further conclusions can be drawn from it? Obviously, to begin with, the inference, which is accompanied by a thrill of admiration, that Iago's powers of dissimulation and of self-control must have been prodigious . . .

There we have the process by which the prodigious Iago is created. But the scrupulous Bradley nevertheless records the passing doubt:

> In fact so prodigious does his self-control appear that a reader might be excused for feeling a doubt of its possibility.

Of course, it is recorded only to be overcome:

> But there are certain observations and further inferences which, apart from a confidence in Shakespeare, would remove this doubt.

Actually, if we are to be saved from these doubts (those of us who are not strengthened by this confidence in Shakespeare), we must refrain from careful observations, comparative notes and scrupulous inferences. Shakespeare's genius carries with it a large facility in imposing conviction locally, and before we ask for more than this we should make sure we know just what is being offered us in the whole. The title tells us where, in this play (it is not, of course, so in all the plays), we are to focus. As for Iago, we know from the beginning that he is a villain; the business of Roderigo tells us that. In the other scenes we have no difficulty in taking him as we are meant to take him; and we don't (at any rate in the reading, and otherwise it's the actor's problem) ask how it is that appearance and reality can have been so successfully divorced. Considered as a comprehensibly villainous person, he represents a not uncommon kind of grudging, cynical malice (and he's given, at least in suggestion, enough in the way of grievance and motive). But in order to perform his function as dramatic machinery he has to put on such an appearance of invincibly

[1] 'And it is a fact too little noticed that he presented an appearance not very different to his wife. There is no sign either that Emilia's marriage was downright unhappy, or that she suspected the true nature of her husband.'

cunning devilry as to provide Coleridge and the rest with some excuse for their awe, and to leave others wondering, in critical reflection, whether he isn't a rather clumsy mechanism. Perhaps the most serious point to be pondered is that, if Othello is to retain our sympathy sufficiently, Iago must, as devil, claim for himself an implicit weight of emotional regard that critical reflection finds him unfit to carry.

'Clumsy', however, is not the right word for anything in *Othello*. It is a marvellously sure and adroit piece of workmanship; though closely related to that judgement is the further one that, with all its brilliance and poignancy, it comes below Shakespeare's supreme – his very greatest – works.

*

I refrained, of set purpose, from reading Professor Stoll on *Othello* and its critics till I had written, as Bradley precipitated it, my own account of the play. Professor Stoll is of course known as, in academic Shakespeare criticism, the adversary of the Bradley approach, and now that I have read what he has to say[1] about *Othello* he seems to me to confirm where the critical centre lies by deviating as badly on his side as Bradley does on the other.

Professor Stoll, having first justified with a weight of scholarship my unscholarly assumption that the view of *Othello* represented by Bradley has, since Coleridge's time, been the generally accepted one, exposes unanswerably and at length the absurdity of that view. His own positive account of the play, however, is no less indefensible than Bradley's. He argues that Othello's lapse into jealousy is to be explained in terms, not of Othello's psychology, but of convention. Profiting by the convention of 'the slanderer believed' (for the use of which Professor Stoll gives a long string of instances) Shakespeare simply imposes jealousy on Othello from the outside: that is Professor Stoll's position.

As we contemplate his string of instances we are moved to insist on certain distinctions the importance of which seems to

1. In *Othello: An Historical and Comparative Study* (*Studies in Language and Literature*, No. 2. University of Minnesota, 1915) and *Art and Artifice in Shakespeare* (1933). Professor Stoll's position appears not to have changed between the two essays, but I find his less developed style the more intelligible.

have passed him by. When Shakespeare uses the 'same' convention as Beaumont and Fletcher, Dryden and Voltaire, his use is apt to be such that only by a feat of abstraction can the convention be said to be the same. Who will bother to argue whether jealousy in Beaumont and Fletcher or any of the others is psychologically defensible or not? The unique power by which Shakespeare compels 'faith in the emotions expressed' and beguiles Bradley and company into their absurdities is, of course, recognized by Professor Stoll, though he cannot recognize with any sureness its nature:

> By the sheer potency of art Othello, Iago, Desdemona, and Emilia maintain, through all their incredible vicissitudes, their individual tone. And inconsistent, unpsychological though they be, their passions speak ever true.[1]

To explain this potency, Professor Stoll, urging us to be content with 'mere art', talks vaguely of 'tact', 'delicacy' and 'poetry', makes play with analogies from music, and quotes Shaw's 'it is the score and not the libretto that keeps the work alive and fresh'. Elsewhere he can recognize that 'No one has more imaginative sympathy than Shakespeare; but', he goes on,

> he employs it by fits and starts, often neglects motivation and analysis, takes a leap as he passes from one 'soul-state' to another, and not content with the inconsistencies of life, falls into the contradictions of convention and artifice.[2]

This is better than talking about 'score' and 'libretto', though a critic who saw that and understood would make distinctions and discriminations that Professor Stoll ignores. The 'sheer potency' of Shakespeare's art, the 'magic' of his 'score' (and where is the 'libretto'?) derives from his imaginative grasp of concrete human situations in their complexity and particularity; his power of realizing a vivid here-and-now of experience as part of an intricate and coherent context. The convincing life of the verse locally and the more inclusive realizing grasp belong together; the one is the index of the other.

There are, no doubt, places in Shakespeare of which one may

1. *Othello: An Historical and Comparative Study*, p. 62.
2. *Op. cit.*, p. 69.

argue that local vividnesses here and there, convincingly living parts, are not related in an inwardly grasped whole, and that Shakespeare has fallen 'into the contradictions of convention and artifice'. That would be an adverse criticism. But before we make it we must make sure what kind of whole Shakespeare is offering us. For instance, it is not intelligent criticism of *Measure for Measure* to say, as a dramatic critic did in *The New Statesman and Nation*:[1]

> The author seems to have lost interest in it about half-way through, and turns a fine story to nonsense. (The Duke's character, if one could take it seriously, would be as curious and complicated as any in Shakespeare – a moralist who tortures people in order to study their behaviour on the rack.)

To 'take seriously' means, it is clear, to regard Shakespeare's Duke as a historical person and judge him by the standards one would apply in actual life. But, for anyone who can read, Shakespeare provides intimation enough that the Duke isn't to be taken in that way – that he moves on a different plane from the other characters. And because of the obviously serious purpose it subserves, and the impressiveness of the total effect it makes possible, we readily accept the convention involved in taking the Duke as we are meant to take him.

But with Othello it is different. By the time he becomes the jealous husband it has been made plain beyond any possibility of doubt or reversal that we are to take him, in the dramatic critic's sense, seriously – at any rate, such a habit of expectation has been set up with regard to him (and he is well established as the main focus of attention) that no development will be acceptable unless the behaviour it imposes on him is reconcilable with our notions of ordinary psychological consistency. Other characters in the play can be 'convincing' on easier terms; we needn't inquire into the consistency of Emilia's behaviour – we accept her as a datum, and not even about Iago are we – or need we be – so psychologically exacting. His combination of honest seeming with devilish actuality we accept as, at least partly, a matter of tacit convention; convention acceptable because of the convincingly handled tragic theme to which it is ancillary.

And the tragic theme is centred in Othello. Dramatic sleight

1. Oct. 16th, 1937.

is not cheating so long as it subserves honesty there. We do not, even when we consider it critically, quarrel with the trick of 'double time', though it involves impossibilities by the criteria of actual life and yet is at the same time necessary to the plausible conduct of the intrigue; but equivalent tricks or illusions passing off on us mutually incompatible acceptances with regard to Othello's behaviour or make-up *would* be cheating – that is, matter for critical condemnation. To impose by convention sudden jealousy on Leontes in *The Winter's Tale* and Posthumus in *Cymbeline* is one thing: we admit the convention for the sake of an inclusive effect – a dramatic design that does not, we recognize (wherever in the scale of Shakespeare's work we may place these plays), anywhere ask us to endorse dramatic illusion with the feeling of everyday reality. But to impose jealousy by mere convention on Othello is another thing. What end would be served? What profit would accrue?

According to Professor Stoll, the profit of 'putting jealousy upon the hero instead of breeding it in him' is an 'enormous emotional effect':

> The end – the enormous emotional effect – justifies the means . . .[1]

This emotional effect, as Professor Stoll enjoys it, he represents as the product of our being enabled, by Shakespeare's art, to have it both ways: Othello succumbing to jealousy before our eyes acquires an intense dramatic value without incurring in our esteem the disadvantages attendant upon being jealous; there he is, patently jealous, yet he is at the same time still the man who couldn't possibly have become jealous like that.

> The villain, by all this contriving of the poet's, bears in this instance, like the ancient Fate or intruding god, the burden of responsibility; and our sympathy with a hero made of no such baseness is almost wholly without alloy.[2]

Professor Stoll, that is, in spite of the difference of his analysis, sees the play as the triumph of sentimentalization that it has appeared to so many admirers:

> . . . no one in Shakespeare's tragedies more bitterly and wildly reproaches himself . . . Yet not of himself suspicious or sensual, he is now

1. *Art and Artifice in Shakespeare*, p. 41.   2. *Op. cit.*, p. 42.

not corrupted or degraded; and amid his misery and remorse he can still hold up his head and declare:

> For nought I did in hate, but all in honour.

> not easily jealous, but, being wrought,
> Perplex'd in the extreme.

He is a more effective tragic figure because he can say that – because, unlike many, he keeps our sympathy and admiration to the end.[1]

The 'emotional effect' of the tragedy upon Professor Stoll is essentially that celebrated in his own way by Bradley, and Professor Stoll's analysis, in fact, does explain in large measure why such a tragedy should be so widely found in *Othello* and found irresistible.

Fortunately we are not reduced to reversing the critical judgement and censuring Shakespeare. The dilemma that Professors Stoll and Bradley resolve in their different but equally heroic ways – the dilemma represented by a 'not easily jealous' Othello who succumbs at once to Iago's suggestions – needn't be allowed to bother us. Both critics seem to think that, if Othello hasn't exhibited himself in the past as prone to sexual jealousy (and his reputation tells us he hasn't), that establishes him as 'not easily jealous', so that his plunge into jealousy would, if we had to justify it psychologically (Bradley, of course, prefers not to recognize it), pose us an insoluble problem. Yet surely, as Shakespeare presents him, it is not so very elusive a datum about Othello, or one that ordinary experience of life and men makes it difficult to accept, that his past history hasn't been such as to test his proneness to sexual jealousy – has, in fact, thereby been such as to increase his potentialities in just that respect.

However, he is likely to remain for many admirers the entirely noble hero, object of a sympathy poignant and complete as he succumbs to the machinations of diabolic intellect.

1. *Op. cit.*, p. 43.

'MEASURE FOR MEASURE'

RE-READING, both of L. C. Knights's essay[1] and of *Measure for Measure*, has only heightened my first surprise that such an argument about what seems to me one of the very greatest of the plays, and most consummate and convincing of Shakespeare's achievements, should have come from the author of *How Many Children Had Lady Macbeth?* For I cannot see that the 'discomfort' he sets out to explain is other in kind than that which, in the bad prepotent tradition, has placed *Measure for Measure* both among the 'unpleasant' ('cynical') plays and among the unconscionable compromises of the artist with the botcher, the tragic poet with the slick provider of bespoke comedy. In fact, Knights explicitly appeals to the 'admitted unsatisfactoriness' of *Measure for Measure*. The 'admitted unsatisfactoriness', I find myself with some embarrassment driven to point out (he quotes Hazlitt and Coleridge, and might have followed up with Swinburne, the *Arden* editor, Sir Edmund Chambers, Mr Desmond MacCarthy, the editors of the *New Cambridge Shakespeare*, and innumerable others), has to be explained in terms of that incapacity for dealing with poetic drama, that innocence about the nature of convention and the conventional possibilities of Shakespearean dramatic method and form, which we associate classically with the name of Bradley.

It is true that Knights doesn't make the usual attack on the character and proceedings of the Duke, and tell us how unadmirable he is, how indefensible, as man and ruler.[2] Nor, in reading

1. In *Scrutiny*, X, 3.
2. 'The Duke hardly seems to be a personage to delight in. It is not merely his didactic platitudes and his somewhat over-done pompousness that get upon one's nerves, but his inner character. We first meet him too timid or too irresolute to enforce his own laws and deputing his duty to another, while he himself plunges into a vortex of scheming and intrigue; concluding by falling in love with a votary. At III, i, 67 does he not transgress against the confessional? Again, he must have known of Angelo's treatment of Mariana, at least we are left to suppose he did [III, i, 228], and was not his (the Duke's) a very shifty way of bringing him to justice, instead of a straight prosecution? Then the freedom with which he lies [IV, iii, 108–15] is not prepossessing. I imagine Shakespeare was not in love with his Duke. "A shy fellow was the Duke".'
– The *Arden* Introduction, p. xxii.

this critic, do we find cause for invoking the kind of inhibition that has certainly counted for a lot in establishing the 'accepted' attitude towards *Measure for Measure* – inhibition about sex: he doesn't himself actually call the play 'unpleasant' or 'cynical'. But that 'sense of uneasiness' which 'we are trying to track down' – what, when we have followed through his investigations, does it amount to? It focuses, he says, upon Claudio, or, rather, upon Claudio's offence:

It is Claudio – who is scarcely a 'character' at all, and who stands between the two extremes – who seems to spring from feelings at war with themselves, and it is in considering the nature of his offence that one feels most perplexity.'

I am moved to ask by the way what can be Knights's critical intention in judging Claudio to be 'scarcely a "character" at all'. I think it worth asking because (among other things) of his judgement elsewhere that Angelo is a 'sketch rather than a developed character-study'. True, he says this parenthetically, while remarking that Angelo is the 'admitted success of the play'; but it is an odd parenthesis to have come from the author of *How Many Children Had Lady Macbeth?* It seems to me to have no point, though an unintentional significance.

But to come back to Claudio, whom Knights judges to be 'not consistently *created*': it is plain that the main critical intention would be rendered by shifting the italics to 'consistently' – he is not 'created' (*i.e.* 'scarcely a "character"') and, what's more significant, not consistent. This inconsistency, this 'uncertainty of handling', we are invited to find localized in the half-dozen lines of Claudio's first address to Lucio – here Knights makes his most serious offer at grounding his argument in the text:

> From too much liberty, my Lucio, liberty:
> As surfeit is the father of much fast,
> So every scope by the immoderate use
> Turns to restraint. Our natures do pursue,
> Like rats that ravin down their proper bane,
> A thirsty evil, and when we drink we die.

What problem is presented by these lines? The only problem I can see is why anyone should make heavy weather of them. Knights finds it disconcerting that Claudio should express vehement self-condemnation and self-disgust. But Claudio has committed a serious offence, not only in the eyes of the law, but in his own eyes. No doubt he doesn't feel that the offence deserves death; nor does anyone in the play, except Angelo (it is characteristic of Isabella that she should be not quite certain about it). On the other hand, is it difficult to grant his acquiescence in the moral conventions that, barring Lucio and the professionals, everyone about him accepts? A Claudio who took an advanced twentieth-century line in these matters might have made a more interesting 'character'; but such an emancipated Claudio was no part of Shakespeare's conception of his theme. Nor, I think Knights will grant, are there any grounds for supposing that Shakespeare himself tended to feel that the prescription of pre-marital chastity might well be dispensed with.

No perplexity, then, should be caused by Claudio's taking conventional morality seriously; that he should do so is not in any way at odds with his being in love, or with the mutuality of the offence. And that he should be bitterly self-reproachful and self-condemnatory, and impute a heavier guilt to himself than anyone else (except Isabella and Angelo) imputes to him, is surely natural: he is not a libertine, true (though a pal of Lucio's); but, as he now sees the case, he has recklessly courted temptation, has succumbed to the uncontrollable appetite so engendered, and as a result brought death upon himself, and upon Juliet disgrace and misery. Every element of the figurative comparison will be found to be accounted for here, I think, and I can't see anything 'odd' or 'inappropriate' about the bitterness and disgust.

Further, Knights's own point should be done justice to: 'The emphasis has, too, an obvious dramatic function, for, by suggesting that the offence was indeed grave, it makes the penalty seem less fantastic; and in the theatre that is probably all one notices in the swift transition to more explicit exposition.' The complementary point I want to make is that nowhere else in the play is there anything to support Knights's diagnostic commentary. The 'uncertainty of attitude' in Shakespeare's handling of Claudio, an uncertainty manifested in a 'dislocation or confusion of feeling', depends on those six lines for its demonstration: it can't be plausibly illustrated from any other producible passage of the text. And I don't think anyone could have passed from those lines to the argument that adduces sonnet 129 and the passage from *Cymbeline*, and ends in references to *Hamlet* and *Troilus and Cressida*, who was not importing into *Measure for Measure* something that wasn't put there by Shakespeare. The importation seems to me essentially that which is provided by what I have called the bad prepotent tradition. Taking advantage of the distraction caused by the problems that propose themselves if one doesn't accept what *Measure for Measure* does offer, that tradition naturally tends to smuggle its irrelevancies into the vacancies one has created. It must be plain that the references to *Hamlet* and *Troilus and Cressida* implicitly endorse the accepted classing of *Measure for Measure* with the 'unpleasant', 'cynical' and 'pessimistic' 'problem' plays.

The strength of the *parti pris* becomes very strikingly apparent when we are told, of the Provost's sympathetic remark,

> Alas!
> He hath but as offended in a dream,

that 'it seems to echo once more the sonnet on lust'. I am convinced it couldn't have seemed to do so to anyone who was not projecting on to the text what it gives him back. When the word 'dream', without any supporting context, can set up such repercussions, we have surely a clear case of possession by the idea or pre-determined bent. The intention of the Provost's remark is plain enough: he is merely saying that the offence (morals are morals, and we don't expect a Provost to say, or think, there has been *no* offence) can't be thought of as belonging to the world of real wrong-doing, where there is willed offending action that effects evil and is rightly held to accountability. The Provost, that is, voices a decent common-sense humanity.

Isabella takes a sterner moral line. But why this should give rise to perplexity or doubt about the attitude we ourselves are to take towards Claudio I can't see. Then I don't agree that she is not sufficiently 'placed'. Without necessarily judging that she is to be regarded with simple repulsion as an 'illustration of the frosty lack of sympathy of a self-regarding puritanism', we surely know that her attitude is not Shakespeare's, and is not meant to be ours. With the Duke it is different. His attitude, nothing could be plainer, *is* meant to be ours – his total attitude, which is the total attitude of the play. He, then, is something more complex than

Isabella; but need it conduce to a 'sense of strain and mental discomfort' when, speaking as a Friar, he shows himself 'disposed to severity towards "the sin" of Claudio and Juliet'; or when, speaking both as a Friar and to Lucio, he says, 'It is too general a vice, and severity must cure it'? To impersonate a reverend friar, with the aim, essential to the plot, of being taken for a reverend friar, and talk otherwise about the given 'natural relation' – we might reasonably have found uncertainty of handling in that. As it is, the disguised Duke acts the part, so that the general confidence he wins, including Isabella's, is quite credible.

The criticism that the Duke's speech, 'Reason thus with life . . .', 'ignores the reality of emotion' was anticipated (as Knights, by mentioning in the same footnote Claudio's 'retort to the equally "reasonable" Isabella', reminds us) by Shakespeare himself. The duly noted superiority of Claudio's speech on death to the Duke's (on which at the same time, I think, Knights is too hard) is significant, and it is, not insignificantly, in the same scene. A further implicit criticism is conveyed through Barnardine, who is not, for all the appreciative commentary of the best authorities, a mere pleasing piece of self-indulgence on Shakespeare's part: of all the attitudes concretely lived in the play, the indifference to death displayed by him comes nearest to that preached by the Friar. Those illusions and unrealities which he dismisses, and which for most of us make living undeniably positive and real, have no hold on Barnardine; for him life is indeed an after-dinner's sleep, and he, in the wisdom of drink and insensibility, has no fear at all of death. And towards him we are left in no doubt about the attitude we are to take: 'Unfit to live or die', says the Duke, voicing the general contempt.

In fact, the whole context, the whole play, is an implicit criticism of that speech; the speech of which the *Arden* editor, identifying the Friar-Duke quite simply and directly with Shakespeare, says representatively, on the page now beneath my eye: 'There is a terrible and morbid pessimism in this powerful speech on "unhealthy-mindedness" that can have only escaped from a spirit in sore trouble.' Actually, no play in the whole canon is remoter from 'morbid pessimism' than *Measure for Measure*, or less properly to be associated in mood with *Hamlet* or *Troilus and Cressida*. For the attitude towards death (and life, of course) that the Friar recommends is rejected not merely by Claudio, but by its total context in the play, the varied positive aspects of which it brings out – its significance being that it does so. In particular this significance appears when we consider the speech in relation to the assortment of attitudes towards death that the play dramatizes. Barnardine is an unambiguous figure. Claudio shrinks from death because, once he sees a chance of escape, life, in spite of all the Friar may have said, asserts itself, with all the force of healthy natural impulse, as undeniably real and poignantly desirable; and also because of eschatological terrors, the significance of which is positive, since they are co-relatives of established positive attitudes (the suggestion of Dante has often been noted). Isabella can exhibit a contempt of death because of the exaltation of her faith. Angelo begs for death when he stands condemned, not merely in the eyes of others, but in his own eyes, by the criteria upon which his self-approval has been based; when, it may fairly be said, his image of himself shattered, he has already lost his life.

The death-penalty of the Romantic comedy convention that Shakespeare starts from he puts to profoundly serious use. It is a necessary instrument in the experimental demonstration upon Angelo:

> hence shall we see,
> If power change purpose, what our seemers be.

The demonstration is of human nature, for Angelo is

> man, proud man,
> Drest in a little brief authority,
> Most ignorant of what he's most assured.
> His glassy essence ...   [II, ii, 117]

Of the nature of the issue we are reminded explicitly again and again:

> If he had been as you, and you as he,
> You would have slipped like him ...   [II, ii, 64]

> How would you be
> If He, which is the top of judgment, should
> But judge you as you are? O! think on that.   [II, ii, 75]

> Go to your bosom;
> Knock there, and ask your heart what it doth know
> That's like my brother's fault; if it confess
> A natural guiltiness such as is his,
> Let it not sound a thought upon your tongue
> Against my brother's life.   [II, ii, 136]

The generalized form in which the result of the experiment may be stated is, 'Judge not, that ye be not judged' – how close in this play Shakespeare is to the New Testament, Wilson Knight (whose essay in *The Wheel of Fire* gives the only adequate account of *Measure for Measure* I know) and R. W. Chambers (see *Man's Unconquerable Mind*) have recognized. But there is no need for us to create a perplexity for ourselves out of the further recognition that, even in the play of which this is the moral, Shakespeare conveys his belief that law, order, and formal justice are necessary. To talk in this connexion of the 'underlying dilemma' of the play is to suggest (in keeping with the general purpose of Knights's paper) that Shakespeare shows himself the victim of unresolved contradictions, of mental conflict or of uncertainty. But, surely, to believe that some organs and procedures of social discipline are essential to the maintenance of society needn't be incompatible with recognizing profound and salutary wisdom in 'Judge not, that ye be not judged', or with believing that it is our duty to keep ourselves alive to the human and personal actualities that underlie the 'impersonality' of justice. Complexity of attitude isn't necessarily conflict or contradiction; and, it may be added (perhaps the reminder will be found not unpardonable), some degree of complexity of attitude is involved in all social living. It is Shakespeare's great triumph in *Measure for Measure* to have achieved so inclusive and delicate a complexity, and to have shown us complexity distinguished from contradiction, conflict and uncertainty, with so sure and subtle a touch. The quality of the whole, in fact, answers to the promise of the poetic texture, to which Knights, in his preoccupation with a false trail, seems to me to have done so little justice.

To believe in the need for law and order is not to approve of any and every law; and about Shakespeare's attitude to the particular law in question there can be no doubt. We accept the law as a necessary datum, but that is not to say that we are required to accept it in any abeyance of our critical faculties. On the contrary it is an obvious challenge to judgement, and its necessity is a matter of the total challenge it subserves to our deepest sense of responsibility and our most comprehensive and delicate powers of discrimination. We have come now, of course, to the treatment of sex in *Measure for Measure*, and I find myself obliged to insist once more that complexity of attitude needn't be ambiguity, or subtlety uncertainty.

The attitude towards Claudio we have dealt with. Isabella presents a subtler case, but not, I think, one that ought to leave us in any doubt. 'What,' asks Knights, 'are we to think of Isabella? Is she the embodiment of a chaste serenity, or is she, like Angelo, an illustration of the frosty lack of sympathy of a self-regarding puritanism'? But why assume that it must be 'either or' – that she has to be merely the one or else merely the other? It is true that, as Knights remarks, *Measure for Measure* bears a relation to the Morality; but the Shakespearean use of convention permits far subtler attitudes and valuations than the Morality does. On the one hand, Isabella is clearly not a simple occasion for our feelings of critical superiority. The respect paid her on her entry by the lewd and irreverent Lucio is significant, and she convincingly establishes a presence qualified to command such respect. Her showing in the consummate interviews with Angelo must command a measure of sympathy in us. It is she who speaks the supreme enunciation of the key-theme:

> man, proud man,
> Drest in a little brief authority . . .

On the other hand, R. W. Chambers is certainly wrong in contending that we are to regard her with pure uncritical sympathy as representing an attitude endorsed by Shakespeare himself.

To begin with, we note that the momentary state of grace to which her influence lifts Lucio itself issues in what amounts to a criticism – a limiting and placing criticism:

> *Lucio:* I hold you as a thing ensky'd and sainted:
> By your renouncement an immortal spirit,
> And to be talked with in sincerity,
> As with a saint.
> *Isab.:* You do blaspheme the good in mocking me.

Lucio: Do not believe it. Fewness and truth, 'tis thus:
          Your brother and his lover have embrac'd:
          As those that feed grow full, as blossoming time
          That from the seedness the bare fallow brings
          To teeming foison, even so her plenteous womb
          Expresseth his full tilth and husbandry.

                                              [I, iv, 34]

This is implicit criticism in the sense that the attitude it conveys,
while endorsed dramatically by the exalted seriousness that is a
tribute to Isabella, and poetically by the unmistakable power of
the expression (it comes, we feel, from the centre), is something
to which she, with her armoured virtue, can't attain. We note
further that this advantage over her that Lucio has (for we feel it to
be that, little as he has our sympathy in general) comes out again
in its being he who has to incite Isabella to warmth and persistence
in her intercession for Claudio. The effect of this is confirmed
when, without demanding that Isabella should have yielded to
Angelo's condition, we register her soliloquizing exit at the end of
Act IV, Sc. ii; it is not credibly an accidental touch:

          Then, Isabel, live chaste, and, brother, die:
          More than our brother is our chastity.

The cumulative effect is such that it would need a stronger argument that R. W. Chambers's to convince us that there oughtn't
to be an element of the critical in the way we take Isabella's parting discharge upon Claudio:

Isab.:   Take my defiance:
          Die, perish! Might but my bending down
          Reprieve thee from thy fate, it should proceed,
          I'll pray a thousand prayers for thy death,
          No word to save thee.
Claud.: Nay, hear me, Isabel.
Isab.:   O! fie, fie, fie.
          Thy sin's not accidental, but a trade.
          Mercy to thee would prove itself a bawd:
          'Tis best that thou diest quickly.

                                              [Going.
Claud.:   O hear me, Isabella!

It is all in keeping that she should betray, in the exalted assertion of her chastity, a kind of sensuality of martyrdom:

> were I under the terms of death,
> The impression of keen whips I'd wear as rubies,
> And strip myself to death, as to a bed
> That longing have been sick for, ere I'd yield
> My body up to shame.
>
> [II, iv, 100]

Finally, it is surely significant that the play should end upon a hint that she is to marry the Duke – a hint that, implying a high valuation along with a criticism, aptly clinches the general presentment of her.

But at this point I come sharply up against the casual and confident assumption that we must all agree in a judgement I find staggering: 'it is significant that the last two acts, showing obvious signs of haste, are little more than a drawing out and resolution of the plot.' The force of this judgement, as the last sentence of Knights's first paragraph confirms, is that the 'drawing out and resolution of the plot', being mere arbitrary theatre-craft done from the outside, in order to fit the disconcerting development of the poet's essential interests with a comedy ending that couldn't have been elicited out of their inner logic, are not, for inter-pretive criticism, significant at all. My own view is clean contrary: it is that the resolution of the plot of *Measure for Measure* is a consummately right and satisfying fulfilment of the essential design; marvellously adroit, with an adroitness that expresses, and derives from, the poet's sure human insight and his fineness of ethical and poetic sensibility.

But what one makes of the ending of the play depends on what one makes of the Duke; and I am embarrassed about proceeding, since the Duke has been very adequately dealt with by Wilson Knight, whose essay Knights refers to. The Duke, it is important to note, was invented by Shakespeare; in *Promos and Cassandra*, Shakespeare's source, there is no equivalent. He, his delegation of authority and his disguise (themselves familiar romantic conven-tions) are the means by which Shakespeare transforms a romantic comedy into a completely and profoundly serious 'criticism of life'. The more-than-Prospero of the play, it is the Duke who initiates and controls the experimental demonstration – the controlled experiment – that forms the action.

There are hints at the outset that he knows what the result will be; and it turns out that he had deputed his authority in full knowledge of Angelo's behaviour towards Mariana. Just what he is, in what subtle ways we are made to take him as more than a mere character, is illuminatingly discussed in *The Wheel of Fire*. Subtly and flexibly as he functions, the nature of the convention is, I can't help feeling, always sufficiently plain for the purposes of the moment. If he were felt as a mere character, an actor among the others, there would be some point in the kind of criticism that has been brought against him (not explicitly, I hasten to add, by Knights – though, in consistency, he seems to me committed to it). How uncondonably cruel, for example, to keep Isabella on the rack with the lie about her brother's death!

I am bound to say that the right way of taking this, and everything else that has pained and perplexed the specialists, seems to me to impose itself easily and naturally. The feeling about the Duke expressed later by Angelo –

> O my dread lord!
> I should be guiltier than my guiltiness,
> To think I can be undiscernible,
> When I perceive your grace, like power divine
> Hath look'd upon my passes,

the sense of him as a kind of Providence directing the action from above, has been strongly established. The nature of the action as a controlled experiment with the Duke in charge of the controls, has asserted itself sufficiently. We know where we have to focus our critical attention and our moral sensibility: not, that is, upon the Duke, but upon the representatives of human nature that provide the subjects of the demonstration. This, we know, is to be carried to the promised upshot –

> hence shall we see,
> If power change purpose, what our seemers be,

which will be, not only the exposure of Angelo, but his exposure in circumstances that develop and unfold publicly the maximum significance.

The reliance on our responding appropriately is the more

patently justified and the less questionable (I confess, it seems to me irresistible) in that we can see the promise being so consummately kept. The 'resolution of the plot', ballet-like in its patterned formality and masterly in stage-craft, sets out with lucid pregnancy the full significance of the demonstration: 'man, proud man', is stripped publicly of all protective ignorance of 'his glassy essence'; the ironies of 'measure for measure' are clinched; in a supreme test upon Isabella, 'Judge not, that ye be not judged' gets an ironical enforcement; and the relative values are conclusively established – the various attitudes settle into their final placing with regard to one another and to the positives that have been concretely defined.

I don't propose to do a detailed analysis of this winding-up – that seems to me unnecessary; if you see the general nature of what is being done, the main points are obvious. I will only refer, in illustration of the economy of this masterpiece in which every touch has significance, to one point that I don't remember to have seen noted. There is (as every one knows) another invention of Shakespeare's besides the Duke – Mariana, and her treatment by Angelo. It wasn't, as R. W. Chambers thinks, merely in order to save Isabella's chastity that Shakespeare brought in Mariana; as the winding-up scenes sufficiently insist, she plays an important part in the pattern of correspondences and responses by which, largely, the moral valuations are established. In these scenes, Angelo's treatment of her takes its place of critical correspondence in relation to Claudio's offence with Juliet; and Claudio's offence, which is capital, appears as hardly an offence at all, by any serious morality, in comparison with Angelo's piece of respectable prudence.

Finally, by way of illustrating how the moral aspect of the play is affected by an understanding of the form and convention, I must glance at that matter of Angelo's escape from death – and worse than escape ('. . . the pardon and marriage of Angelo not merely baffles the strong indignant claim of justice', etc.) – which has stuck in the throats of so many critics since Coleridge. One has, then, to point out as inoffensively as possible that the point of the play depends upon Angelo's not being a certified criminal-type, capable of a wickedness that marks him off from you and me:

> Go to your bosom;
> Knock there, and ask your heart what it doth know

> That's like my brother's fault: if it confess
> A natural guiltiness such as is his,
> Let it not sound a thought upon your tongue
> Against my brother's life.

> If he had been as you, and you as he,
> You would have slipp'd like him . . .

There is a wider application than that which is immediately intended by the speaker. If we don't see ourselves in Angelo, we have taken the play very imperfectly. Authority, in spite of his protest, was forced upon him, and there are grounds for regarding him as the major victim of the experiment. He was placed in a position calculated to actualize his worst potentialities; and Shakespeare's moral certainly isn't that those potentialities are exceptional. It is not for nothing that Isabella reluctantly grants:

> I partly think
> A due sincerity govern'd his deeds
> Till he did look on me.

If any further argument should seem necessary for holding it possible, without offending our finer susceptibilities, to let Angelo marry a good woman and be happy, it may be said in complete seriousness that he has, since his guilty self-committals, passed through virtual death; perhaps that may be allowed to make a difference. It is not merely that immediate death has appeared certain, but that his image of himself, his personality as he has lived it for himself as well as for the world, having been destroyed, he has embraced death:

> I am sorry that such sorrow I procure:
> And so deep sticks it in my penitent heart
> That I crave death more willingly than mercy:
> 'Tis my deserving, and I do entreat it.

The bright idea of the recent 'Marlowe' production, the idea of injecting point, interest and modernity into the play by making him a study in neurotic abnormality, strained and twitching from his first appearance, was worse than uncalled-for. But then, if you can't accept what Shakespeare does provide, you have, in some way, to import your interest and significance.

THE CRITICISM
OF SHAKESPEARE'S LATE PLAYS

A Caveat

I HAVE before me two essays on *Cymbeline*. In the later[1] of them Fr. A. A. Stephenson both criticizes the account of the play offered by F. C. Tinkler in the earlier,[2] and offers a positive account of his own. With the criticisms I find myself pretty much in agreement; but I also find myself as unconvinced by the new interpretation as by Tinkler's – or any other that I have read. Fr. Stephenson, judging that Tinkler's attempt to explain the play in terms 'of critical irony' and 'savage farce' doesn't cover the admitted data, himself observes, and argues from, what he takes to be a significant recurrence of 'valuation-imagery'. But while developing his argument he at the same time – and this is the curious fact that seems to me to deserve attention – makes a firm note of another set of characteristics, and draws an explicit conclusion:

the inequalities, the incongruities, the discontinuity, the sense of different planes, the only spasmodic and flickering life in *Cymbeline*. It must, I think, be recognized that *Cymbeline* is not an 'organic whole', that it is not informed and quickened by an idea-emotion in all its parts.

The stress laid on these characteristics of the play seems to me much more indisputably justified than that laid on the valuation-imagery. So much so, in fact, that the question arises: Why didn't both Fr. Stephenson and Tinkler (whose argument also derives from observation of these characteristics) rest in the judgement that the play 'is not an "organic whole", that it is not informed and quickened by an idea-emotion in all its parts'? Why must they set out to show that it is, nevertheless, to be paradoxically explained in terms of a pressure of 'significance' –

significance, according to Fr. Stephenson, of a kind that cannot be conveyed?

That two such intelligent critics, bent on conclusions so different, should countenance one another in this kind of proceeding suggests some reflections on the difficulties and temptations of Shakespeare criticism – and especially of criticism of the late plays – at the present time. We have left Bradley fairly behind. We know that poetic drama is something more than drama in verse, and that consideration of the drama cannot be separated from consideration of the poetry. We are aware of subtle varieties of possibility under the head of convention, and we know we must keep a vigilant eye open for the development of theme by imagery and symbolism, and for the bearing of all these on the way we are to take character, action and plot. Shakespeare's methods are so subtle, flexible and varied that we must be on our guard against approaching any play with inappropriate preconceptions as to what we have in front of us. By assuming that the organization is of a given kind we may incapacitate ourselves for seeing what it actually is, and so miss, or misread, the significance. What a following-through of F. C. Tinkler's and Fr. Stephenson's account will, I think, bring home to most readers is that we may err by insisting on finding a 'significance' that we assume to be necessarily there.

I have put the portentous word in inverted commas in this last use of it, in order not to suggest a severity of judgement that is not intended. The play contains a great variety of life and interest, and if we talk of 'inequalities' and 'incongruities' it should not be to suggest inanity or nullity: out of the interplay of contrasting themes and modes we have an effect as (to fall back on the usefully corrective analogy) of an odd and distinctive music. But the organization is not a matter of a strict and delicate subservience to a commanding significance, which penetrates the whole, informing and ordering everything – imagery, rhythm, symbolism, character, episode, plot – from a deep centre: *Cymbeline* is not a great work of art of the order of *The Winter's Tale*.

The Winter's Tale presents itself as the comparison with which to make the point, in that it belongs with *Cymbeline* to the late group of plays – plays that clearly have important affinities, though my purpose here is to insist on the differences. In academic

tradition *The Winter's Tale* is one of the 'romantic' plays; the
adjective implying, among other things, a certain fairy-tale licence
of spirit, theme and development – an indulgence, in relation to
reality, of some of the less responsible promptings of imagination
and fancy. Thus we have the sudden, unheralded storm of jealousy
in Leontes, the part played by the oracle, the casting-out and preservation of the babe, the sixteen-year gap in the action, the
pastoral scene (regarded as a pretty piece of poetical by-play) and,
finally, the return to life after sixteen years' latency of Galatea-
Hermione, in the reconciliation-tableau. But all this has in the
concrete fulness of Shakespeare's poetry an utterly different
effect from what is suggested by the enumeration. *The Winter's
Tale*, as D. A. Traversi shows so well in his *Approach to Shakespeare*, is a supreme instance of Shakespeare's poetic complexity –
of the impossibility, if one is to speak with any relevance to the
play, of considering character, episode, theme, and plot in abstraction from the local effects, so inexhaustibly subtle in their
inter-play, of the poetry, and from the larger symbolic effects to
which these give life.

Properly taken, the play is not romantically licentious, or loose
in organization, or indulgent in a fairy-tale way to human fondness. What looked like romantic fairy-tale characteristics turn out
to be the conditions of a profundity and generality of theme. If we
approach expecting every Shakespearean drama to be of the same
kind as *Othello*, we criticize Leontes' frenzy of jealousy as disconcertingly sudden and unprepared. But if our preconceptions
don't prevent our being adverted by imagery, rhythm, and the
developing hints of symbolism – by the subtle devices of the
poetry and the very absence of 'psychology' – we quickly see
that what we have in front of us is nothing in the nature of a novel
dramatically transcribed. The relations between character, speech
and the main themes of the drama are not such as to invite a
psychologizing approach; the treatment of life is too generalizing
(we may say, if we hasten to add 'and intensifying'); so large a
part of the function of the words spoken by the characters is so
plainly something other than to 'create' the speakers, or to advance an action that can profitably be considered in terms of the
interacting of individuals. The detail of Shakespeare's processes
this is not the place for discussing; anyone who wants hints for the

analysis will find all that can be asked in D. A. Traversi's book. It is enough here to remind the reader of the way in which the personal drama is made to move upon a complexity of larger rhythms – birth, maturity, death, birth ('Thou mettest with things dying, I with things new-born'); Spring, Summer, Autumn . . .

> Sir, the year growing ancient.
> Not yet on summer's death, nor on the birth
> Of trembling winter . . .

– so that the pastoral scene is something very much other than a charming superfluity. The power and subtlety of the organization – and this is a striking instance of Shakespeare's ability to transmute for serious ends what might have seemed irremediably romantic effects – are equal to absorbing into the profoundly symbolic significance of the whole even the *coup de théâtre* with which Pauline justifies her sixteen years of double-living and funereal exhortation.

As Fr. Stephenson points out, there is no such organization in *Cymbeline*. The romantic theme remains merely romantic. The reunions, resurrections and reconciliations of the close belong to the order of imagination in which 'they all lived happily ever after'.[1] Cloten and the Queen are the wicked characters, step-mother and son, of the fairy-tale: they don't strike us as the expression of an adult intuition of evil. Posthumus's jealousy, on the other hand (if I may supplement Fr. Stephenson's observation: 'the "evil" characters, in particular, do not receive full imaginative realization'), is real enough in its nastiness, but has no significance in relation to any radical theme, or total effect, of the play. And here there is opportunity for a brief aside in illustration

---

1. 'A ce moment parut doña Luz, l'air timide. (Dès qu'il l'aperçut, le général la prit par la main.)

"Ma nièce, lui-dit-il, le visage joyeux, tu peux aimer sans crainte Cœur-Loyal, il est vraiment mon fils. Dieu a permis que je le retrouve au moment où j'avais renoncé à jamais au bonheur!"

La jeune fille poussa un cri de joie et abandonna sa main à Rafael, qui tomba à ses pieds. En même temps le général s'approcha de sa femme et dans la réunion qui suivit on oublia tous les malheurs du passé en songeant à l'avenir qui promettait tant de joie.'

Les Trappeurs de l'Arkansas, Gustave Aimard.

of the variety of Shakespeare's dramatic modes. Jealousy is a theme common to *The Winter's Tale*, *Othello* and *Cymbeline*. In *The Winter's Tale* there is no psychological interest; we don't ask (so long as we are concerning ourselves with Shakespeare): What elements in Leontes' make-up, working in what way, explain this storm? The question is irrelevant to the mode of the play. *Othello*, on the other hand, it would not be misleading to describe as a character-study. The explosive elements have been generated between the very specifically characterized Othello and his situation, and Iago merely touches them off. Posthumus's case actually answers to the conventional account of Othello's: the noble hero, by nature far from jealous, is worked on and betrayed by devilish Italian cunning – Iachimo is, quite simply, the efficient cause that Iago, in the sentimentalized misreading of *Othello*, is seen as being. Posthumus suffers remorse for his murderous revulsion, but we are not to consider him degraded by his jealousy, or seriously blamable. Simply, he is a victim. He falls in with a villain who, out of pure malice, deceives him about Imogen, and, after strange vicissitudes, fairy-tale fortune brings the lovers together again to enjoy a life of happiness. Shakespeare, that is, has taken over a romantic convention and has done little to give it anything other than a romantic significance.[1]

Why then should two such intelligent critics as those in question not settle down in the obvious judgement that the play challenges? I have already suggested that the answer should be sought in terms of a reaction against what may be called the Bradley–Archer[2] approach to Shakespeare. In the case of *Cymbeline* the assumption that a profound intended significance must be discovered in explanation of the pecularities of the play is fostered by the presence of varied and impressive evidence of the Shakespearean genius.

Strength could be adduced in a wealth of illustration. I myself have long carried mental note of a number of passages from *Cymbeline* that seemed to me memorable instances of Shake-

1. In *Pericles* he took over a romantic play, and the three acts that are clearly his are remarkable for the potency of the transmuting 'significance'.
2. See *The Old Drama and the New* by William Archer. T. S. Eliot comments interestingly on the book in the essay called 'Four Elizabethan Dramatists' (*Selected Essays*).

speare's imagery and versification. Two in particular I will mention. One is Posthumus's description of the battle [V. iii, lines 14 to 51]. It is a remarkable piece of vigorous dramatic felicity. The precisely right tone, a blend of breathless excitement, the professional soldier's dryness, and contempt (towards the Lord addressed), is perfectly got. There are some fine examples of Shakespearean compression and ellipsis; and here, surely, is strength in imagery:

> and now our cowards,
> Like fragments in hard voyages, become
> The life of the need: having found the back-door open
> Of the unguarded hearts, heavens, how they wound!

In 'like fragments in hard voyages' and the 'back-door' we have, in imagery, the business-like and intense matter-of-factness, at once contemptuous and, in its ironical dryness, expressive both of professional habit and of controlled excitement, that gives the speech its highly specific and dramatically appropriate tone. The other passage is Posthumus's prison speech in the next scene [V, iv, 3–29], so different in tone and movement:

> Most welcome, bondage! for thou art a way,
> I think, to liberty: yet am I better
> Than one that's sick of the gout; since he had rather
> Groan so in perpetuity than be cured
> By the sure physician, death, who is the key
> To unbar these locks.

This doesn't belong to 'romantic comedy', nor does the dialogue with the gaoler at the end of the scene. And here, and in the many vigorously realized passages, we have the excuse for the attempt, in spite of 'the inequalities, the incongruities, the discontinuity, the sense of different planes', to vindicate the play (for that, paradoxically, is Fr. Stephenson's aim as well as Tinkler's) in terms of a profound significance. But surely there should be no difficulty in recognizing that, wrestling with a job undertaken in the course of his exigent profession, Shakespeare might, while failing to find in his material a unifying significance such as might organize it into a profound work of art, still show from place to place, when prompted and incited congenially, his characteristic realizing genius?

Cymbeline, then, is not like *The Winter's Tale* a masterpiece. *The Tempest* is by more general agreement a masterpiece than *The Winter's Tale*, but it is a very different kind of thing (to complete briefly the hint of comparison I threw out above). Lytton Strachey in his essay on 'Shakespeare's Final Period' (see *Books and Characters*), gives us an opening: 'There can be no doubt that the peculiar characteristics which distinguish *Cymbeline* and *The Winter's Tale* from the dramas of Shakespeare's prime are present here in still greater degree. In *The Tempest*, unreality has reached its apotheosis.' Lytton Strachey's 'unreality', strongly derogatory in intention, has to be understood, of course, in relation to the Bradley–Archer assumptions of his approach. Actually, it seems to me that *The Tempest* differs from *The Winter's Tale* in being much closer to the 'reality' we commonly expect of the novelist. The 'unreality', instead of penetrating and transmuting everything as in *The Winter's Tale*, is in *The Tempest* confined to Prospero's imagery and its agents. Prospero himself, the Neapolitan and Milanese nobility and gentry, Stephano and Trinculo, the ship's crew – all these belong as much to the 'reality' of the realistic novelist as the play of *Othello* does. Prospero manages the wreck, lands the parties and directs their footsteps about the island to the final convergence, but they strike us, in their behaviour and conversation, as people of the ordinary everyday world. The courtiers are Elizabethan quality, and Gonzalo's attempt to distract the king and raise the tone of the conversation with a piece of advanced thought from Montaigne is all in keeping. Even Caliban (though sired by the devil on a witch) leads the modern commentator, quite appropriately, to discuss Shakespeare's interest in the world of new discovery and in the impact of civilization on the native.

The 'unreality' functions in Ariel and in the power (as it were a daydream actualized) that enables Prospero to stage the scene of repentance and restitution. But the nature of this power as a licence of imagination stands proclaimed in the essential symbolism of the play; and not only does Prospero finally renounce magic, break his staff and drown his book, but the daydream has never been allowed to falsify human and moral realities. That Alonso should, without the assistance of magic, suffer pangs of conscience is not in the least incredible; on the other hand, we note that the sinister pair, Sebastian and Antonio, remain what they were. They may be fairly set over against Ferdinand and Miranda, and they represent a potent element in that world to which the lovers are returning, and in which, unprotected by magic, they are to spend their lives.

> O brave new world,
> That has such people in't!

– that is both unironical and ironical. Shakespeare's power to present acceptably and movingly the unironical vision (for us given in Miranda and Ferdinand) goes with his power to contemplate the irony at the same time.

Rightly, then, is *The Tempest* accounted a masterpiece; but I am not sure that it deserves the relative valuation it commonly enjoys. The judgement that *The Winter's Tale* is a masterpiece would not, I think, in general be as readily concurred in; and it is true that *The Tempest* has nothing in it to trouble in the same way the reader who finds difficulty in arriving at an unqualified acceptance of the statue business as part of a total unromantic response. But the perfection (or something like it) of *The Tempest* is achieved within limits much narrower than those of *The Winter's Tale*; and the achievement by which, in *The Tempest*, the time-gap of *The Winter's Tale* is eliminated ought not to be allowed to count improperly in the comparative valuation. With the absence of the time-gap goes also an absence of that depth and richness of significance given, in *The Winter's Tale*, by the concrete presence of time in its rhythmic processes, and by the association of human growth, decay and rebirth with the vital rhythms of nature at large. The range, the depth, the effect that I have described as both generalizing and intensifying, for which *The Winter's Tale* is remarkable, are missing in *The Tempest*. Not that while reading *The Tempest* we are at all inclined to judge that this inspired poetry and this consummate art reveal any falling-off in the poet's creative vigour; yet we may perhaps associate the mood expressed in Prospero's farewell to *his* art and in the 'insubstantial pageant' speech (the mood in which Shakespeare can in the symbolic working of the drama itself so consciously separate his art from the life it arranges and presents – life that is 'such stuff as dreams are made on') – perhaps we may associate this mood with

an absence of that effect as of the sap rising from the root which
The Winter's Tale gives us. No doubt it might as truly be said of
Florizel and Perdita as it has been of Ferdinand and Miranda, that
they are lovers seen by one who is himself beyond the age of
love, but Florizel and Perdita are not merely two individual
lovers; they are organic elements in the poetry and symbolism
of the pastoral scene, and the pastoral scene is an organic part
of the whole play.

LITERATURE AND SOCIETY [1]

TWO or three years back, or at any time in the Marxizing decade, having been invited to discourse on 'Literature and Society', I should have known what was expected of me – and what to expect. I should have been expected to discuss, or to give opportunities for discussing, the duty of the writer to identify himself with the working-class, the duty of the critic to evaluate works of literature in terms of the degree in which they seemed calculated to further (or otherwise) the proper and pre-destined outcome of the class-struggle, and the duty of the literary historian to explain literary history as the reflection of changing economic and material realities (the third adjective, 'social', which I almost added here, would be otiose). I should have been braced for such challenges as the proposition that D. H. Lawrence, though he

was unquestionably aware of and tried to describe the outside forces that were undermining the bourgeois society into which he made his way . . . saw those forces from a bourgeois viewpoint, as destroyers to be combated. Consequently he misrepresented reality.[2]

What was wrong with his work was that he 'shared the life of a social class which has passed its prime'.

I assume that the expectation I should have had to address myself to in those not so very remote days isn't entertained at all generally on the present occasion, and I assume it gladly. But that does leave me with a large undirected formula on my hands: 'Literature and Society' might, in fact, seem to be daunting and embarrassing in the wealth of possibilities it covers. However, certain major interests of my own respond to it quite comfortably and I had no difficulty in concluding that I should be expected to do what, in accordance with those interests, it would suit me to do: that is, to try and define on what grounds and in what ways

1. This is the substance of an address given to the Students' Union of the London School of Economics and Politics.
2. *The Mind in Chains*, edited by C. Day Lewis.

the study of literature – literature as it concerns me, who am avowedly in the first place a literary critic – should, I think, be seen as intimately relevant to what may be presumed to be the major interest of students at the London School of Economics.

For if the Marxist approach to literature seems to me unprofitable, that is not because I think of literature as a matter of isolated works of art, belonging to a realm of pure literary values (whatever they might be); works regarding the production of which it is enough to say that individuals of specific creative gifts were born and created them. No one interested in literature who began to read and think immediately after the 1914 war – at a time, that is, co-incident with the early critical work of T. S. Eliot – can fail to have taken stock, for conscious rejection, of the Romantic critical tradition (if it can be called that): the set of ideas and attitudes about literary creation coming down through the nineteenth century. That tradition laid all the stress on inspiration and the individual genius. How do masterpieces arrive? Gifted individuals occur, inspiration sets in, creation results. Mr Eliot, all of whose early prose may be said to have been directed against the Romantic tradition, which till then had not been effectively challenged, lays the stress on the other things (or some of them) besides individual talent and originative impulse from within that have to be taken account of when we try to understand any significant achievement in art. Of course, it was no discovery that there are these things to be taken account of: criticism and literary history had for generations dealt in influences, environments and the extra-literary conditions of literary production. But we are apt to be peculiarly under the influence of ideas and attitudes of which we are not fully conscious, they prevail until rejected, and the Romantic set – an atmosphere of the unformulated and vague – may be said to have prevailed until Mr Eliot's criticism, co-operating with his poetry, made unconsciousness impossible and rejection inevitable.

Something like the idea of Tradition so incisively and provocatively formulated by him plays, I think, an essential part in the thinking of everyone today who is seriously interested in literature. If I say that idea represents a new emphasis on the social nature of artistic achievement, I ought to add at once that the word 'social' probably doesn't occur in the classical essay, *Tradition and*

the Individual Talent (the word that takes Mr Eliot's stress is
'impersonal'). The 'society' implied in this 'social' – and (which
is, of course, my point) in the idea of Tradition – is not the
Marxist concept; and the difference is what I have my eye on.
But let me first remind you of the idea as Mr Eliot formulates it.
The individual writer is to be aware that his work is of the Literature to which it belongs and not merely added externally to it.
A literature, that is, must be thought of as essentially something
more than an accumulation of separate works: it has an organic
form, or constitutes an organic order, in relation to which the
individual writer has his significance and his being. 'Mind' is the
analogy (if this is the right word) used:

He must be aware that the mind of Europe – the mind of his own
country – a mind which he learns in time to be much more important
than his own private mind – is a mind which changes . . .

and so on.

Something, I said, in the nature of this way of thinking seems to
me inevitable for anyone who thinks about literature at all. The
ways in which it is at odds with Marxist theories of culture are
obvious. It stresses, not economic and material determinants, but
intellectual and spiritual, so implying a different conception
from the Marxist of the relation between the present of society
and the past, and a different conception of society. It assumes that,
enormously – no one will deny it – as material conditions count,
there is a certain measure of spiritual autonomy in human affairs,
and that human intelligence, choice and will do really and effectively operate, expressing an inherent human nature. There is a
human nature – that is how, from the present point of view, we
may take the stress as falling; a human nature, of which an understanding is of primary importance to students of society and
politics. And here is the first way that presents itself of indicating
the kind of importance literature – the literary critic's literature –
should be recognized to have for such students: the study of it is,
or should be, an intimate study of the complexities, potentialities
and essential conditions of human nature.

But that by itself is too large a proposition to take us anywhere.
Let me, by way of moving towards more discussible particularity, make another obvious note on the difference between the

Marxist kind of attitude toward literature and that represented by the idea of Tradition I've invoked. It's true that this latter stresses the social aspect of creative achievement as the Romantic attitude didn't: but it allows for the individual aspect more than the Marxist does. This is inevitably a crude way of putting it – as you'll see, that 'inevitably' is my point. But to postpone that for a moment: you can't be interested in literature and forget that the creative individual is indispensable. Without the individual talent there is no creation. While you are in intimate touch with literature no amount of dialectic, or of materialistic interpretation, will obscure for long the truth that human life lives only in individuals: I might have said, the truth that it is only in individuals that society lives.

The point I wanted to make is this: you can't contemplate the nature of literature without acquiring some inhibition in respect of that antithesis, 'the individual and society', and losing any innocent freedom you may have enjoyed in handling it; without, that is, acquiring some inhibiting apprehensions of the subtleties that lie behind the antithesis.

An illustration presents itself readily. I have spoken of the 'Romantic' attitude, and the phrase might be called misleading, since the actual poets of the Romantic period – Wordsworth, Coleridge, Byron, Shelley, Keats – differ widely among themselves. No general description worth offering will cover them. Though as influences they merge later in a Romantic tradition, they themselves do not exemplify any common Romanticism. What they have in common is that they belong to the same age; and in belonging to the same age they have in common something negative: the absence of anything to replace the very positive tradition (literary, and more than literary – hence its strength) that had prevailed till towards the end of the eighteenth century. It is this tradition, the Augustan, that I want to consider briefly first.

It originated in the great changes in civilization that make the second part of the seventeenth century look so unlike the first, and its early phase may be studied in the works of John Dryden. The conventions, standards and idiom of its confident maturity offer themselves for contemplation in *The Tatler* and *The Spectator*. The relevant point to be made about it for the present purpose is that it laid a heavy stress on the social. Its insistence that man is a social being was such as to mean in effect that all his activities, inner as well as outer, that literature took cognizance of, were to belong to an overtly social context. Even the finest expressions of the spirit were to be in resonance with a code of Good Form – for with such a code the essential modes and idioms of Augustan culture were intimately associated. The characteristic movements and dictions of the eighteenth century, in verse as well as prose, convey a suggestion of social deportment and company manners.

An age in which such a tradition gets itself established is clearly an age in which the writer feels himself very much at one with society. And the Augustan heyday, the Queen Anne period, was a period very confident of its flourishing cultural health. But we should expect such an insistence on the social to have in time a discouraging effect on the deeper sources of originality, the creative springs in the individually experiencing mind. We should expect to find evidence of this in the field of poetry, and we find it. This is no place to pretend to give a fair account of the Augustan decline, which was a complex affair: I'm merely stressing an aspect that is relevant to my present purpose. Where, then, a tradition like that I have adumbrated prevails, there is bound before long to be a movement of protest in minds of the kind that ought to be creative. They will feel that conventional expression – that which, nevertheless, seems natural and inevitable to the age – imposes a conventional experience, and that this, suppressing, obtruding, muffling, and misrepresenting, is at odds with their own. There will be a malaise, a sense of blunted vitality, that would express iteself to this effect if it were fully conscious. Full consciousness is genius, and manifests itself in technical achievement, the new use of words. In the seventeen-eighties it is William Blake.

Blake in his successful work says implicitly: 'It is I who see and feel. I see only what I see and feel only what I feel. My experience is mine, and in its specific quality lies its significance'. He may be said to have reversed for himself the shift of stress that occurred at the Restoration. But to such a reversal there is clearly a limit. Blake uses the English language, and not one of his own invention; and to say that he uses it is not to say that it is for him a mere instrument. His individuality has developed in terms of the language, with the ways of experiencing, as well as of handling experience, that it involves. The mind and sensibility that he has to express are of the language.

I may seem here to be handling a truism of the kind that there's no point in recalling. But I believe that the familiar truths that we contemplate when we contemplate the nature of language – in the way, that is, in which we have to when we take a critical interest in literature – have the familiarity of the familiar things that we tend to lose sight of when we begin to think. And what I have just been touching on is perhaps the most radical of the ways in which the literary critic's interest in literature leads to a new recognition of the essentially social nature of the individual – and (I may add) of the 'reality' he takes for granted.

In any case, I want to pass at once to an order of consideration that will probably seem to have more discussible bearings on the normal pre-occupations of the student of society. The measure of social collaboration and support represented by the English language didn't make Blake prosperously self-sufficient: he needed something more – something that he didn't get. This is apparent in a peculiar kind of difficulty that his work offers to the critic. I am thinking of the difficulty one so often has in deciding what kind of thing it is one has before one.

> A petty sneaking knave I knew –
> O! Mr Cromek, how do ye do?

– that is clearly a private blow-off. *The Tyger* is clearly a poem (in spite of the bluffed-out defeat in the third stanza).[1] But again and again one comes on the thing that seems to be neither wholly private nor wholly a poem. It seems not to know what it is or where it belongs, and one suspects that Blake didn't know. What he did know – and know deep down in himself – was that he had no public: he very early gave up publishing in any serious sense. One obvious consequence, or aspect, of this knowledge is the carelessness that is so apparent in the later prophetic books. Blake had ceased to be capable of taking enough trouble. The uncertainty I have just referred to is a more radical and significant

1. The second interrogative sentence of the stanza Blake made a number of attempts at completing before he threw up the problem.

form of the same kind of disability. In the absence, we may put it, of adequate social collaboration (the sense, or confident prospect, of a responsive community of minds was the minimum he needed) his powers of attaining in achieved creation to that peculiar impersonal realm to which the work of art belongs and in which minds can meet – it is as little a world of purely private experience as it is the public world of the laboratory – failed to develop as, his native endowment being what it was, they ought to have done.[1]

The inevitable way in which serious literary interest develops towards the sociological is suggested well enough here. What better conditions, one asks, can one imagine for a Blake? Can one imagine him in a tradition that should have nurtured his genius rather than have been something it had to escape from, and in a society that should have provided him with the best conceivable public? But what is the best conceivable public? And so one is led on to inquire into the nature and conditions of cultural health and prosperity.

I will illustrate with a line of reflection that has occupied me a good deal. Harking back from Blake one notes that the establishment of the Augustan tradition was associated with – indeed, it involved – a separation, new and abrupt, between sophisticated culture and popular. Anticipating the problem of bringing home as convincingly and vividly as possible to (say) students of modern social and political questions what is meant by saying that there was, in the seventeenth century, a real culture of the people, one thinks first of Dryden's contemporary, Bunyan. If *The Pilgrim's Progress* is a humane masterpiece, that is in spite of the bigoted

[1] The following, both in its curiously striking qualities – it clearly comes from a remarkable poet – and in what I take to be its lack of self-sufficiency as a poem, seems to me a representatively suggestive document of the case I have been trying to describe:

> Truly, my Satan, thou art but a dunce,
> And dost not know the garment from the man;
> Every harlot was a virgin once,
> Nor canst thou ever change Kate into Nan.
>
> Tho' thou art worship'd by the names divine
> Of Jesus and Jehovah, thou art still
> The Son of Morn in weary night's decline,
> The lost traveller's dream under the hill.

sectarian creed that Bunyan's allegory, in detail as in sum, directs itself to enforcing. In spite of his aim, a humane masterpiece resulted because he belonged to the civilization of his time, and that meant, for a small-town 'mechanick', participating in a rich traditional culture.

It is on the reader approaching as a literary critic that this truth compels itself (others seem to miss it).[1] Consider, not one of the most striking illustrations of Bunyan's art, such as the apologia and self-characterization of By-Ends,[2] but a passage representative in a routine kind of way:

Christian: Did you hear no talk of neighbour Pliable?
Faithful: Yes, Christian, I heard that he followed you till he came at the Slough of Despond, where, as some said, he fell in; but he would not be known to have so done; but I am sure he was soundly bedabbled with that kind of dirt.
Christian: And what said the neighbours to him?
Faithful: He hath, since his going back, been had greatly in derision, and that among all sorts of people; some do mock and despise him; and scarce will any set him on work. He is now seven times worse than if he had never gone out of the city.
Christian: But why should they be so set against him, since they also despise the way that he forsook?
Faithful: Oh, they say, hang him, he is a turncoat! he was not true to his profession. I think God has stirred up even his enemies to hiss at him, and make him a proverb, because he hath forsaken the way.
Christian: Had you no talk with him before you came out?
Faithful: I met him once in the streets, but he leered away on the other side, as one ashamed of what he had done; so I spoke not to him.
Christian: Well, at my first setting out, I had hopes of that man; but now I fear he will perish in the over-throw of the city; for it is happened to him according to the true proverb, *The dog is turned to his own vomit again; and the sow that was washed, to her wallowing in the mire.*

The relation of this to the consummate art of the By-Ends passage is plain; we have the idiomatic life that runs to saw and proverb, and runs also to what is closely akin to these, the kind

1. See, e.g., two books discussed below (see p. 204). *John Bunyan: Maker of Myths*, by Jack Lindsay, and *John Bunyan: Mechanick Preacher*, by William York Tindall.
2. See page 207 below.

of pungently characterizing epitome represented by 'turncoat' (which, with a capital letter, might have appeared in By-Ends' list of his kindred). The vitality here is not merely one of raciness; an art of civilized living is implicit, with its habits and standards of serious moral valuation.

This then is what the literary critic has to deduce from his reading. If he finds that others, interested primarily in social reform and social history, do not seem properly impressed by such evidence, he can, by way of bringing home to them in how full a sense there is, behind the literature, a social culture and an art of living, call attention to Cecil Sharp's introduction to *English Folk-Songs from the Southern Appalachians*. Hearing that the English folk-song still persisted in the remoter valleys of those mountains Sharp, during the war of 1914, went over to investigate, and brought back a fabulous haul. More than that, he discovered that the tradition of song and dance (and a reminder is in place at this point of the singing and dancing with which the pilgrims punctuate their progress in the second part of Bunyan's Calvinistic allegory) had persisted so vigorously because the whole context to which folk-song and folk-dance belong was there too: he discovered, in fact, a civilization or 'way of life' (in our democratic parlance) that was truly an art of social living.

The mountaineers were descended from settlers who had left this country in the eighteenth century.

The region is from its inaccessibility a very secluded one . . . the inhabitants have for a hundred years or more been completely isolated and shut off from all traffic with the rest of the world. Their speech is English, not American, and, from the number of expressions they use that have long been obsolete elsewhere, and the old-fashioned way in which they pronounce many of their words, it is clear that they are talking the language of a past day. They are a leisurely, cheery people in their quiet way, in whom the social instinct is very highly developed . . . They know their Bible intimately and subscribe to an austere creed, charged with Calvinism and the unrelenting doctrines of determinism or fatalism . . . They have an easy unaffected bearing and the unselfconscious manners of the well-bred . . . A few of those we met were able to read and write, but the majority were illiterate. They are however good talkers, using an abundant vocabulary racily and picturesquely.

That the illiterate may nevertheless reach a high level of culture will surprise only those who imagine that education and cultivation are convertible terms. The reason, I take it, why these mountain people, albeit unlettered, have acquired so many of the essentials of culture, is partly to be attributed to the large amount of leisure they enjoy, without which, of course, no cultural development is possible, but chiefly to the fact that they have one and all entered at birth into the full enjoyment of their racial inheritance. Their language, wisdom, manners and the many graces of life that are theirs, are merely racial attributes which have been gradually acquired and accumulated in past centuries and handed down generation by generation, each generation adding its quota to what it received . . .

. . . Of the supreme value of an inherited tradition, even when unenforced by any formal school education, our mountain community in the Southern Highlands is an outstanding example.

Correlation of Cecil Sharp's introduction with Bunyan should sufficiently confirm and enforce the significance attributed to Bunyan above. And Bunyan himself shows how the popular culture to which he bears witness could merge with literary culture at the level of great literature. The converse, regarding the advantages enjoyed by the literary writer, the 'intellectual', need not be stated: they are apparent in English literature from Shakespeare to Marvell. We see Marvell – it is, of course, for this reason I name him – as pre-eminently refined, European in sophistication, and intimately related to a tradition of courtly urbanity; but his refinement involves no insulation from the popular – the force of which judgement is brought out by contrast with Pope. In prose, compare Halifax with Dryden. Halifax (the Trimmer) is 'easy', 'natural' and urbane, a master of the spoken tone and movement; in short he is unmistakably of the Restoration; but his raciness and idiomatic life relate him as unmistakably to Bunyan. I don't think I am being fanciful when I say that when Dryden gets lively, as in the Preface to *All for Love*, he tends towards the Cockney; he assimilates, in fact, with L'Estrange. At least, his polite idiomatic ease is wholly of the coffee-house, that new organ of metropolitan culture the vibration of which seems essentially to exclude any intimate relations with Bunyan's world. The exclusive, or insulating, efficacy of the politeness of Augustan verse, even in Pope, whose greatness manifests itself in his power of transcending the

Augustan, is at any rate obvious; and Pope's politeness belongs to the same world as the politeness of Addison's prose. Where, in short, Augustan convention and idiom, with their social suggestion, prevail, sophisticated culture cuts itself off from the traditional culture of the people.

The eighteenth century, significantly, had a habit of attempting the naïve, and, characteristically, evoked its touching simplicities of low life in modes that, Augustan tone and movement being inescapable, evoked at the same time the elegant and polite. It is one of the manifestations of Blake's genius that he, unique in this, can – the evidence is apparent here and there in *Poetical Sketches* (1783) – be genuinely, in verse that has nothing Augustan about it, of the people (popular London in his time was clearly still something of a 'folk'). The mention of this aspect of Blake serves to bring out by contrast the significance of Wordsworth's kind of interest in rustic life. It is essentially – in so far as it is more than nominal – an interest in something felt as external to the world to which he himself belongs, and very remote from it: the reaction that Wordsworth represents against the Augustan century doesn't mean any movement towards re-establishing the old organic relations between literary culture and the sources of vitality in the general life. By Wordsworth's death, the Industrial Revolution had done its work, and the traditional culture of the people was no longer there, except vestigially.

No one, then, seriously interested in modern literature can feel that it represents a satisfactory cultural order. But if anyone should conclude that it ought therefore – the literature that the literary critic finds significant – to be contemned, and that a really significant contemporary literature would have the Marxizing or Wellsian kind of relation to social, political and economic problems, he may be reminded that, but for the persisting literary tradition, the history I have so inadequately sketched would have been lost, and our notions of what a popular culture might be, and what relations might exist between it and a 'highbrow' culture, would have been very different. And it needs stressing that where there isn't, in the literary critic's sense, a significant contemporary literature, the literary tradition – the 'mind' (and mind includes memory) – is not fully alive. To have a vital literary culture we must have a literature that is a going concern;

and that will be what, under present conditions of civilization, it has to be. Where it is can be determined only by the literary critic's kind of judgement.

What one has to suggest in general by way of urging on students of politics and society the claims of literary studies (I don't mean the ordinary academic kind) to be regarded as relevant and important is that thinking about political and social matters ought to be done by minds of some real literary education, and done in an intellectual climate informed by a vital literary culture. More particularly, of course, there are, capable of endless development and illustration, the hints for the social historian and the sociologist I have thrown out in the course of my argument. These all involve the principle that literature will yield to the sociologist, or anyone else, what it has to give only if it is approached as literature. For what I have in mind is no mere industrious searching for 'evidence', and collecting examples, in whatever happens to have been printed and preserved. The 'literature' in question is something in the definition of which terms of value-judgement figure essentially, and something accessible only to the reader capable of intelligent and sensitive criticism.

I am thinking, in this insistence, not of the actual business of explicit valuation, but of the ability to respond appropriately and appreciatively to the subtleties of the artist's use of language and to the complexities of his organizations. And I am not thinking merely of poetry. It is to poetry, mainly, that I have made my illustrative references, but if one were enumerating the more obvious kinds of interest that literature has to offer the sociologist, prose fiction, it is plain, would figure very largely. There seems to be a general view that anyone can read a novel; and the uses commonly made of novels as evidence, sociological or other, would seem to illustrate that view. Actually, to use as evidence or illustration the kinds of novel that are most significant and have most to offer requires an uncommon skill, the product of a kind of training that few readers submit themselves to. For instance, the sociologist can't learn what D. H. Lawrence has to teach about the problems of modern civilized man without being a more intelligent critic than any professional literary guide he is likely to find. Nor, without being an original critic, adverted and sensitized by experience and the habit of critical analysis, can the social psychologist learn what Conrad has to teach about the social nature of the individual's 'reality'.

Then there are kinds of inquiry where the literary-critical control cannot be so delicate and full, but where, at the same time, the critic's experience and understanding have their essential rôle. Hints are to be found in Gilbert Murray's *Rise of the Greek Epic* – a book that has a still greater value when pondered along with Dame Bertha Phillpotts' *Edda and Saga*. She, towards the end of chapter viii, throws out some peculiarly good incitements to inquiry. Observing that the Saga literature was democratic ('it had to interest all classes, because all classes listened to it') she says:

> But though it was democratic in the sense that it appealed to the whole people, [it] was mainly the creation of the intellectual classes, and it obviously brought about a general levelling-up of interests and culture. This is an effect of oral literature which it is easy to overlook. Printing . . . makes knowledge very easy to avoid.

And she makes – is it acceptable? (and if not, why not?) – an optimistic suggestion about broadcasting.

These instances must suffice – I choose them for their suggestive diversity. Instead of offering any further, I will end by making a general contention in other terms. Without the sensitizing familiarity with the subtleties of language, and the insight into the relations between abstract or generalizing thought and the concrete of human experience, that the trained frequentation of literature alone can bring, the thinking that attends social and political studies will not have the edge and force it should.

SOCIOLOGY AND LITERATURE

THAT 'spirit of the age' doesn't amount to much of an explanation where changes of literary taste are concerned, and that there are sociological lines of inquiry capable of yielding profit – in these suggestions one readily concurs: they are not new, and were not when Dr Schücking's essay, *The Sociology of Literary Taste*, was first published in German, in 1931. And I cannot, after several re-readings, find substantially more to bring away from it. That anyone could write the most casual note relevant to Dr Schücking's title without proposing any more definite inquiry than he does, or making any more of an attempt to distinguish between possible inquiries, is remarkable. But then, the apparent casualness of his whole procedure is very remarkable. He throws out the most vague of general suggestions and proceeds to demonstrate them with a random assortment of 'evidence' in this way (p. 10):

Elsewhere, with the general understanding less, the conditions were still worse. Chaucer had his Visconti – the unscrupulous John of Gaunt. He ate the bread of a court at which French taste and the rather stale theories of love of past centuries were still accepted; and a good part of his literary activity ran on these lines. They still left room for the play of his sense of grace and elegance, his taste and wit and irony, but not for the real element in his popularity, his wonderful sense of the Thing as It Is, which made him at the end of his life the most vivid portrayer of the Middle Ages. But by then his relations with the court had probably grown far less intimate, and it may be that these descriptions were written for recital to an audience of burghers. Such examples might be multiplied.

This kind of thing, of course, is not a use of evidence at all, and no amount of it can forward our knowledge or understanding of anything. If you are to conduct a profitable argument about the 'sociological medium of literature' you must have a more inward acquaintance with the works of literature from which you argue than can be got from a literary history or a text-book. There is indeed a most interesting and significant inquiry to be made into the sociological background of Chaucer, but it is of a kind that can hardly fall within Dr Schücking's ken. It is what, in spite of the reference to 'the philologists', Raleigh suggests here (in one of the extracts from his lecture-notes published posthumously as *On Writing and Writers*):

It is impossible to overpraise Chaucer's mastery of language. Here at the beginning, as it is commonly reckoned, of Modern English literature, is a treasury of perfect speech. We can trace his themes, and tell something of the events of his life. But where did he get his style – from which it may be said that English literature has been (in some respects) a long falling away?

What is the ordinary account? I do not wish to cite individual scholars, and there is no need. Take what can be gathered from the ordinary text-books – what are the current ideas? Is not this a fair statement of them?

'English was a despised language little used by the upper classes. A certain number of dreary works written chiefly for homiletic purposes or in order to appeal to the humble people, are to be found in the half-century before Chaucer. They are poor and flat and feeble, giving no promise of the new dawn. Then arose the morning star! Chaucer adopted the despised English tongue and set himself to modify it, to shape it, to polish it, to render it fit for his purpose. He imported words from the French; he purified the English of his time from its dross; he shaped it into a fit instrument for his use.'

Now I have no doubt that a competent philologist examining the facts could easily show that this account *must* be nonsense, from beginning to end. But even a literary critic can say something certain on the point – perhaps can even give aid by divination to the philologists, and tell them where it will best repay them to ply their pickaxes and spades.

No poet makes his own language. No poet introduces serious or numerous modification into the language that he uses. Some, no doubt, coin words and revive them, like Spenser or Keats in verse, Carlyle or Sir Thomas Browne in prose. But least of all great English poets did Chaucer mould and modify the speech he found. The poets who take liberties with speech are either prophets or eccentrics. From either of these characters Chaucer was far removed. He held fast by communal and social standards for literary speech. He desired to be understood of the people. His English is plain, terse, homely, colloquial English, taken alive out of daily speech. He expresses his ideal again and again . . .

Chaucer has expressed his views on the model literary style so clearly and so often, and has illustrated them so well in his practice, that no mistake is possible. His style is the perfect courtly style; it has all the qualities of ease, directness, simplicity, of the best colloquial English, in short, which Chaucer recognized, three centuries before the French Academy, as the English spoken by cultivated women in society. His 'facound', like Virginia's, 'is ful womanly and pleyn'. He avoids all 'counterfeited terms', all subtleties of rhetoric, and addresses himself to the 'commune intente'.

. . . Now a style like this, and in this perfection, implies a society at the back of it. If we are told that educated people at the Court of Edward III spoke French and that English was a despised tongue, we could deny it on the evidence of Chaucer alone. His language was shaped for him, and it cannot have been shaped by rustics. No English style draws so much as Chaucer's from the communal and colloquial elements of the language. And his poems made it certain that from his youth up he had heard much admirable, witty talk in the English tongue.

Investigations of the kind suggested could be prosecuted – they are, indeed, likely to be conceived – only by a more sensitively critical reader of English poetry than most scholars show themselves to be, even when they are born to the language. A point that has to be made is that Dr Schücking's dealings with German literature seem to be no more inward than his dealings with English. He certainly betrays no sense of not being qualified to deal with English, and his confident reference to Thackeray as 'the greatest English novelist of the nineteenth century' (p. 7) is representative. But if the critical quality of his approach to literature can be brought home in a quotation, this is perhaps the one:

The deepening of the cleavage between public and art through Naturalism. The aesthetic movement in Germany was of no great importance. Of more note was the German movement of Naturalism. In Germany naturalism (or realism) came remarkably late. In France its most eminent representative, Emile Zola, had written his most famous novels in the 'seventies; he sought admittance to the Academy in 1888. About the same time (1886) Tennyson indignantly hurled his lame imprecations (now of great historic interest) in *Locksley Hall sixty years after* against the new movement, which had already had in the 'seventies a typical representative in Henry James. Tolstoy's *Anna Karenina* was begun in 1874; Ibsen's *League of Youth* dates from 1869.

It is bad enought to bracket the Tolstoy of *Anna Karenina* with

Zola, as this passage seems to do. But to be capable of referring to Henry James as a 'typical representative' of Naturalism, or a typical representative of anything – what considerable conclusions are compatible with such an approach?

There can be no pleasure in elaborating this kind of commentary. Enough has been said as a preliminary to making the point Dr Schücking's book provides an opportunity for making – the more suitable an opportunity because of the drive in sociology with which, in its English publication, it is associated. It is an elementary point, but one that seems unlikely to get too much attention as the Sociology of Literature forges ahead: no 'sociology of literature' and no attempt to relate literary studies with sociological will yield much profit unless informed and controlled by a real and intelligent interest – a first-hand critical interest – in literature. That is, no use of literature is of any use unless it is a real use; literature isn't so much material lying there to be turned over from the outside, and drawn on, for reference and exemplification, by the critically inert.

There are, indeed, many different kinds of possible sociological approach to literature and of literary approach to sociology, but to all of them the axiom just enunciated applies. To Dr Schücking's offer it most patently applies. You cannot make changes in taste the centre of your inquiry without implicitly undertaking, as an essential part of your work, a great deal of perception, discrimination and analysis such as demand a sensitive, trained and active critic. You can, of course, collect some kinds of relevant material without being, critically, very deeply engaged: there is, for instance, the economic history of literature. (Dr Schücking, by the way, doesn't mention Beljame's admirable book,[1] nor does he the work of A. S. Collins.)[2] But as soon as you start using it in a 'sociological' handling of literature, as, for instance, in *Fiction and the Reading Public*, you are committed to being essentially and

1. *Le public et les hommes de lettres au XVIII siècle*, by Alexandre Beljame (translated as *Men of Letters and the English Public in the XVIIIth Century*).

2. Nor does he appear to know Courthope's *History of English Poetry* or Leslie Stephen's *English Literature and Society in the XVIIIth Century*, both of which are half a century old. Leslie Stephen's classic is brief and modest, but in the ready fulness of ordered knowledge and with the ease of a trained and vigorous mind he really *does* something; something as relevant to Dr

constantly a critic if your use of the information and of the literature is to amount to anything.

This is so, even if your concern is primarily with the condition of the literary market – so long, that is, as your concern is with the effect of these on literature. And any serious inquiry into changes of 'taste' (a more complex and less delimitable field of interest than perhaps Dr Schücking realizes) tends inevitably to develop into a consideration of the most radical ways in which the use of individual talent is conditioned – into the kind of inquiry, for instance, suggested above into the art and language of Chaucer. Everyone interested in literature must have noted a number of inquiries of that order asking to be undertaken. It is an order of inquiry that, properly undertaken, would pre-eminently justify a 'sociology of literature'; but it could hardly propose itself except to a mind taking the most inward kind of critical interest in the relevant literature. That a German scholar should miss it where Chaucer is concerned is not surprising. That Shakespeare, though Dr Schücking makes a great deal (relatively) of the Elizabethan theatre as a sociological theme, shouldn't propose it to him brings home more strikingly the disability of an external approach. This suggests fairly enough all the significance he sees (p. 12):

New fields lay open. An infinitely wider sphere of activity showed itself. Literature was written no longer with an eye to the approval of a particular aristocratic patron, who might easily demand, in consequence of his conservative outlook, that traditions should be respected; and the work of the artist was no longer directed by a small and exclusive social group, whose atmosphere was the breath of his life. The

---

Schücking's confused and ambitious gesturings as this suggests: 'Briefly, in talking of literary changes, I shall have, first, to take note of the main intellectual characteristics of the period; and secondly, what changes took place in the audience to which men of letters addressed themselves, and how the gradual extension of the reading class affected the development of the literature addressed to them'. The possibilities of a 'sociology of literary taste' are incomparably better presented by Leslie Stephen's book (written late in life as lectures, which he was too ill to deliver, or to correct for publication) than by Dr Schücking's inconsequent assortment of loosely thrown out and loosely thought adumbrations.

artist depended instead indirectly on the box-office receipts, and directly on the theatre managers who ordered plays from him.

But in the theatre the works that won applause were precisely those which through their closeness to life and their realistic psychology were bound to be foreign to the taste of the aristocratic world. Thus the shackles of tradition could here be struck off and a wealth of varied talents could find scope.

What wealth of 'sociological' interest presented by Shakespearean drama and the Elizabethan theatre has been missed here there is no need to insist; this is a field that has had much attention in recent years. Its significance for an understanding of the nature of a national culture and of the conditions of vitality in art will not be quickly exhausted. There are other fields less obviously inviting attention and offering less obvious rewards. There is that marked out by L. C. Knights in his paper on 'The Social Background of Metaphysical Poetry' (see *Scrutiny*, Vol. XIII, 207) – one to which it is very much to be hoped that he will devote a book. If it is asked of such an inquiry whether it is primarily sociological or literary it will be enough to answer that it represents the kind of sociological interest into which a real literary, or critical, interest in literature develops, and that, correlatively, the sociologist here will be a literary critic or nothing.

For to insist that literary criticism is, or should be, a specific discipline of intelligence is not to suggest that a serious interest in literature can confine itself to the kind of intensive local analysis associated with 'practical criticism' – to the scrutiny of the 'words on the page' in their minute relations, their effects of imagery, and so on: a real literary interest is an interest in man, society and civilization, and its boundaries cannot be drawn; the adjective is not a circumscribing one. On the other hand, a living critical inwardness with literature, and a mind trained in dealing analytically with it, would have improved much work undertaken in fields for which these qualifications are not commonly thought of as among the essential ones, if they are thought of as relevant at all. Here is a passage from a distinguished historian – one distinguished among historians for the humane cultivation he brings to his work (he is, moreover, discussing the quality of English civilization in the seventeenth century):

Since thought among common people had now reached a momentary perfection for the purposes of religious and imaginative literature, the English language was for those purposes perfect. Whether in the Bible, the play-book, the street ballad, the broad-sheet or report of the commonest dialogue of daily life, it was always the same language, ignorant of scientific terms, and instinct with a poetical feeling about life that was native to the whole generation of those who used it. Its fault, corresponding to the state of thought in that age, is want of exactness and of complexity in ideas, that renders it unfit for psychology or for close analysis of things either material or spiritual.

A footnote to this paragraph runs:

If Mill or Darwin, Browning or Mr Meredith had tried to express their ideas in the English of the seventeenth century they would have failed. The extreme simplicity of Hamlet's thought is only concealed by the obscurity of his motives and the richness of his poetical diction.

G. M. Trevelyan's *England Under the Stuarts* (which I re-read with gratitude at fairly frequent intervals – the quotation comes from page 54) was written, of course, a good many years ago, and literary fashions since then have changed in ways calculated to help, in respect of the particular point, a similarly cultivated writer who should embark on a similar undertaking. Nevertheless, the passages are sufficiently striking: the appreciation of seventeenth century civilization that goes with them is clearly a seriously limited one. And one would be agreeably surprised to find a historian who was essentially any better provided with the kind of qualification under discussion.

On the same author's recent *English Social History* I have heard the comment that it is disappointing in that it does little more than add to some economic history that almost every educated person knows some information about English life that any educated person has gathered, and could supplement, from his acquaintance with English literature. Whether this is a fair comment or not (and the book was clearly designed for a given kind of public – it belongs with that higher advertising of England which has employed so many distinguished pens of late), it is certain that a social historian might make a much greater, more profound and more essential use of literature than *English Social History* exemplifies; a use that would help him to direct his inquiries by some sharper definition of aims and interests than is

represented by Mr Trevelyan's account of 'social history' in his
Introduction:

Social history might be defined negatively as the history of a people
with the politics left out.

Positively, we have:

But social history does not merely provide the required link between
economic and political history. It has also its own positive value and
peculiar concern. Its scope may be defined as the daily life of the inhabitants of the land in past ages: this includes the human as well as the
economic relation of different classes to one another, the character of
family and household life, the conditions of labour and of leisure, the
attitude of man to nature, the culture of each age as it arose out of these
general conditions of life, and took ever-changing forms in religion,
literature and music, architecture, learning and thought.

A social historian who appreciated the nature of the vitality
of the English language and of English literature in the seventeenth century – and such appreciation itself leads to sociological
inquiries – would, in defining and developing his interests, be
sensitized by more positively and potently realized questions than
any that have given life, form and significance to *English Social
History*: questions as to the conditions of a vigorous and spiritually
vital culture, the relations between the sophisticated and the
popular, and the criteria by which one might attempt to judge the
different phases of a national civilization. To say this is not to en-
visage with complaisance a habit of naïve comparative valuation.
But social history will have shape and significance – will have
significant lines and contours – only so far as informed by the life
and pressure of such questions; and as intent preoccupations it is
towards comparative valuation that they press, even if they
actually issue in none that is explicit, definitive and comprehensive. What, as civilization to live in and be of, did England
offer at such and such a time? As we pass from now to then, what
light is thrown on human possibilities – on the potentialities and
desirabilities of civilized life? In what respects might it have been
better to live then than now? What tentative conception of an
ideal civilization are we prompted towards by the hints we
gather from history? It is with such questions in mind – which is
not to say that he will come out with answers to them – that a

social historian, in so far as history is anything more than an assemblage of mechanically arranged external information, must define the changes and developments that he discerns. Some such questions were no doubt in Mr Trevelyan's mind. But they hadn't a sufficient concrete charge; they were not sufficiently informed with that kind of appreciation of the higher possibilities of a civilization which, in the earlier book, would have made it impossible for him to pronounce that the English of the seventeenth century was inadequate to the complexities and subtleties of Browning and Meredith, or to suggest that one has disposed of the language of Shakespeare in saying that 'the extreme simplicity of Hamlet's thought is only concealed by the obscurity of his motives and the richness of his poetical diction'.

Mr Trevelyan, as I have said, is distinguished among historians by his general culture. But his use of literature is nowhere more than external (see, *e.g.*, his use of Chaucer in *England in the Age of Wycliffe*): he knows that literature exists – it nowhere amounts to evidence of much more than that. The possible uses of literature to the historian and the sociologist are many in kind, and all the important ones demand that the user shall be able, in the fullest sense, to read. If, for instance, we want to go further than the mere constatation that a century and a half ago the family counted for much more than it does now, if we want some notion of the difference involved in day-to-day living – in the sense of life and its dimensions and in its emotional and moral accenting – for the ordinary cultivated person, we may profitably start trying to form it from the novels of Jane Austen. But only if we are capable of appreciating shade, tone, implication and essential structure – as (it is necessary to add) none of the academically, or fashionably, accredited authorities seems to be.

On the other hand, the understanding of literature stands to gain much from sociological interests and a knowledge of social history. And this is an opportunity to mention, for illustration, Mr Yvor Winters' *Maule's Curse*, a book that deserves to be distinguished, seeing how few good books of literary criticism appear. In it Mr Winters, by relating the key American authors with the New England background and the heritage of Puritanism, throws a truly revealing light on their work and on the evolution of American literature.

BUNYAN THROUGH MODERN EYES

MR LINDSAY is Marxist and psycho-analytic. The arrival of his book[1] reminded me of one on Bunyan that came out some years ago, and in this earlier book[2] now open before me – it is by William York Tindall – I read (p. 94):

> For the saints too the class struggle needed the dignity of divine auspices, and as the miserable of today look for their sanction to Karl Marx and *The Communist Manifesto*, their seventeenth-century predecessors looked to Jesus and the Bible.
> The religious man may remain only half-aware, or by virtue of a rationalization, quite unaware of the social or economic motives which determine his sectarian allegiance.

Mr Lindsay and Mr Tindall, then, in their modes of approach have something in common. But whereas Mr Lindsay is mainly concerned to show that Bunyan's religion was merely a self-un-comprehending reaction to the class-war, Mr Tindall is mainly concerned to show that Bunyan was merely one of a mob – a large, ludicrous and Hudibrastic mob of preaching and scribbling fanatics:

> Bunyan was one of a great number of eloquent tinkers, cobblers and tailors; he thought what they thought, felt what they felt, and wrote according to their conventions; he was one of hundreds of literary mechanicks, and he can be considered unique only by his survival to our day as the sole conspicuous representative of a class of men from whom he differed less in kind than in degree. (viii.)

While Mr Lindsay's 'merely' has the intention of exalting, the intention as well as the effect of Mr Tindall's is the reverse. It is true he speaks of Bunyan's 'genius', but what this consists in he gives no sign that he knows or cares. As for the superiority in 'expression': 'The qualities of style for which Bunyan is esteemed today', he says, 'his raciness, earthiness, and familiarity were common to his kind, and are not easily to be distinguished from

1. *John Bunyan: Maker of Myths.*
2. *John Bunyan: Mechanick Preacher.*

those of other mechanicks'. And any other superiority there may be doesn't impress Mr Tindall. His set attitude expresses itself in the heavy Gibbonian affectation that (inspired, no doubt, by Lytton Strachey) he practises, with complacent insistence, as his own style:

The ingenious speculations of Mr Gerald Owst have been valuable in suggesting the sermons of Bunyan's time as the principal sources of his similitudes ... Apparently at the impulse of the Spirit, Bunyan condescended to employ and to imitate for his imperishable works the materials of pamphlets, which are now as remote as they were once familiar, and of oral sermons, which are now, perhaps, recorded only in heaven. (p. 196.)

I still bear something of a grudge against *The New Republic* for having persuaded me, by a eulogistic review, to spend seventeen and six on such a book. The book has, nevertheless, a use. Mr Tindall – and in this he has the advantage over Mr Lindsay – is a scholar; his book represents a disciplined and laborious research, and makes a 'genuine contribution to knowledge' – one in which, moreover, in spite of the obtuseness and the offensive tone, we may see some value. In demonstrating so thoroughly that Bunyan was one of a host, and how much he belonged to his environment, Mr Tindall does, if not for himself, illuminate Bunyan's distinctive genius. And at the same time he tells us something about the genius of the English people in that age.

It is a richly fantastic background of fanaticism, bigotry and ignorance that is displayed for us in his account of the sectarian England of Bunyan's time. Here, for instance, is a passage he quotes from a broadside called *Divine Fire-Works*:

I have seen the Lord. The King;
Who appeared unto me
On (Innocents Day) the 28 of the last moneth.
He spake to me and with me ...
Then was I raised to sit up in my bed (in my shirt) smoaking like a
    furnace ...
Fear not it is I. Blu I.

Whereupon the Spirit within me (with exceeding joy) exceedingly
    groaned; & with a loud voice out-sounded
        O the Blu! O the Blu! O the Blu!
And the worm, and no man said, what Blu ...

That, of course, is a lunatic extreme; but lunatic extremes, Mr Tindall brings home to us, were common – were, one is inclined to say, what sectarian enthusiasm tended towards. Bunyan, of course, was a Baptist (Particular Open-Communion) and not a Quaker, Ranter or antinomian extremist. But Mr Tindall convincingly exhibits the world of fissiparous sects as one, and Bunyan and his works as essentially of it.

Where, then, did *The Pilgrim's Progress* get its classical quality from? Mr Tindall talks vaguely about Bunyan's 'art', and apparently sees in this nothing but a vividness and 'earthy vigour' of style. But it is not merely vividness and vigour (though these it certainly has) that make *The Pilgrim's Progress* a classic – a classic in the fullest sense. And it is not merely a certain superiority in vividness and vigour so unemphatically conceded by Mr Tindall to Bunyan that explains the following facts:

By 1692, according to Charles Doe, about one hundred thousand copies of *Pilgrim's Progress* had been sold; it had been translated into foreign tongues, and had surpassed by ninety thousand copies the combined sale of Benjamin Keach's two most popular allegories.

The England of the Sects, in thus distinguishing in favour of Bunyan, confirms the conclusions about it that we are in any case led to by *The Pilgrim's Progress* itself – *The Pilgrim's Progress* being, as Mr Tindall demonstrates, so completely and essentially representative (so essentially unoriginal, the implication almost is), and Bunyan so completely and essentially one of the mob of scribbling and preaching fanatics. That England, plainly, cannot be taken full account of in Hudibrastic (or Strachey-Gibbonian) terms; something besides fanaticism, bigotry and ignorance has to be invoked. For what makes *The Pilgrim's Progress* a great book, one of the great classics, is its humanity – its rich, poised and mature humanity. And this is not the less impressive for our being, here and there, by the allegorical intent of this and that incident, reminded of the uglier and pettier aspects of the intolerant creed, the narrow Calvinistic scheme of personal salvation, that Bunyan explicitly sets out to allegorize.

The Pilgrim's Progress, in fact, is the fruit of a fine civilization; the enthusiasts and mechanick preachers were not out of touch with a traditional wisdom. Bunyan as a popular homilist was, as

Mr G. R. Owst (in *Literature and Pulpit in Mediaeval England*) has sufficiently shown, in a tradition that goes uninterruptedly back beyond the Reformation to the Middle Ages. If one observes that this tradition owes its vitality to a popular culture it must be only to add that the place of religion in the culture is obvious enough. The same people that created the English language for Shakespeare's use speaks in Bunyan, though it is now a people that knows its Authorized Version.

Mr Tindall, however, has no use for these super-subtleties; he can explain Bunyan's art more simply:

To Bunyan the name By-Ends connoted ends other than that of salvation by imputed righteousness. . . . By-Ends is the product of the resentment against the Anglicans of an enthusiastic evangelist and despised mechanick . . . Bunyan's fortunate discovery that through these controlled debates between his hero and these caricatured projections of his actual enemies he could experience the pleasures of combat without the complications of reality invests *Pilgrim's Progress* with the character of a controversial Utopia. (60–62.)

And that's what Mr Tindall sees in By-Ends. There seems some point in quoting here what should be one of the best-known passages of Bunyan:

Christian: Pray, who are your kindred there, if a man may be so bold?

By-Ends: Almost the whole Town; and in particular, my Lord *Turnabout*, my Lord *Timeserver*, my Lord *Fair-speech*, (from whose ancestors that Town first took its name), also Mr *Smoothman*, Mr *Facing-bothways*, Mr *Anything*; and the Parson of our Parish, Mr *Two-tongues*, was my Mother's own Brother by Father's side; and to tell you the truth, I am become a Gentleman of good Quality; yet my Great Grandfather was but a Waterman, looking one way and rowing another; and I got most of my estate by the same occupation.

Christian: Are you a married man?

By-Ends: Yes, and my Wife is a very virtuous woman, the Daughter of a virtuous woman; she was my Lady *Faining's* daughter, therefore she came of a very honourable Family, and is arrived to such a pitch of breeding, that she knows how to carry it to all, even to Prince and Peasant. 'Tis true we somewhat differ in Religion from those of the stricter sort, yet but in two small points: First, we never strive against Wind and Tide: Secondly, we are always most zealous when Religion goes in his Silver Slippers; we love much to walk with him in the Street, if the Sun shines, and the People applaud him.

That is plainly traditional art and, equally plainly the life in it is of the people (not the less so for there being literary associations too). The names and racy turns are organic with the general styles and the style, concentrating the life of popular idiom, is the expression of popular habit – the expression of a vigorous humane culture. For what is involved is not merely an idiomatic raciness of speech, expressing a strong vitality, but an art of social living, with its mature habits of valuation. We must beware of idealizing, but the fact is plain. There would have been no Shakespeare and no Bunyan if in their time, with all its disadvantages by present standards, there had not been, living in the daily life of the people, a positive culture which has disappeared and for which modern revolutionaries, social reformers and Utopists do not commonly project any serious equivalent.

Contemplating one aspect of this past order Mr Tindall remarks that

the economic opinions of Bunyan, Baxter and the Quakers were the last moral vestiges of the Middle Ages.

This aspect causes some embarrassment to Mr Lindsay, who as a Marxist has to recognize that Bunyan (though of course we have to cheer him for standing up for his class) was wrong in opposing the development of the new economic order and trying to hold up the dialectic and hinder the growth of a proletariat: it was the rising bourgeoisie, trading, industrialist and capitalist, that was 'doing the work of history'. But Mr Lindsay has no difficulty in making Bunyan's religious preoccupations respectable by reducing them, with the help of psycho-analysis and history, to explanation in terms of class-relations and methods of production. This last is an ugly sentence; but Mr Lindsay's idiom doesn't lend itself to elegant or lucid summary. Here are representative passages (the argument of the book consists of the repetitive development – if that is the word, and perhaps the musical sense conveys the right suggestion – of such formulations):

The sense of unity, developed by the productive advance with its intensified socialization of method, cannot in such conditions be actualized. What would actualization mean? It would mean that social relationships would be made as harmoniously coherent as the method of production. But that is impossible in a class-society.

Therefore the sense of unity is abstracted.

So it is felt that if only a perfectly concordant scheme of son-father relationship can be imagined, this abstraction will balance the loss of unity in actual life. The religious intuition thus glosses over, emotionally cements, the discord between social relationship and productive methods. (38.)

Bunyan, according to Mr Lindsay (p. 192),

wanted to get outside the cramping, distorting social discord of his day into the fuller life of fellowship.

Though Mr Lindsay talks of 'fuller life' he proffers emptiness; like most Marxist writers who undertake to explain art and culture, he produces the effect of having emptied life of content and everything of meaning.

It is impossible in any case to believe that the classless society produced by the process that the Marxist's History has determined on could have a cultural content comparable with that represented by *The Pilgrim's Progress*. And Mr Lindsay almost goes out of his way to bring home to us without realizing it the problem of the religious sanction:

The world of light is not the land of death. It is the future of fellowship. The tale tells of the passage from privation and obstruction to light and joy and plenty. The heaven-symbol is brought down from beyond-death; it becomes a symbol of what earth could be made by fellowship.

Thus the allegory, which superficially is a story of how to die, is a stimulus to further living. (192.)

It's all quite simple – for Mr Lindsay. But Bunyan, he points out, is muddled; he can't really see that it's as simple as that. For instance:

He makes Christiana wade over the river at the end and leave her children behind. The picture is ridiculous. Here are husband and wife rushing off to death as the consummation of their purpose, yet the children are left to wander about on the banks of the death-river before they too are allowed to get over into heaven.

Bunyan here confessed his sense that something was wrong about the idea of death as the goal of life. (193.)

Mr Lindsay, of course, has no sense of betraying here the shallowness of his own ideas of life and death. But who with any wisdom to offer, worth listening to, could have published that as his reaction to the incomparable end of Part Two of *The Pilgrim's Progress*, where the pilgrims, waiting by the river, receive one by one the summons to cross? – Incomparable, for where else in prose can a like sustained exaltation be found?

When the time was come for them to depart, they went to the Brink of the River. The last words of Mr Dispondency were, *Farewell Night, welcome Day.* His daughter went through the River singing, but none could understand what she said.

Then it came to pass a while after, that there was a Post in the town that enquired for Mr Honest. So he came to his house where he was, and delivered to his hand these lines. *Thou art commanded to be ready against this day seven-night to present thyself before thy Lord at his Father's house.* And for a Token that my Message is true, *All thy Daughters of Musick shall be brought low.* Then Mr Honest called for his Friends, and said unto them, I die, but shall make no Will. As for my Honesty, it shall go with me; let him that comes after be told of this. When the day that he was to be gone was come, he addressed himself to go over the River. Now the River at the time overflowed the Banks in some places, but Mr Honest in his life-time had spoken to one Good-conscience to meet him there, the which he also did, and lent him his hand, and so helped him over. The last words of Mr Honest were, Grace reigns. So he left the World.

So it goes on, for pages, without a false or faltering note. It would be useless arguing with anyone who contended that the inspiration here was essentially a Utopian vision of what 'the earth might be made by fellowship'. Whatever of that element there may be in it, the whole effect is something far more complex and mature. It is something, clearly, that could not be reproduced today. Yet *The Pilgrim's Progress* must leave us asking whether without something corresponding to what is supremely affirmed in that exaltation, without an equivalently sanctioned attitude to death that is at the same time 'a stimulus to further living' (the contradiction that Mr Lindsay sees), there can be such a thing as cultural health.

LITERARY CRITICISM AND PHILOSOPHY

I MUST thank Dr Wellek[1] for bringing fundamental criticism to my work, and above all for raising in so complete a way an issue that a reviewer or two had more or less vaguely touched on – an issue of which no one can have been more conscious than myself, who had seen the recognition of it as an essential constituent of what I naturally (whatever the quality of my performance) hoped for: an appreciation of my undertaking. Dr Wellek points out, justly, that in my dealings with English poetry I have made a number of assumptions that I neither defend nor even state: 'I could wish', he says, 'that you had made your assumptions more explicitly and defended them systematically'. After offering me a summary of these assumptions, he asks me to 'defend this position abstractly and to become conscious that large ethical, philosophical and, of course, ultimately, also aesthetic *choices* are involved'.

I in my turn would ask Dr Wellek to believe that if I omitted to undertake the defence he desiderates it was not from any lack of consciousness: I knew I was making assumptions (even if I didn't – and shouldn't now – state them to myself quite as he states them) and I was not less aware than I am now of what they involve. I am interested that he should be able to say that, for the most part, he shares them with me. But, he adds, he would 'have misgivings in pronouncing them without elaborating a specific defence or a theory in their defence'. That, I suggest, is because Dr Wellek is a philosopher; and my reply to him in the first place is that I myself am not a philosopher, and that I doubt whether in any case I could elaborate a theory that he would find satisfactory. I am not, however, relying upon modesty for my defence. If I profess myself so freely to be no philosopher it is because I feel that I can afford my modesty; it is because I have pretensions –

1. This is a reply to criticisms of my book *Revaluation*, contributed by Dr René Wellek to *Scrutiny* for March, 1937.

pretensions to being a literary critic. And I would add that even if
I had felt qualified to satisfy Dr Wellek on his own ground I
should have declined to attempt it in that book.

Literary criticism and philosophy seem to me to be quite
distinct and different kinds of discipline – at least, I think they
ought to be (for while in my innocence I hope that philosophic
writing commonly represents a serious discipline, I am quite sure
that literary-critical writing commonly doesn't). This is not to
suggest that a literary critic might not, as such, be the better for a
philosophic training, but if he were, the advantage, I believe,
would manifest itself partly in a surer realization that literary
criticism is not philosophy. I pulled up just short of saying 'the
two disciplines . . .', a phrase that might suggest too great a
simplification: it is no doubt possible to point to valuable writing
of various kinds representing varying kinds of alliance between
the literary critic and the philosopher. But I am not the less sure
that it is necessary to have a strict literary criticism somewhere and
to vindicate literary criticism as a distinct and separate discipline.

The difficulty that one who approaches with the habit of one
kind of discipline has in duly recognizing the claims of a very
different kind – the difficulty of reconciling the two in a working
alliance – seems to me to be illustrated in Dr Wellek's way of referring to the business of literary criticism: 'Allow me', he says,
'to sketch your ideal of poetry, your "norm" with which you
measure every poet . . .' That he should slip into this way of
putting things seems to me significant, for he would on being
challenged agree, I imagine, that it suggests a false idea of the procedure of the critic. At any rate, he gives me an excuse for making,
by way of reminder, some elementary observations about that
procedure.

By the critic of poetry I understand the complete reader: the
ideal critic is the ideal reader. The reading demanded by poetry is
of a different kind from that demanded by philosophy. I should
not find it easy to define the difference satisfactorily, but Dr
Wellek knows what it is and could give at least as good an account
of it as I could. Philosophy, we say, is 'abstract' (thus Dr Wellek
asks me to defend my position 'more abstractly'), and poetry
'concrete'. Words in poetry invite us, not to 'think about' and
judge but to 'feel into' or 'become' – to realize a complex ex-

perience that is given in the words. They demand, not merely a fuller-bodied response, but a completer responsiveness – a kind of responsiveness that is incompatible with the judicial, one-eye-on-the-standard approach suggested by Dr Wellek's phrase: 'your "norm" with which you measure every poet'. The critic – the reader of poetry – is indeed concerned with evaluation, but to figure him as measuring with a norm which he brings up to the object and applies from the outside is to misrepresent the process. The critic's aim is, first, to realize as sensitively and completely as possible this or that which claims his attention; and a certain valuing is implicit in the realizing. As he matures in experience of the new thing he asks, explicitly and implicitly: 'Where does this come? How does it stand in relation to . . . ? How relatively important does it seem?' And the organization into which it settles as a constituent in becoming 'placed' is an organization of similarly 'placed' things, things that have found their bearings with regard to one another, and not a theoretical system or a system determined by abstract considerations.

No doubt (as I have admitted) a philosophic training might possibly – ideally would – make a critic surer and more penetrating in the perception of significance and relation and in the judgement of value. But it is to be noted that the improvement we ask for is of the critic, the critic as critic, and to count on it would be to count on the attainment of an arduous ideal. It would be reasonable to fear – to fear blunting of edge, blurring of focus and muddled misdirection of attention: consequences of queering one discipline with the habits of another. The business of the literary critic is to attain a peculiar completeness of response and to observe a peculiarly strict relevance in developing his response into commentary; he must be on his guard against abstracting improperly from what is in front of him and against any premature or irrelevant generalizing – of it or from it. His first concern is to enter into possession of the given poem (let us say) in its concrete fulness, and his constant concern is never to lose his completeness of possession, but rather to increase it. In making value-judgements (and judgements as to significance), implicitly or explicitly, he does so out of that completeness of possession and with that fulness of response. He doesn't ask, 'How does this accord with these specifications of goodness in poetry?'; he aims to make fully conscious and articulate the immediate sense of value that 'places' the poem.

Of course, the process of 'making fully conscious and articulate' is a process of relating and organizing, and the 'immediate sense of value' should, as the critic matures with experience, represent a growing stability of organization (the problem is to combine stability with growth). What, on testing and re-testing and wider experience, turn out to be my more constant preferences, what the relative permanencies in my response, and what structure begins to assert itself in the field of poetry with which I am familiar? What map or chart of English poetry as a whole represents my utmost consistency and most inclusive coherence of response?

From this consistency and this coherence (in so far as I have achieved them) it should, of course, be possible to elicit principles and abstractly formulable norms. Dr Wellek's first criticism of me is (to give it its least exceptionable force) that I haven't proceeded to elicit them: that, having written the book I undertook to write, I haven't gone on to write another book in which I develop the theoretical implications of the first (for it would be essentially a matter of two books, even if there were only one binding). To this I make again my modest reply that I doubt, in any case, my capacity to satisfy Dr Wellek in this respect. And I add again that I do not think my modesty has any adverse bearing on my qualifications for writing the book I did undertake to write. The cogency I hoped to achieve was to be for other readers of poetry – readers of poetry as such. I hoped, by putting in front of them, in a criticism that should keep as close to the concrete as possible, my own developed 'coherence of response', to get them to agree (with, no doubt, critical qualifications) that the map, the essential order, of English poetry seen as a whole did, when they interrogated their experience, look like that to them also. Ideally I ought perhaps (though, I repeat, I should not put my position in quite the terms Dr Wellek ascribes to me) to be able to complete the work with a theoretical statement. But I am sure that the kind of work that I have attempted comes first, and would, for such a theoretical statement to be worth anything, have to be done first.

If Dr Wellek should still insist that I ought, even if I declined to elaborate the philosophy implicit in my assumptions, at any rate to have been more explicit about them, I can only reply that I think I have gone as far in explicitness as I could profitably attempt to go, and that I do not see what would be gained by the kind of explicitness he demands (though I see what is lost by it). Has any reader of my book been less aware of the essential criteria that emerge than he would have been if I had laid down such general propositions as: 'poetry must be in serious relation to actuality, it must have a firm grasp of the actual, of the object, it must be in relation to life, it must not be cut off from direct vulgar living, it should be normally human . . .'? If, as I did, I avoided such generalities, it was not out of timidity; it was because they seemed too clumsy to be of any use. I thought I had provided something better. My whole effort was to work in terms of concrete judgements and particular analyses: 'This – doesn't it? – bears such a relation to that; this kind of thing – don't you find it so? – wears better than that', etc. If I had to generalize, my generalization regarding the relation between poetry and 'direct vulgar living' or the 'actual' would run rather in the following way than in that suggested by Dr Wellek: traditions, or prevailing conventions or habits, that tend to cut poetry in general off from direct vulgar living and the actual, or that make it difficult for the poet to bring into poetry his most serious interests as an adult living in his own time, have a devitalizing effect. But I cannot see that I should have added to the clarity, cogency or usefulness of my book by enunciating such a proposition (or by arguing it theoretically). Again, I did not say that the language of poetry 'should not flatter the singing voice, should not be merely mellifluous', etc. I illustrated concretely in comparison and analysis the qualities indicated by those phrases, pointed to certain attendant limitations, and tried to show in terms of actual poetic history that there were serious disadvantages to be recognized in a tradition that insisted on such qualities as essential to poetry. In fact, though I am very much aware of the shortcomings of my work, I feel that by my own methods I have attained a relative precision that makes this summarizing seem intolerably clumsy and inadequate. I do not, again, argue in general terms that there should be 'no emotion for its own sake, no afflatus, no mere generous emotionality, no luxury in pain and joy'; but by choice, arrangement and analysis of concrete examples I give those phrases (in so far, that is, as I have achieved my purpose) a precision of meaning they couldn't have got in any other way. There is, I hope, a chance that I may in this way have advanced theory, even if I haven't done the theorizing. I know that the cogency and precision I have aimed at are limited; but I believe that any approach involves limitations, and that it is by recognizing them and working within them that one may hope to get something done.

Dr Wellek has a further main criticism to bring against me: it is that my lack of interest in philosophy makes me unfair to the poets of the Romantic period. I hope he will forgive me if I say that his demonstration has, for me, mainly the effect of demonstrating how difficult it is to be a philosopher and a literary critic at the same time. The positive aim of his remarks he sums up as being 'to show that the romantic view of the world . . . underlies and pervades the poetry of Blake, Wordsworth and Shelley, elucidates many apparent difficulties, and is, at least, a debatable view of the world'. – 'The romantic view of the world', a view common to Blake, Wordsworth, Shelley and others – yes, I have heard of it; but what interest can it have for the literary critic? For the critic, for the reader whose primary interest is in poetry, those three poets are so radically different, immediately and finally, from one another that the offer to assimilate them in a common philosophy can only suggest the irrelevance of the philosophic approach.

My attitude towards Blake Dr Wellek, I think, misunderstands. He certainly misrepresents my verdict on the particular poem, the *Introduction to Songs of Experience*. The comparison with *Ash-Wednesday* has a context in the chapter to which the note challenged by Dr Wellek is appended, and, so far from arguing that Blake's poem is 'so ambiguous as to have no "right sense" ', I have in that note the explicit aim of showing how Blake, with his astonishingly original technique, achieves something like the extraordinary precision of *Ash-Wednesday*. And in general, where Blake is concerned, my intention is the reverse of a slighting one. My view of the poem, in fact, seems to me more favourable than that implied by Dr Wellek, who says: 'Actually I think the poem has only one possible meaning, which can be ascertained by a study of the whole of Blake's symbolical philosophy'. I myself, a literary critic, am interested in Blake because it is possible to say with reference to some of his work that his symbolical philosophy is one thing, his poetry another. I know that even in his best poetry symbolism appears, and I was aware of symbolism in the poem I picked on; but I judged that I might fairly avoid a large discussion that seemed inessential to the point I was proposing to make.

I will say now, though, that when in Blake's poetry his symbols function poetically they have, I believe, a life that is independent of his 'symbolical philosophy': for instance, 'Earth', 'starry pole', 'dewy grass' and 'wat'ry shore', in the *Introduction* to *Songs of Experience*, seem to me to have a direct evocative power. Knowledge of Blake's arbitrary assignment of value to a symbol may often help to explain why he should have written as he has done here, there and elsewhere; I do not believe that it will ever turn what was before an unsuccessful poem into a good one. And I think *Hear the voice of the Bard* decidedly a good one. Dr Wellek's account of it seems to me to justify my assumption that I could fairly discuss the poem without talking about symbols; for I cannot see that his account tends to invalidate mine. I cannot, in fact, see why he should suppose it does. Or rather, I see it is because he assumes that what we are elucidating is a text of symbolical philosophy – written as such and to be read as such.

The confidence of his paraphrase made me open my eyes. It is a philosopher's confidence – the confidence of one who in the double strength of a philosophic training and a knowledge of Blake's system ignores the working of poetry. The main difference, one gathers, between the philosopher and the poet is that to the poet there may be allowed, in the interests of rhythm and mere formal matters like that, a certain looseness, a laxity of expression; 'Delete "and" (in line 7) which was inserted only because of the rhythm and the sense is quite clear' – Yes, immediately clear, if one derives from a study of 'the whole of Blake's symbolical philosophy' the confidence to perform these little operations. But I myself believe that in this poem Blake is using words with very unusual precision – the precision of a poet working as a poet.

And it is this precision that Dr Wellek ignores in his paraphrase and objects to my noticing:

In spite of his fall Man might yet control the universe ('the starry pole') . . . The next 'that' cannot possibly refer to God, but to the soul or to Man, who after his rebirth might control the 'starry pole'. There is no need to evoke Lucifer.

'Man' capable of controlling the universe may surely be said to have taken on something of God and may be, I suggest, in Blake's syntax – in his peculiar organization of meaning – not so sharply distinguishable from God as Dr Wellek's notion of 'clear sense' and 'one possible meaning' demands. And if 'fallen, fallen light' does not for Dr Wellek bring into the complex of associations Lucifer –

> from morn
> To noon he fell, from noon to dewy eve,
> A summer's day, and with the setting sun,
> Dropt from the zenith like a falling star
> On Lemnos, the Aegean isle

– then I think we have an instance of the philosopher disabling the critic; an instance of the philosophical approach inducing in the reader of poetry a serious impercipience or insensitiveness. Blake is not referring to abstract ideas of Man and rebirth; he works in the concrete, evoking by a quite unproselike (that was my point) use of associations a sense of a state of desolation that is the more grievous by contrast with an imagined state of bliss in which Man, in harmonious mastery of his full potentialities, might be godlike – an unfallen and unsinful Lucifer (Milton, we remember, was of the Devil's party without knowing it).

The twinkling stars in Blake mean always the light of Reason and the watery shore the limit of matter or of Time and Space. The identification of Earth and Man in this poem is explicitly recognized by Blake in the illustration to this very poem which represents a masculine figure lying upon the 'watery shore' and, with the 'starry floor' as a background, painfully lifting his head.

I would call Dr Wellek's attention to the poem, *Earth's Answer*, immediately following that which is under discussion. It opens:

> Earth raised up *her* head
> From the darkness dread and drear.
> Her light fled,
> Stony dread!
> And her locks cover'd with grey despair.

Prison'd on wat'ry shore.
Starry Jealousy does keep my den:
Cold and hoar,
Weeping o'er,
I hear the father of the ancient men.

I quote these stanzas as a way of suggesting to him that his neat and confident translation of symbols will not do (I am not saying that 'Reason' and 'Jealousy' could not be reconciled), and that even an argument from one of Blake's illustrations may not be as coercive as Dr Wellek supposes.

Again, where Wordsworth is concerned, Dr Wellek seems to misunderstand my intention. 'So contrary to your own conclusion' (p. 164), he says, 'I would maintain the coherence, unity, and subtlety of Wordsworth's thought'. – Well, I had heard of and read about Wordsworth's thought, which, indeed, has received a great deal of notice, but my business was with Wordsworth's poetry; I never proposed, and do not propose now, to consider him as a philosophic thinker. When I look up p. 164 in my book I find this as the only passage Dr Wellek can be referring to: 'His philosophizing (in the sense of the Hartleian studies and applications) had not the value he meant it to have; but it is an expression of his intense moral seriousness and a mode of that essential discipline of contemplation which gave consistency and stability to his experience'. In saying that Wordsworth's philosophizing hadn't the value he meant it to have I was pointing out that it hadn't the relation he supposed to his business as a poet, and my analysis still seems to me conclusive. Dr Wellek merely says in general terms that it isn't conclusive for him: 'I cannot see why the argument of Canto II of the *Prelude* could not be paraphrased'. – It can, I freely grant, be very easily paraphrased if one brings to it a general knowledge of the kind of thought involved and an assumption that poets put loosely what philosophers formulate with precision. For would Dr Wellek in prose philosophy be satisfied with, or even take seriously, such looseness of statement and argument as Wordsworth's in his philosophic verse? If so, he has a very much less strict criterion for philosophy as philosophy than I have for poetry as poetry. Even if Wordsworth had a philosophy, it is as a poet that he matters, and if we remember that even where he offers 'thought' the strength of what he gives is the poet's, we shall, as critics, find something better to do than supply precision and completeness to his abstract argument.

I do not see what service Dr Wellek does either himself or philosophy by adducing chapter V of *Science and the Modern World*. That an eminent mathematician, logician and speculative philosopher should be so interested in poetry as Professor Whitehead there shows himself to be is pleasing; but I have always thought the quality of his dealings with poetry to be exactly what one would expect of an authority so qualified. I will add, perhaps wantonly and irrelevantly, that the utterances of Professor Whitehead's quoted by Dr Wellek look to me like bad poetry; in their context no doubt they become something different, but I cannot see why even then they should affect a literary critic's view of Wordsworth and Shelley.

When Dr Wellek comes to Shelley he hardly makes any serious show of sustaining his case against me and the weakness of his own approach is most clearly exposed. He is so interested in philosophy that he pays no real attention to my analyses of poetry. Take, for instance, his suggested interpretations of points in the *Ode to the West Wind*: it is not merely that they are, it seems to me, quite unacceptable; even if they were otherwise, they would make no substantial difference to my carefully elaborated analysis of the way in which Shelley's poetry works. And why should Dr Wellek suppose that he is defending Shelley in arguing that 'the tangled boughs of Heaven and Ocean may allude to "the old mystical conception of the two trees of Heaven and Earth intertwining"'? Not that I attack the *Ode to the West Wind*; I merely illustrate from it the characteristic working of Shelley's poetry.

Nor do I attack *Mont Blanc*. When Dr Wellek says, 'I cannot see the slightest confusion in the opening paragraph of *Mont Blanc*', he seems to me to be betraying an inappreciation of Shelley – an inappreciation explained by the approach intimated in his next sentence: 'It states an epistemological proposition quite clearly'. Now to me the opening paragraph of *Mont Blanc* evokes with great vividness a state of excited bewilderment and wonder. The obvious Wordsworthian element in the poem suggests a comparison with Wordsworth, and, regarding as I do the two poets, not as stating epistemological propositions or asserting general conceptions, but as reacting characteristically to similar concrete occasions, the comparison I actually make seems to me justified. When Dr Wellek tells me that the passage I quote from the *Prelude* 'has philosophically nothing to do with the introduction of Shelley's *Mont Blanc*', he merely confirms my conviction that philosophy and literary criticism are very different things.

Having described certain Shelleyan habits I go on to point out that these carry with them a tendency to certain vices; vices such that, in diagnosing them, the literary critic finds himself becoming explicitly a moralist. I conduct the argument very carefully and in terms of particular analysis, and I cannot see that Dr Wellek makes any serious attempt to deal with it. I cannot see why he should think that his alternative interpretation of the third stanza of *When the lamp is shattered* makes that poem less bad in any of the ways in which I have judged it adversely. But I do see that, *not* reading as a literary critic, he fails to respond with his sensibility to the peculiarly Shelleyan virtue, the personal voice of the last stanza, and so fails to realize the force of my radical judgement on the poem (I cannot recapitulate the whole argument here).

Actually, of course, Dr Wellek's attention is elsewhere than on Shelley's poetry and my analysis. 'These notes', he slips into saying, 'are made only to support my main point that Shelley's philosophy, I think, is astonishingly unified, and perfectly coherent' – I do not consider it my business to discuss that proposition, and Dr Wellek has given me no grounds for judging Shelley's poetry to be anything other than I have judged it to be. If, in reply to my charge that Shelley's poetry is repetitive, vaporous, monotonously self-regarding and often emotionally cheap, and so, in no very long run, boring, Dr Wellek tells me that Shelley was an idealist, I can only wonder whether some unfavourable presumption has not been set up about idealism. Again, it is no consolation for disliking the characteristic Shelleyan vapour to be told:

This fusing of the spheres of the different senses in Shelley is exactly paralleled in his rapid transitions and fusions of the emotions, from pleasure to pain, from sorrow to joy. Shelley would like us similarly to ignore or rather to transcend the boundaries of individuality between persons just as Indian philosophy or Schopenhauer wants us to overcome the curse and burden of the *principium individuationis*.

Of course, according to that philosophy, poetry may be a mistake or illusion, something to be left behind. But Dr Wellek will hardly bring it against me that I have been unfair to Shelley's poetry out of lack of sympathy with such a view.

Unfairness to poets out of lack of interest in their philosophy he does, of course, in general charge me with. His note concludes:

> Your book . . . raises anew the question of the poet's 'belief' and how far sympathy with this belief and comprehension of it is necessary for an appreciation of the poetry. A question which has been debated a good deal, as you know, and which I would not like to solve too hastily on the basis of your book.

I will only comment, without wishing to question the justice of this conclusion, that Dr Wellek seems to me to assume too easily that the poet's essential 'belief' is what can be most readily extracted as such from his works by a philosopher.

HENRY JAMES AND THE FUNCTION
OF CRITICISM

TO form a just idea of Mr Quentin Anderson's contribution to the understanding of Henry James one needs to have read his essay in *The Kenyon Review* for Autumn, 1946. He had room there to develop his case at length, and the interested reader of the briefer presentment that, at the Editors' invitation, he wrote for *Scrutiny* (September and December, 1947) ought to know that the fuller treatment exists and may, by those who have no access to it, be taken as, in an important respect, finally convincing.

Mr Anderson has established, I think, a very interesting fact. Not only are there decided manifestations in James's work of a strong and sympathetic interest on his part in his father's system; in certain of his books, generally considered as constituting his 'major phase', the system is present to such effect that, unadverted and uninformed, the reader is without the key to the essential intention – the intention that makes the given book what it is and explains what James saw it as being. The fact, then, has its bearings for criticism.

The statement of these is not a simple matter. Moreover, Mr Anderson seems to me to have started with radical misconceptions as to what they could be. But I should like at the outset to make quite plain my sense of the positive value of his work. His argument regards mainly the late novels and stories. These, of course, are very highly rated by the fashionable admirers of James, who, indeed, assumed them to be the supreme expression of his genius, but seem quite incapable of suggesting either any intelligible grounds for the assumption or any clear idea of the kind of thing we are supposed to be admiring. Novels are novels; James's distinction, we gather, is that he handles with great refinement the relations between 'civilized' individuals – representative members of a Victorian or Edwardian house-party: these late books (that appears to be the assumption) are especially alembicated specimens

of the same variety of 'the novel'. Well, Mr Anderson shows that
The Wings of the Dove and *The Golden Bowl* are, in intention,
allegories about Man, and by both intention and method much
more closely related to *Everyman* than to 'the novel of manners'.
If this fact can be brought to general notice its disconcerting
effect may be salutary. It may even induce some receptivity in
respect of the truth that even in his earlier work James is not a
mere novelist of manners; so that ultimately it will become impossible for critics to tell us, as Mr David Garnett does, that
James's characters are 'ordinary people' . . . 'just as much alive
as the people we meet in hotels or at the houses of our friends,
but no more'.

But to return to my disagreements with Mr Anderson: he
doesn't, I've suggested, deal satisfactorily with the critical bearings of the fact he establishes. The fact itself, I think, is less clear-
cut and measurable than he supposes. '*The Ambassadors*, *The
Wings of the Dove*, and *The Golden Bowl* were planned as a single
poem embracing the history of mankind. They represent three
stages in the experience of the race which are paralleled by three
stages in the moral career of an individual'. And Mr Anderson in
his essay in *The Kenyon Review*, gives a detailed account of the
three works as allegorizing faithfully and comprehensively the
blend of Swedenborg and Fourier (for that's what it is, though Mr
Anderson himself doesn't put it that way) elaborated by Henry
James senior. I am not convinced that the younger James even in
intention identified himself as completely with his father's system
as that – I can't believe it, if only because the system, taken as a
whole, seems to me pretty meaningless, except as satisfying the
particular emotional and moral needs of the leisure-class American
idealist who elaborated it.

But what I have to insist on is that intention in the important
sense can only be determined by the tests applied in literary
cricitism. The analysis and judgement of works of literary art
belong to the literary critic, who *is* one in so far as he observes a
disciplined relevance in response, comment and determination of
significance. He is concerned with the work in front of him as
something that should contain within itself the reason why it is so
and not otherwise. The more experience – experience of life and
literature together – he brings to bear on it the better, of course;

and it is true that extraneous information may make him more percipient. But the business of critical intelligence will remain what it was: to ensure relevance of response and to determine what is actually *there* in the work of art. The critic will be especially wary how he uses extraneous knowledge about the writer's intentions. Intentions are nothing in art except as realized, and the tests of realization will remain what they were. They are applied in the operation of the critic's sensibility; they are a matter of his sense, derived from his literary experience, of what the living thing feels like – of the difference between that which has been willed and put there, or represents no profound integration, and that which grows from a deep centre of life. These tests may very well reveal that the deep animating intention (if that is the right word) is something very different from the intention the author would declare.

My main criticism of Mr Anderson is that he is not, in his interpretation of James, actively enough a literary critic: his use of his key seems to be something apart from his critical sensibility. Doesn't he assume his value-judgements, and rest inertly on the conventional consensus that rates the late novels so high? I may be wrong in this general suggestion, but I am sure that his commentary on *The Ambassadors* implies an indefensible valuation. Why should he assume that the reader tends, almost irresistibly (though mistakenly) to identify himself with Strether? I can only comment that I haven't been in the least tempted so to identify myself, or to spend any moral or intellectual energy determining the worth or significance of Strether's resolution to 'have got nothing for himself'. For all the light Mr Anderson throws on possible intentions, *The Ambassadors* still seems to me so feeble a piece of word-spinning that I should have been inclined to dismiss it as merely senile if James hadn't himself provided an explanation in telling us that it had been conceived as a short story. What Mr Anderson points to is a set of preoccupations that helps us to understand how James should have been so mistakenly led into fluffing out the story to the bulk and pretensions of a major work.

I suspect that *The Ambassadors*, which to me remains wholly boring, doesn't belong so essentially with the other late 'great' novels as Mr Anderson thinks – and as, perhaps, James himself in elaborating it, intended. But before I leave Strether I have a comment to make on the kind of significance Mr Anderson attributes to him. Strether represents, we are told, self-righteousness. What Mr Anderson's argument, so far as I understand it, seems to compel one to point out is that self-righteousness and moral neutrality are not exhaustive alternatives. We can resolve to eschew self-righteousness, and yet, without inconsistency, believe we have a duty of moral discrimination. It is true that our judgements ought to come from an impersonal centre in us, and that we shouldn't have been able to make them but for a truth the statement of which would be a generalized form of Mr Anderson's proposition: 'If James had not felt in himself the very impulses which he saw crystallized in American manners he would not have understood American manners'. This possibility of impersonality and this measure of 'community of consciousness' are implied in the existence of art.

Difficult as they are for discussion and definition, these truths are profoundly familiar. It is only here and there, in the individual focus, that consciousness exists, and yet, as the experience of great literature brings home to us very forcibly, and the more forcibly the more we ponder it, that is not the last word: the individual focus of consciousness is not an insulated unit, whose relation with others are merely external and susceptible of statement in Benthamite terms.

It is difficult to see what more can be conveyed by the phrase in which Mr Anderson summarizes the elder James, 'We all share the same consciousness', than a reminder of these familiar truths. Clearly, it can't be literally true: when the lorry breaks your leg you feel the pain and I don't. And what the special Jamesian intention may be is not given definition and cogency by any success of concrete presentment in the younger James's art.

But at this point there is a discrimination to be made: both *The Wings of the Dove* and *The Golden Bowl* seem to me much more interesting than *The Ambassadors*, and interesting in the general way suggested by Mr Anderson. They are no more specimens of 'the novel' than *Everyman* is a specimen of naturalistic drama. Thanks to the light brought by Mr Anderson we can see, for instance, in the peculiar impressiveness of Mrs Lowder of *The Wings of the Dove*, 'Britannia of the Market-Place', a triumph of morality art. Yet that light makes no essential difference to my own final judgements about the book, which remains, as preponderantly as before, fussily vague and intolerably sentimental. Milly Theale, for all the elaboration of indirectnesses with which James sets about generating her, remains an empty excuse for unctuous sentimentality. Kate Croy continues to engage more of our sympathy than suits the author's purpose.

The Golden Bowl had always seemed the most interesting of the late novels. Helped by Mr Anderson, we can give a better account of its relative strength – though not, I think, a less disabling account of its total unsatisfactoriness. Adverted of the morality intention, we can refrain from dismissing Adam Verver *tout court* as the American millionaire denatured and sentimentalized. Adam, we can see, stands for America in certain of its aspects – on the one hand (going with the loosening of tradition) a characteristic innocence combined with generous goodwill, and, on the other, the supremacy of wealth that makes possible the purchase of what America hasn't been able to produce, represented by Prince Amerigo and the fabulous collection of *objets d'art* that is to be housed in American City. What precisely the allegorical intention amounts to in full it is difficult to determine – to say which is to make a radical criticism. Certainly it doesn't merely amount to the elder James's system. For not only is American City a penal Botany Bay for Charlotte[1]; about the withdrawal there of the Ververs there is an unmistakable pathos.

1. Mr Anderson's account of American City is different:
   > She is led off in a silken halter to become the cicerone of the temple of the divine-natural humanity. Appearance, the sum of all the objects of art which *represent* the divinity, is to be housed in America, the spiritual realm.

But how does he explain James's presenting Madame Merle's banishment in this unambiguous light (the quotation comes from the late revised version – and in any case Mr Anderson contends that James based his work from the outset on an acceptance of his father's apocalyptic philosophy)? –

> 'It's my husband who doesn't get on with me', said Isabel.
> 'I could have told him he wouldn't. I don't call that crowing over *you*', Mrs Touchett added. 'Do you still like Serena Merle?' she went on.
> 'Not as I once did. But it doesn't matter, for she's going to America'.
> 'To America? She must have done something very bad'.
> 'Yes – very bad'.

What we are not reconciled to by any awareness of intentions is the outraging of our moral sense by the handling of the adultery theme – the triangle, or rather quadrilateral, of personal relations. We remain convinced that when an author, whatever symbolism he intends, presents a drama of men and women, he is committed to dealing in terms of men and women, and mustn't ask us to acquiesce in valuations that contradict our profoundest ethical sensibility. If, of course, he can work a revolutionary change in that sensibility, well and good, but who will contend that James's art in those late novels has that power? In *The Golden Bowl* we continue to find our moral sense outraged.

Actually we can see that James doesn't realize what violent accommodations he is demanding of us, for his own sense of life is in abeyance. This, in spite of all our attempts to say what can be said in favour of *The Wings of the Dove* and *The Golden Bowl*, is the judgement we rest at. And what, in fact, Mr Anderson has done is to further the diagnosis of James's late phase. It had already been plain that the hypertrophy of technique, the overdoing, was correlated with a malnutrition. James paid the penalty of living too much as novelist, and not richly enough as a man. He paid the price, too, of his upbringing – of never having been allowed to take root in any community, so that for all his intense critical interest in civilization, he never developed any sense of society as a system of functions and responsibilities. And he spent his life, when not at house-parties of a merely social kind (he was un-aware, it would seem, of the Victorian country-house at its func-tional best), dining out and writing. The deep consciousness that he had no public and no hope of real critical attention would confirm the dispositions tending to life-impoverishment in his art. It is in this late period that the inherited symbolism assumes control, and we can see why this should be so: it moves into the place once occupied in force by the system of interests belonging to the novelist as novelist – the system of interests derived from his most vital experience. We can see too that in coming so to power it both increases, and disguises from James, the separation of his art from life.

The system of symbolism, in short, doesn't represent the structure of interests behind his operative sensibility; it doesn't belong with his creativeness. It is from the beginning, in fact, associated with an odd weakness, which, we can now see, it helps to explain – for, as Mr Anderson enables us to perceive, an intention to be indentified with it asserts itself as an intrusive presence even in James's early phase. A representative instance may be seen in *The American*, with its symbolically named hero, Christopher Newman, who, starting from nothing, has rapidly made his pile in the West, and yet is offered to us as embodying a guileless integrity that places him at a disadvantage in dealing with a corrupt and self-seeking aristocratic Europe. If we ask how James can have been guilty of so preposterous an unreality, the answer lies in the paternal spell. The system of the elder James had at its centre, as its living principle, an optimistic and idealistic Americanism. The relation to reality of the satisfaction it gave him is suggested by a passage quoted by Mr Matthiessen in *The James Family* (p. 286):

They (the English) are an intensely vulgar race, high and low.... They are not worth studying. The prejudices one has about them, even when they are unjust, are scarcely worth correcting.... They belong, all their good and their evil, to the past humanity, to the infantile development of the mind, and they don't deserve, more than any other European nation, the least reverence from a denizen of the new world.

The younger James – while he remained a good novelist, at any rate – was not as simple-minded as that. He knew that he preferred living in France and England to living in America, and in that drama of critical-constructive interplay between different traditions which provides the organization of so much of his best work, he shows himself capable of intelligent and convincing discriminations in favour of America. He evinces, nevertheless, a deep-seated desire to produce a transcendent and aboriginally pure American superiority – a desire, we can see, related to his filial devotion. James himself places *The American* as 'romantic' and the romanticism is a matter of the insurrectionary repotence of this desire, which comes out again, to take another familiar instance, in his *Daisy Miller* (who is real enough – so real that the implicit valuation of her presents the reader with a problem).

In James's creative phases the manifestations of the impulse are sporadic and anomalous. In *The Wings of the Dove* and *The Golden*

Bowl it rules unchastened and unchecked. We are to take Milly Theale as superlatively a Princess, and as a supremely fit object of awed and compassionate reverence, merely because she is an American heiress on a fabulous scale (she isn't even represented as intelligent). As for Adam Verver of *The Golden Bowl*, it may be true that he isn't to be taken as merely a more preposterous Christopher Newman, but both Newman and Verver, it is plain, are intimately associated with the optimistic Fourier-cum-Swedenborg Americanism in which the elder James (whose freedom from economic cares had been earned by his father) indulged his idealism and his sheltered ignorance of the more rigid facts of life. The younger James, yielding to the paternal inspiration, and preoccupied with elaborating in its interest the ambiguities and evasions of his late technique, had himself lost touch with concrete life.

The optimism, Mr Anderson reminds us, was incompatible with tragic art; that suggests its relation to James's greatness. Consider *Washington Square*, *The Portrait of a Lady*, *The Awkward Age* . . .: these works are characteristic expressions of his essential genius, and they are tragic. If the optimism had prevailed we shouldn't have had them. Plainly, however intense may have been James's interest in his father's system, his relation to it can't ever have been quite what Mr Anderson suggests, and in so far as James did at any time incline to the optimism this was at odds with his essential genius. And it is surely significant that nowhere in the *Notebooks*, in the copious discussing of themes for novels and stories, is there the least reference to any symbolic intention.

It is true that a great artist's consciousness is in a profound way representative and never unconditioned by the age and culture to which he belongs. But it doesn't at all follow, as Mr Anderson seems to suggest, that James, because he was born in America, had, as great artist, to share that optimism. His strength was both American and more than American, and it enabled him, when he was a great artist, to transcend the optimism. He was, it is clear, also drawn to it. It seems to me equally clear that this weakness was closely correlated with another that looks like its antithesis. I am thinking of the very unpleasantly sentimental morbidity exemplified by *The Altar of the Dead*. And that morbidity seems in its turn to be related to the curious suggestion of abnormality, the preoccupation with indefinite evil, of which *The Turn of the Screw* is the best-known illustration.

I must before closing say that the facts adduced by Mr Anderson make no difference at all to my appreciation of those works of James which made him for me a great writer. I ought perhaps to confess that I couldn't antecedently have believed that facts of that kind would, in the nature of things, make any notable difference: the works I admired were what they clearly were, and the grounds of my admiration were such as I certainly hadn't put there myself. The works I am thinking of are *The Europeans*, *Washington Square*, *The Bostonians*, *The Portrait of a Lady*, *The Awkward Age*, *What Maisie Knew* and a number of *nouvelles* having virtues of the same order as the major works. I see no possibility at all of questioning the nature and conditions of the value of these things.

What strikes us first about them as we read them is the vivid concreteness of the rendering of this world of individual centres of consciousness we live in – a rendering such as seems to imply a kind of interest and a habit of discrimination that bear no relation to any Swedenborgian ethos. Then, the organization that, when we have completed the reading of the given book, is seen to give it significance as a work of art involves no reference to any such symbolism as Mr Anderson described. What we have, for instance, in *The Europeans* and *The Portrait of a Lady* is a characteristic (as I see it) critical and constructive interplay, done in dramatic terms, between different cultural traditions; an interplay in which discriminations for and against are made in respect of both sides, American and European, and from which emerges the suggestion of an ideal positive that is neither. James here is unmistakably preoccupied with the thought of a possible world in which the country house, with its external civilization, shall also be a centre of the life of the spirit; in which manners shall be the index of an inner fineness; and in which the man of the world and the inveterate diner-out who is also an intellectual novelist shall be able to find congenial society and a public capable of appreciating his novels. The characters and the action are 'symbolic' (to use the treacherous word) in a Shakespearean way, and the discriminations made invoke criteria of personality and moral quality that the cultivated reader recognizes, and can accept, immediately.

The organization, again, of a representative success like *The Lesson of the Master*, is no more to be explained in terms of Swedenborgian mysticism. The relations between the young author and the veteran clearly dramatize the complex debate that has gone on in James himself, between the special exacting claims of his art, and his fears, both as man and artist, of missing the full experience of life.

THE WILD, UNTUTORED PHOENIX

LAWRENCE is placed – is, in fact, distinctly *passé*; we are no longer (if we ever were) very much impressed by him. He had, of course, a kind of genius, but to take him seriously as an intellectual and spiritual force, a force that could affect our attitude towards life and the problems of our time – it's amusing to think that there were once earnest souls who did so. Today, while recognizing the queerly limited gifts he dissipated, we hardly bother to smile at his humourless fanaticisms.

At least, that's the impression one gets from the literary world today (I mean the milieu in which fashions are set and worn and the higher reviewing provided for). Lawrence is decidedly out of favour – in fact, he was never in, for it was without permission that he won his fame, and he was patently not the kind of writer who would ever earn permission. *Phoenix* is an admirable reminder of the qualities that make our ruling literary intellectuals feel that his fame had better be encouraged to fade as quickly as possible.

Here, for instance, in this collection of dispersed papers, he appears as an incomparable reviewer (presenting, that is, a standard that our higher literary editors couldn't be expected to take seriously). We remember that neglected critical masterpiece, *Studies in Classical American Literature*, and may very well go on to ask what kind of gift it was that made D. H. Lawrence the finest literary critic of our time – a great literary critic if ever there was one. We know it can't have been intelligence; for Mr Quennell's view[1] that (in contrast to the superlatively intelligent Mr Aldous Huxley) he was, though a genius, muddle-headed is generally accepted (and did not Mr Eliot find in Lawrence 'an incapacity for what we ordinarily call thinking'?)[2]

Yet here, in these reprinted reviews, we have Lawrence dealing under ordinary reviewing conditions (he needed the money) with books of all kinds – H. G. Wells, Eric Gill, Rozanov, Dos Passos,

1. See *The English Novelists*, edited by Derek Verschoyle.
2. *After Strange Gods*, p. 58.

Hemingway, Baron Corvo, fiction, poetry, criticism, psychology
– and giving almost always the impression of going straight to
the centre with the masterly economy, the sureness of touch, of
one who sees exactly what it is in front of him and knows
exactly what he thinks of it. Here he is on H. G. Clissold-Wells:

His effective self is disgruntled, his ailment is a peevish, ashy indifference to *everything*, except himself, himself as centre of the universe. There is not one gleam of sympathy with anything in all the
book, and not one breath of passionate rebellion. Mr Clissold is too
successful and wealthy to rebel and too hopelessly peeved to sympathize.
What has got him into such a state is a problem; unless it is his insistence on the Universal Mind, which he, of course, exemplifies. The
emotions are to him irritating aberrations. Yet even he admits that even
thought must be preceded by some obscure physical happenings, some
kind of confused sensation or emotion which is the necessary coarse
body of thought and from which thought, living thought, arises or
sublimates.
This being so, we wonder that he so insists on the Universal or racial
mind of man, as the only hope of salvation. If the mind is fed from the
obscure sensations, emotions, physical happenings inside us, if the mind
is really no more than an exhalation of these, is it not obvious that
without a full and subtle emotional life the mind itself must wither; or
that it must turn itself into an automatic sort of grind-mill, grinding
upon itself.

His critical poise is manifested in (*pace* Mr Eliot) a lively ironic
humour – a humour that for all its clear-sighted and mocking
vivacity is quite without animus. For, idiosyncratic as Lawrence's
style is, it would be difficult to find one more radically free from
egotism.

Professor Sherman once more coaxing American criticism the way
it should go.
Like Benjamin Franklin, one of his heroes, he attempts the invention of a creed that shall 'satisfy the professors of all religions, and
offend none'.
He smites the marauding Mr Mencken with a velvet glove, and
pierces the obstinate Mr More with a reproachful look. Both gentlemen, of course, will purr and feel flattered . . .
So much for the Scylla of Mr Mencken. It is the first essay in the

book. The Charybdis of Mr P. E. More is the last essay: to this monster the professor warbles another tune. Mr More, author of the *Shelburne Essays*, is learned, and steeped in tradition, the very antithesis of the nihilistic stink-gassing Mr Mencken. But alas, Mr Moore is remote: somewhat haughty and supercilious at his study table. And even, alasser! with all his learning and remoteness, he hunts out the risky Restoration wits to hob-nob with on high Parnassus; Wycherley, for example; he likes his wits smutty. He even goes and fetches out Aphra Behn from her disreputable oblivion, to entertain her in public.

The humour seems to me that of a man whose insight into human nature and human experience makes egotism impossible, and I find myself, in fact, in thus attributing to him an extraordinary self-awareness and intelligence about himself, seeming to contradict Mr Eliot, who denies him 'the faculty of self-criticism' (*op. cit.*, p. 59). Lawrence does indeed characteristically exhibit certitude and isn't commonly to be found in a mood of hesitation or self-condemnation (though his art is largely a technique of exploration – exploration calling for critical capacity as well as courage); but in purity of interest and sureness of self-knowledge he seems to me to surpass Mr Eliot, even though he pays no respect to criteria that Mr Eliot indicates as essential.

A man like Lawrence, therefore, with his acute sensibility, violent prejudices and passions, and lack of intellectual and social training . . . (*After Strange Gods*, p. 59.)

I have already intimated that the acuteness of Lawrence's sensibility seems to me (whatever Bloomsbury may have decided) inseparable from the play of a supremely fine and penetrating intelligence. And if one is to agree that Lawrence lacked intellectual and social training, one would like to be shown someone who didn't or doesn't. It's true that he didn't go to Oxford or Harvard, and that his family was of a social class the sons of which, at that time, had little chance of getting to one of the ancient universities. But few readers of the memoir of Lawrence by E. T.[1] will, I imagine, however expensive their own education, claim with any confidence that they had a better one than Lawrence had.

At school, and later at University College, Nottingham, what-

1. *D. H. Lawrence*, by E. T.

ever their faults (and he says some stringent things about the
College), he got sufficient stimulus and sufficient guidance to the
sources and instruments of knowledge to be able, in intercourse,
social and intellectual, with his friends to carry on a real education.
They discussed their way eagerly over an extraordinary range of
reading, English and French, past and contemporary (Lawrence
hit on the *English Review*, then in its great days), and it is difficult
to imagine adolescents who should have read more actively and to
greater profit. For, belonging as they did to the self-respecting
poor in a still vigorous part of the country, not only was their
intellectual education intimately bound up with a social training
(what respectable meaning Mr Eliot, denying a 'social training'
to Lawrence, can be giving the phrase I can't guess); they enjoyed
the advantage of a still persistent cultural tradition that had as its
main drive the religious tradition of which Mr Eliot speaks so
contemptuously. And the setting of family life (quite finely
civilized and yet pressed on by day-to-day economic and practical exigencies) in which these young people met and talked was
in sight of – in immediate touch with – on one side the colliery
(Lawrence's father was a miner) and on the other the farm
(Miriam's father was a small farmer). It seems to me probable that
D. H. Lawrence at twenty-one was no less trained intellectually
than Mr Eliot at the same age; had, that is, read no less widely
(even if lacking Greek), was no less in command of his capacities
and resources and of the means of developing further, and had as
adequate a sense of tradition and the nature of wisdom. And it
seems to me probable that, even if less sophisticated than Mr
Eliot, he was not less mature in experience of life.

Some can absorb knowledge, the more tardy must sweat for it.
Shakespeare acquired more essential history from Plutarch than most
men could from the whole British Museum.

Lawrence was not Shakespeare, but he had genius, and his
genius manifests itself in an acquisitiveness that is a miraculous
quickness of insight, apprehension and understanding. The 'information' that Mr Eliot doesn't deny him ('a lack not so much of
information as . . .') is more than mere information; he had an
amazing range and wealth of living knowledge. He knew well at
least four languages besides his own, and it is characteristic of him

that in reviewing Cunninghame Graham's *Pedro de Valdivia* he not only shows a wide general knowledge of the Spanish conquests, but, referring to the original Spanish particular instances of Cunninghame Graham's rendering, censures him for 'the peculiar laziness or insensitiveness to language which is so great a vice in a translator'. What those qualified to judge think of Lawrence's dealings with painting I don't know, but he certainly shows an extremely wide and close acquaintance with it, deriving from an obviously intense interest. This appears notably, not only in the *Introduction to these Paintings*, but also in the *Study of Thomas Hardy*.

This long *Study of Thomas Hardy*, perhaps, represents the kind of thing that Mr Eliot has especially in mind when he charges Lawrence with 'an incapacity for what we ordinarily call thinking'. It is an early work, and hasn't much to do with Hardy. Lawrence frankly admits that he is using Hardy as an occasion and a means, and that his real purpose is to explore, refine and develop certain ideas and intuitions of his own. I found the study difficult to read through; it is diffuse and repetitive, and Lawrence has dealt with the same matters better elsewhere. Yet in the persistent integrity of this exploration the genius is manifest, and without this kind of work we couldn't have had the later ease, poise and economy, and the virtues in general that compel Mr Eliot to say:

As a criticism of the modern world, *Fantasia of the Unconscious* is a book to keep at hand and re-read.

If Lawrence's criticism is sound that seems to me to be because of the measure in which his criteria are sound, and because they and their application represent, if not what we 'ordinarily call thinking', an extraordinarily penetrating, persistent and vital kind of thinking. He says (p. 611):

What good is our intelligence to us, if we will not use it in the greatest issues? Nothing will excuse us from the responsibility of living; even death is no excuse. We have to live. So we may as well live fully. We are doomed to live. And therefore it is not the smallest use running into *pis allers* and trying to shirk the responsibility of living. We can't get out of it.

And therefore the only thing is to undertake the responsibility with good grace.

It is Lawrence's greatness that he was in a position to say this; he was, in fact, intelligent as only the completely serious and disinterested can be. Those who plume themselves on being intelligent but find this notion of intelligence uncongenial will prefer Mr Wyndham Lewis – even a Wyndham Lewis who comes out for Hitler.

I was reminded of Mr Wyndham Lewis by this in *Phoenix* (p. 271):

> Wyndham Lewis gives a display of the utterly repulsive effect people have on him, but he retreats into the intellect to make his display. It is a question of manners and manners. The effect is the same. It is the same exclamation: They stink! My God, they stink!

The Lawrence who thus places Wyndham Lewis seems to me the representative of health and sanity. Mr Eliot's reactions to Lawrence are, of course, at a different level from those referred to at the end of the last paragraph, the common petty reactions of the literary world, and the case that Mr Eliot argues does, at its most respectable, demand serious attention. But it is odd that he should, in pronouncing Lawrence 'spiritually sick', be able at the same time to invoke Wyndham Lewis's 'brilliant exposure' and 'conclusive criticism' of any side of Lawrence.

I hadn't intended to end on this note. But my attention has just been drawn to Mr Eliot's essay in *Revelation*. He treats Lawrence there still more respectfully than in *After Strange Gods*, but can say:

> For Babbitt was by nature an educated man, as well as a highly well-informed one; Lawrence, even had he acquired a great deal more knowledge and information than he ever came to possess, would always have remained uneducated. By being 'educated' I mean having such an apprehension of the contours of the map of what has been written in the past, as to see instinctively where everything belongs, and approximately where anything new is likely to belong; it means, furthermore, being able to allow for all the books one has not read and the things one does not understand – it means some understanding or one's own ignorance.

Irving Babbitt, all one's divinations about whom have been confirmed by the reminiscences and memoirs of him that have appeared since his death! Babbitt, who was complacently deaf and blind to literature and art, and completely without understanding of his incapacity; who, being thus in sensibility undeveloped or dead, can hardly, without misplacing a stress, be called intelligent! Even as Mr Eliot quotes him and comments on him he appears as the born academic (is that what 'by nature an educated man' means?), obtuse – Mr Eliot seems almost to bring out the word – obtuse in his dogged and argumentative erudition.

How can Mr Eliot thus repeatedly and deliberately give away his case by invoking such standards? It is an amazing thing that so distinguished a mind can so persistently discredit in this way a serious point of view.

1937

MR ELIOT, MR WYNDHAM LEWIS
AND LAWRENCE

AFTER STRANGE GODS, like the last set of printed lectures, is clearly not a book the author would choose to have written, and one is tempted to pass it by with a glance at the circumstances of production. Yet the weaknesses, the embarrassing obviousness of which is partly to be explained by those circumstances, cannot, after all, be dismissed as having no significance. Mr Eliot is too distinguished, his preoccupations have too representative an importance, and the sub-title of the book, recalling as it does an old and notorious promise, invites us to consider their presentment here as embodying a certain maturity of reflection.

His themes are orthodoxy and tradition, and, as one would expect, he says some memorable things. Tradition, for example, he describes admirably as 'the means by which the vitality of the past enriches the life of the present'. And when he describes 'the struggle of our time' as being 'to concentrate, not to dissipate; to renew our association with traditional wisdom; to re-establish a vital connexion between the individual and the race . . .', one again assents with pleasure. But when he goes on, 'the struggle, in a word, against Liberalism', it seems an odd summary.

Mr Eliot's stress in this book, of course, falls explicitly upon the religious needs of the age. And, with conscious inadequacy, holding on to what one is sure of, one agrees that 'to re-establish a vital connexion between the individual and the race' means reviving, in a civilization that more and more, at higher and lower levels, fosters the chauffeur-mentality, what it may be crude to call the religious sense – the sense that spoke in Lawrence when he said, 'Thank God I am not free, any more than a rooted tree is free'. It is the sense, perhaps it may be said, a perception of the need to cultivate which made Dr I. A. Richards, in the book in which he speculates about a future in which we shall 'have learned enough about our minds to do with them what we will' and 'the question "What sort of mind shall I choose to be?"' would turn into an experimental matter' (*Practical Criticism*, p. 347), invent his 'ritual for heightening sincerity' (*ibid.*, p. 290) – that invention the crudities of which Mr Eliot is, if not excessively, perhaps unnecessarily severe upon in *The Use of Poetry and the Use of Criticism*.

What would be the drift of Mr Eliot's comments on the present kind of fumbling inadequacy one knows well enough. The relevance of this, for instance, is plain: 'when morals cease to be a matter of tradition and orthodoxy – that is, of the habits of the community formulated, corrected and elevated by the continuous thought and direction of the Church – and when one man is to elaborate his own, then *personality* becomes a thing of alarming importance.' Mr Eliot has no need to talk hesitantly about the 'need for a religious sense'; he adheres to a religion, and can point to his Church and recite its dogmas.

Nevertheless, those of us who find no such approach to tradition and orthodoxy possible can only cultivate the sense of health we have. 'The number of people in possession of any criteria for distinguishing between good and evil', writes Mr Eliot, 'is very small'. As we watch his in use, we can only test them by reference to our own surest perceptions, our own most stable grounds of discrimination. When, for instance, he says that he is 'applying moral principles' to literature, we cannot accept those principles as *alternatives* to the criteria we know. 'What we can try to do', he says, 'is to develop a more critical spirit, or rather to apply to authors critical standards that are almost in desuetude.' The first phrase is strictly accurate: we could recover such standards only by the development – *as* the development – of a more critical spirit out of the capacity for discrimination that we have already. To put it another way: moral or religious criticism cannot be a substitute for literary criticism; it is only by being a literary critic that Mr Eliot can apply his recovered standards to literature. It is only by demonstrating convincingly that his application of moral principles leads to a more adequate criticism that he can effect the kind of persuasion that is his aim. In these lectures, if he demonstrates anything, it is the opposite: one can only report that the criticism seems painfully bad – disablingly inadequate, often irrelevant and sometimes disingenuous.

And it has, more generally, to be said that since the religious preoccupation has become insistent in them Mr Eliot's critical writings have been notable for showing less discipline of thought and emotion, less purity of interest, less power of sustained devotion and less courage than before. All this must be so obvious to those who read him (except to the conventional and academic who, having reviled him, now acclaim him) that there is no need to illustrate – the only difficulties in doing so would be to select and to stop. Mr Eliot himself can hardly be happy when he contemplates his recent references to, say, Arnold and Professor Housman, and his references in the present book to Hopkins and Meredith.

These comments one makes, in all humility, as essential to the issue; they are to enforce the point of saying that it is not as a substitute or an alternative that what Mr Eliot nowadays offers us could recommend itself, but only as a completion, and this it is far from seeming. One may at any rate venture that health – even religious health – demands a more active concern for other things than formal religion than Mr Eliot now shows or encourages. Indeed, it seems reasonable to restate in terms of Mr Eliot's situation his expressions of fear regarding Lawrence, fear that Lawrence's work 'will appeal not to what remains of health in them ["the sick and debile and confused"], but to their sickness.'

There is hardly any need to be more explicit: it must be plain why for those preoccupied with orthodoxy, order and traditional forms, Lawrence should be especially a test. I do not – need it be said? – mean a 'test' in the sense that one knows beforehand what the 'right' reaction is (it will certainly not be acceptance). What one demands is a truly critical attitude – a serious attempt to discriminate and evaluate after an honest and complete exposure to Lawrence. Mr Eliot has in the past made me indignant by endorsing, of all things, Mr Middleton Murry's *Son of Woman* while at the same time admitting to a very imperfect acquaintance with Lawrence's work. *After Strange Gods* exhibits something much more like a critical attitude; there has obviously been a serious attempt to understand in spite of antipathy.

It is characteristic of the more interesting heretics, in the context in which I use the term, that they have an exceptionally acute perception, or profound insight, of some part of the truth; an insight more important often than the inferences of those who are aware of more, but less acutely aware of anything. So far as we are able to redress the balance, effect the compensation, ourselves, we may find such authors of the greatest value.

This is not explicitly said of Lawrence; but it suggests fairly Mr Eliot's implied estimate of him: he is spoken of with respect, as (what he obviously is) 'a very much greater genius' than Hardy, and there is 'a very great deal to be learned' from him. We are decidedly far away from the imagined 'frightful consequences' of Lawrence the don at Cambridge, 'rotten and rotting others'. It would, indeed, have been ungracious to recall this unhappy past if Mr Eliot's attitude now had been consistently or in general effect critical, to be agreed or disagreed with. But it is not; its main significance still lies in its being so largely and revealingly un-critical – and so equivocally so.

The first [aspect of Lawrence] is the ridiculous: his lack of sense of humour, a certain snobbery, a lack not so much of information as of the critical faculties which education should give, an incapacity for what we ordinarily call thinking. Of this side of Lawrence, the brilliant exposure by Wyndham Lewis in *Paleface*, is by far the most conclusive criticism that has been made.

The charge of snobbery (repeated elsewhere in this book and accompanied by a most unfortunate tone) may be passed by; what damage it does is so obviously not to the object. But why, one asks, this invocation of Mr Wyndham Lewis? With all his undeniable talent, is he qualified to 'expose' any side of Lawrence? No man who can read will acclaim Lawrence as a philosopher, but 'incapacity for what we ordinarily call thinking' – does not this apply far more to Mr Wyndham Lewis than to Lawrence? Mr Lewis stands, in a paradoxically high-pitched and excited way, for common sense; he offers us, at the common-sense level, percep-tions of an uncommon intensity, and he is capable of making 'brilliant' connexions. But 'what we ordinarily call thinking' is just what he is incapable of – consider for instance the list of names brought together under the 'Time-philosophy' in *Time and Western Man*. His pamphleteering volumes are not books; their air of sustained and ordered argument is a kind of bluff, as the reader who, having contrived to read one through, can bring himself to attempt a summary of it discovers. If, on the other hand,

Lawrence does not offer intellectual order or definition or an intellectual approach, to speak of him as incapable of thinking is to mislead. In the same way the phrases, 'lack of intellectual and social training' and 'soul destitute of humility', seem to me misleading in suggestion; and I think that, if Mr Eliot goes on reading Lawrence – and especially the *Letters* and *Phoenix* – in a serious attempt to understand, he may come to wonder whether such phrases are quite consistent with humility in the critic.

When we look up Mr Wyndham Lewis's 'brilliant exposure' of Lawrence in *Paleface*, we discover that it is an 'exposure' of Lawrence and Mr Sherwood Anderson together. Now the primitivistic illusion that Mr Wyndham Lewis rightly attacks was indeed something that Lawrence was liable to (and could diagnose). Just how far, in any critical estimate, the stress may be fairly laid there is a matter for critical difference. But that Lawrence's importance is not anything that can be illuminated by assimilating him, or any side of him, to Mr Sherwood Anderson is plain on Mr Eliot's own showing: 'Lawrence lived all his life, I should imagine, on the spiritual level; no man was less a sensualist. Against the living death of material civilization he spoke again and again, and even if these dead could speak, what he said is unanswerable.' If Lawrence was this, how comes Mr Eliot to be using Mr Wyndham Lewis against him? – Mr Wyndham Lewis, who, though he may stand for Intelligence, is as unqualified to discriminate between the profound insight and the superficial romantic illusion, as anyone who could have been hit on. His remarkable satiric gift is frustrated by an unrestrained egotism, and Mr Eliot might have placed him along with Mr Pound among those whose Hells are for the other people: no one could with less injustice be said to be destitute of humility.

Mr Eliot no doubt thought he was merely using Mr Wyndham Lewis to mark off a weaker side of Lawrence from 'the extra-ordinarily keen sensibility and capacity for profound intuition' which made Lawrence so irreconcilable and potent an enemy of the idea that 'by tolerance, benevolence, inoffensiveness and a re-distribution or increase of purchasing power, combined with devotion on the part of an *elite* to Art, the world will be as good as anyone could require . . .' Mr Eliot, unhappily, was mistaken.

From the two sentences of supreme praise quoted in the last paragraph he goes on: 'As a criticism of the modern world, *Fantasia of the Unconscious* is a book to keep at hand and re-read. In contrast to Nottingham, London or industrial America, his capering redskins of *Mornings in Mexico* seem to represent Life' – *Mornings in Mexico* is Mr Wyndham Lewis's text, and it is one of the very inferior books. If it represented Lawrence and the *Fantasia* deserved to be bracketed with it, or if the 'capering redskins' (betraying phrase) represented Lawrence's 'capacity for profound intuition', then Lawrence would not deserve the praise Mr Eliot gives him – so equivocally.

This equivocalness, this curious sleight by which Mr Eliot surreptitiously takes away while giving, is what I mean by the revealingly uncritical in his attitude towards Lawrence. It is as if there were something he cannot bring himself to contemplate fairly. And the index obtruded in that over-insistence on Lawrence's 'sexual morbidity' refuses to be ignored. It is an odd insistence in one whose own attitudes with reference to sex have been, in prose and poetry, almost uniformly negative – attitudes of distaste, disgust and rejection. (Mr Wyndham Lewis's treatment of sex, it is worth noting, is hard-boiled, cynical and external.) The preoccupation with sex in Lawrence's work is, perhaps, excessive by any standard of health, and no doubt psychologists, if they like, can elicit abnormalities. But who can question his own account of the preoccupation? 'I always labour at the same thing, to make the sex relation valid and precious, not shameful.' And who can question that something as different as this from Mr Eliot's bent in the matter is necessary if the struggle 'to re-establish a vital connexion between the individual and the race' is to mean anything?

Lawrence's concern for health far transcends what is suggested by any talk of sex. His may be 'not the last word, only the first'; but the first is necessary. His justification is given in these remarks from *After Strange Gods* (p. 18):

We become conscious of these items, or conscious of their importance, usually only after they have begun to fall into desuetude, as we are aware of the leaves of a tree when the autumn wind begins to blow them off – when they have separately ceased to be vital. Energy may be wasted at that point in a frantic endeavour to collect the leaves as they fall and gum them on to the branches: but the sound tree will put forth new leaves, and the dry tree should be put to the axe. . . . Our second danger is . . . to aim to return to some previous condition which we imagine as having been capable of preservation in perpetuity, instead of aiming to stimulate the life which produced that condition in its time.

The tree will not put forth new leaves unless the sap flows. The metaphor, of course, is susceptible of more than one translation, but the very choice of it is nevertheless an involuntary concession to Lawrence. To 'stimulate the life' in Lawrence's way is not all that is needed, but is nevertheless, as the phrase itself conveys, indispensable.

It is the way our sympathy flows and recoils that really determines our lives. And here lies the importance of the novel, properly handled. It can inform and lead into new places the flow of our sympathetic consciousness, and it can lead our sympathy away in recoil from things gone dead. Therefore the novel, properly handled, can reveal the most secret places of life – for it is in the *passional* secret places of life, above all, that the tide of sensitive awareness needs to ebb and flow, cleansing and refreshing.

Mr Eliot complains of a lack of moral struggle in Lawrence's novels; here we have Lawrence's reply, and his justification of the earlier description of him as an 'extremely serious and improving' writer. No one will suggest that in Lawrence we have all we need of moral concern, but, as *After Strange Gods* reminds us, a preoccupation with discipline – the effort towards orthodoxy – also has its disabilities and dangers. These are manifest in the obvious and significant failures in touch and tone. It may be prejudice that makes one find something distasteful in the habitual manner of Mr Eliot's references during the past half-dozen years to Baudelaire and Original Sin. But such disasters as that 'curtain' to the second lecture in the present volume leave no room for doubt.

No one who sees in what way Lawrence is 'serious and improving' will attribute the sum of wisdom, or anything like it, to him. And for attributing to him 'spiritual sickness' Mr Eliot can make out a strong case. But it is characteristic of the world as it is that health cannot anywhere be found whole; and the sense in which Lawrence stands for health is an important one. He stands at any rate for something without which the preoccupation (necessary as it is) with order, forms and deliberate construction, cannot produce health.

1934

THE LOGIC OF CHRISTIAN
DISCRIMINATION

I HAVE already had reason for concluding that Christian Discrimination is a decidedly bad thing. Bro. George Every's little book, *Poetry and Personal Responsibility*, has the air of having been designed defiantly to justify that conclusion. It can be recommended for a brief perusal as showing unambiguously what in the concrete Christian Discrimination is, and where its logic leads.

One might, after looking through the book, start by asking why Mr Every has devoted so much time to poetry, and to creative literature in general, since (I hope I may be forgiven for saying) he shows no compelling interest in it, and no aptitude for its study. The answer he would give us is to be found in the first sentence of his Preface:

This book is intended as an introduction to contemporary poetry, considered as the sensitive spot in the modern mind, where a new response to life, a new outlook upon the world, is taking shape.

He follows it up with a sentence that hardly clarifies the idea, and wouldn't, I think, have been left standing if anyone had asked him what he meant by it:

The best poem is the most sensitive not only to the thoughts and feelings of the author, but to those of other people with whom he is in constant communication.

Still, I see what's in his mind. It's the idea that, in the given form, derives its currency from I. A. Richards:

The poet is the point at which the growth of the mind shows itself.

But though this is the idea that seems to Mr Every to explain his dealings with poetry, he doesn't, as to be consistent he should, go on to try and be a critic. He knows beforehand, in a general kind of way, what new responses to life and what 'new outlook upon the world' are to be looked for as making a writer significant and important. They go with his conviction that the most important activity today is to promote a Christian revival. He nowhere begins to come near the business of literary criticism, and it is difficult to see what, apart from names, asserted importances, and impressive generalities his pupils (the substance of the book was given as lectures) can have got from him:

... the younger poets who came to light in 1937–42, such voices as Dylan Thomas, David Gascoyne, Alex Comfort, and Sidney Keyes, have never suffered from any illusions about the future of our civilization. For them the urgent problem is the imminence of death, the need of some significance that can be attached to dying in a world where there is no common belief in immortality.

This suggests well enough his principles of selection and association and the nature of his commentary. It is true that he does a good deal of quoting, but the pieces of verse he quotes get no critical examination, and don't as a rule support the implicit assumption that the author matters as a poet. Mr Every's indifference to the essential critical judgement appears at its most naked in his astonishing collocations. He can glide with perfect aplomb, in a paragraph, from *Little Gidding* to Miss Anne Ridler and Sidney Keyes without a hint of any perception on his part that, for any serious treatment of his theme, something of a change of level has occurred, and that he cannot still be dealing with significance of the same order. Here is a characteristic passage:

Our greatest living novelist, Mr E. M. Forster, deserted the novel twenty-five years ago for other forms of literature. Rex Warner seems to have done the same. Miss Elizabeth Bowen and Mr Desmond Hawkins have not added to their early output, which had great promise for the future. The reputation of Miss Compton-Burnett, so far chiefly among her fellow-writers, rests on a departure from the naturalistic novel into stylized conversation. Her characters are elongated and foreshortened in the manner of sculpture by Mr Henry Moore, a family group or a reclining woman. No other modern novelist cuts so close to the bone of life. As her prose recalls the verse of T. S. Eliot's plays, especially *The Family Reunion*, so her treatment of the novel as a form of poetry makes a convenient introduction to novels by two poets, Herbert Read and Charles Williams.

Christian Discrimination, then, absolves Mr Every from the literary critic's kind of discrimination. This comment will not disturb him; he has provided for it, and disabled it, he feels. Tell him that, if poetry matters because it is the 'sensitive spot in the modern mind . . . where a new response to life is taking shape', then to detect 'poetry' and to discriminate between that which can properly be considered as such and that in which any journalist or extension-lecturer recognizes the *Zeitgeist* becomes a task of great delicacy and importance, the due execution of which only the fostering of the highest critical standards and the observance of the most scrupulous critical discipline can hope to ensure – tell him this, and Mr Every replies (his immediate audience being of the W.E.A. type):

> The error of the *Scrutiny* writers was to look for the intelligentsia in the same places where aesthetes were recruited in the days of the Yellow Book and the Rhymers' Club, among intelligent and well-informed young men and women at the older universities, who were prepared to adopt literature as a vocation. Such people develop very easily into pedants, and pedantry can be reared on a diet of contemporary literature as well as on perfectly safe classics. The minority who in any age are really responsive to new developments in literature and the arts should always include a proportion of people who are not themselves engaged in the practice of literature, who care for art because it helps them to make sense of their lives.

Mr Every doesn't actually bring out the word 'highbrow', but his tactic amounts to nothing more and nothing less than the launching of that appeal to the natural man and the natural man's dislike of the suggestion that perhaps in more important matters than football, billiards, and golf there are qualifications that can only be gained by discipline and experience, developing natural aptitude. For what can be meant by 'the minority should always include a proportion of people who are not themselves engaged in the practice of literature'? The minority is what it is; that it should be bigger is always desirable; but it will not be enlarged by pretending that confidence based on lack of cultivated literary experience and lack of trained aptitude in analysis and judgement – for what does 'not engaged in the practice of literature' mean? – can be counted on to distinguish and respond to the significantly new in literature.

Mr Every's intention and drift are unmistakable. He writes:

> The border between literary criticism and the evaluation of a writer's ideas had been obscured by the critics of the 'twenties, and especially by

Dr Leavis, in the interests of 'significant form'. Now to his great distress criticism seemed to be becoming completely immersed in theological and sociological polemic.

The doctrine of 'significant form' maintains that, where visual art is in question, value-judgements, or judgements of significance, that appeal to the values and interests of general living, are irrelevant; the experience of art is *sui generis* and unrelated to the rest of life, being the concern of an aesthetic sense that is insulated from the rest of one's organization. The true aesthetic appreciator can only ejaculate, since the 'significance' of 'significant form' is to be ineffable; signifying nothing that can be discussed or indicated, it just *is*. Mr Every imputes a literary transposition of that doctrine to me. That is his way (and does he, on reflection, find it honest?) of dealing with my insistence that theological, sociological, political, or moral commentaries and judgements on works of literature should be relevant, and that the business of ensuring relevance is a delicate one, calling for literary experience, cultivated scruple, trained skill, and the literary critic's concern with the quality of the life that is concretely present in the work in front of him.

Having thus absolved himself from the duty of making the essential discriminations, Mr Every can facilitate the business of pushing his own special line of goods by accepting with a large and reassuring catholicity, as established values, most of the current names. Auden, Dylan Thomas, David Gascoyne, Alex Comfort, Herbert Read, Ronald Duncan, Edith Sitwell, a whole team of Christian poets, and not only Sidney Keyes, the boy war-casualty whom by some caprice it has been agreed to immortalize as a symbol of lost Genius (I can see no ground for his reputation), but his friend John Heath-Stubbs: in all these, and how many more, one gathers, one can study, in the same sense as one can in D. H. Lawrence and T. S. Eliot, the 'sensitive spot where a new response to life is taking shape'.

Mr Every's own line of goods is of course Christian. Dr Sitwell writes emotionally, with characteristic afflatus, about Christ, therefore she can be acclaimed as a great (if not yet quite a Christian) poet, of major significance in terms of the critic's concern with the 'sensitive spot'. Of his own discovery and fostering Mr Every offers us, as poet and intellectual of established standing (we are to assume), Mr Norman Nicholson – a writer in whom, I am bound to say, I can see no vestige of any gift, but only intentions and pretensions that have gathered assurance from assiduous encouragement and from the sense of swimming, shoal-supported, with the tide. But then, I can see no reason for being interested in Charles Williams, whom we are offered as a major power, and Mr Nicholson's inspirer.

Mr Every gives us a whole chapter on 'The Poetic Influence of Charles Williams':

Today critics are failing in their understanding of the younger poets because they are not aware of his later work.

Williams, Mr Every, without producing any arguments or evidence tending to make the valuation in the least plausible, confidently sets up as a great poet – a peer, at least, of Eliot. In what sense this is Christian Discrimination comes out with almost disarming naïveté here:

Admiring Milton, he rejected Eliot, until the arch-classicist and ultramodern was revealed as an Anglo-Catholic lay theologian. In 1935–36 Eliot and he wrote plays in succession to one another for the same Canterbury festival, *Murder in the Cathedral* and *Thomas Cranmer*. From that time on their mutual influence grew. In the long run Williams influenced Eliot more, because his own 'effortless originality' was less open to any influence than Eliot's negative capacity, his infinite receptiveness.

The passages of Williams' verse quoted by Mr Every serve only to convince one that, however sound the poet's orthodoxy, he hadn't begun to be a poet, and that the critic is mistaken in supposing himself to be interested in poetry. But Mr Every can assure us, as one who knows (having it on the highest authority), that it was Williams' creative influence that changed Mr Eliot's attitude towards Milton:

The influence of Eliot is seen in repulsion as well as in attraction. In answer to the challenge thrown down by his attack on the Chinese wall, Milton's grand manner of verse, Charles Williams built a Chinese wall of his own to resist the decay of words. This wall in the end prevailed to modify Eliot's judgement where critical arguments failed. In one instance at least the imitation of Milton had been of use.

It is one of the most revealing of contemporary fashions to suppose that Mr Eliot has seriously and radically changed his mind about Milton, and that the utterances giving colour to this view have significant critical bearings on his poetic development. I can only repeat that those who subscribe to this fashion can, it seems plain to me, never have taken an intelligent interest in his poetry, and never had any but a conventional respect for his genius. Mr Eliot, it is true, has referred in a commendatory way to Charles Williams' introduction to the 'World's Classics' Milton. Having taken the tip and looked at it I am obliged to report that I found it the merest attitudinizing and gesturing of a man who had nothing critically relevant to say. It may be an example of Christian Discrimination; I am sure it is not good literary criticism. As for Charles Williams' influence, all that we learn and divine of it leads me to the conclusion that here, in the milieu to which he belonged, we have a subject worth attention from the inquirer into the 'sociology' of contemporary literature. It seems to me that there is some danger of his verse-constructions being imposed on the student in succession to *The Testament of Beauty*.

What I want to say very earnestly to Bro. George Every is that, in so far as he is truly concerned for religion, I think he is doing his cause a great deal of harm. Charles Williams is ostensibly inspired by Christian doctrine, but if you approach as a literary critic, unstiffened by the determination to 'discriminate Christianly', or if you approach merely with order sensitiveness and good sense, you can hardly fail to see that Williams' preoccupation with the 'horror of evil' is evidence of an arrest at the schoolboy (and -girl) stage rather than of spiritual maturity, and that his dealings in 'myth', mystery, the occult, and the supernatural belong essentially to the ethos of the thriller. To pass off his writings as spiritually edifying is to promote the opposite of spiritual health.

More generally, to debase the currency and abrogate the function of criticism, as Mr Every offers to do, can only, I am convinced, do harm by the standards of any real concern for religion. What, one may ask, does Mr Every offer his disciples in return for the great poet to whom he denies them access? He offers them (they were in the first place extension-lecturees, theological students, and training teachers) pretentious phrases, vague and muddled ideas, a confused exaltation of self-importance, and help towards believing that to feel vaguely excited and impressed is to have grappled with serious problems. On the other hand, to take, in any measure, what Mr Eliot's poetry has to give is to be educated into a new understanding of the nature of precision in thought, and at the same time to experience intimately an emotional and spiritual discipline. And this holds, irrespective of whether or not the reader subscribes to Christian doctrine.

As for Christian Discrimination, it needs to be said that there can be no substitute for the scrupulous and disinterested approach of the literary critic. If Christian belief and Christian attitudes have really affected the critic's sensibility, then they will play their due part in his perceptions and judgements, without his summoning his creeds and doctrines to the job of discriminating and pronouncing. If, on the other hand, he does, like Bro. George Every, make a deliberate and determined set at 'discriminating Christianly', then the life of the spirit will suffer damage, more or less severe, in the ways that Bro. George Every's work merely exemplifies with a peculiarly rich obviousness. It is fair to add (if I may use a phrase that was once reported to me as having been applied by the Editor of *The Criterion* to something quite different) that he represents the most active and formidable of contemporary 'gang-movements'.

KEYNES, LAWRENCE AND CAMBRIDGE

FOR the repugnance felt by Lawrence towards Mr David Garnett's friends, and the Cambridge-Bloomsbury milieu in general, Mr Garnett has a simple explanation: jealousy. 'He was a prophet who hated all those whose creeds protected them from ever becoming his disciples'. That Lawrence had gifts Mr Garnett readily perceived. In fact, he has 'never met a writer who appeared to have such genius. I greatly admired, and still admire, his short stories, his poems and several of his novels, particularly his first novel, *The White Peacock*'. (So, by way of paying one's tribute to James, one might say: 'Yes, tremendous! I particularly admire *The American*'. Or, a greater genius being in question: 'I particularly admire *Two Gentlemen of Verona*'). 'But', Mr Garnett continues,

I was a rationalist and a scientist, and I was repelled by his intuitive and dogmatic philosophy, whereas the ideas of my friends from Cambridge interested and attracted me.

It was thus inevitable that sooner or later Lawrence would spew me out of his mouth, since I could never take his philosophy seriously.

Keynes too, attempting his own explanation, invokes jealousy. But he feels that more is needed. His Memoir (the second of the pair that Mr Garnett introduces) is a piece of retrospective self-searching in which he asks whether he and his friends may not have provided Lawrence with some valid grounds for judging them adversely. Keynes, no one will question, was a distinguished mind, and the distinction is there, perhaps, in the very effort at self-criticism and a due humility. But the significance of what he offers is not what he is conscious of; it lies in the inadequacy of the effort, and in the justification he brings Lawrence when he least intends it, or suspects it.

The virtually intact complacency he exposes to our view gives us, at the outset, the assumptions on which the inquiry is to proceed: 'But when all that has been said, was there something true and right in what Lawrence felt?' The 'but' leaves the assumptions with us as implicitly granted, following as it does on this:

Lawrence was jealous of the other lot; and Cambridge rationalism and cynicism, then at their height, were, of course, repulsive to him. Bertie gave him what must have been, I think, his first glimpse of Cambridge. It overwhelmed, attracted and repulsed him – which was the other emotional disturbance. It was obviously a civilization, and not less obviously uncomfortable and unattainable for him – very repulsive and very attractive.

'It was obviously a civilization' – shocked as the provincial and puritanical Lawrence must inevitably have been, he 'obviously' can't but have admired and envied. That Lawrence, judging out of his experience of something incomparably more worthy to be called a 'civilization', loathed and despised what was in front of him merely because he saw just what it was, is inconceivable to Keynes.

The Memoir is devoted to explaining the serious substance underlying the 'brittle stuff' of the conversation in which Lawrence couldn't be brought to join. Such 'brittle stuff' continued, even in the maturer years of the *elite*, to be a large part of the 'civilization' – at least one gathers so from the way in which Keynes (it is 1938) announces his theme:

if it will not shock the Club too much, I should like in this contribution to its proceedings to introduce for once mental or spiritual, instead of sexual, adventures, to try and recall the principal impacts on one's virgin mind and to wonder how it has all turned out, and whether one still holds by that youthful religion.

The 'religion' was derived from G. E. Moore, and the Memoir is largely taken up with describing his influence. 'Influence' here, of course, means what was made of him, not in any field of disciplined study, but at the level of undergraduate 'civilization'. That Moore himself deserves the high terms in which Keynes speaks of him no one will wish to question. But the 'influence' – I well remember the exasperated despair with which its manifestations (in mild forms, I now see) filled me when I met them, just after the 1914 war, in friendly seniors who had been formed in that climate at the beginning of the century. Keynes, looking

back, describes the intellectualities of the coterie and its religion
with a certain amused irony; but it is not the detached irony of a
mature valuation. Still in 1938 he takes them seriously; he sees
them, not as illustrating a familiar undergraduate phase which
should in any case be left behind as soon as possible, and which the
most intelligent men should escape, but as serious and admirable
– even, it would seem, when cultivated well beyond undergraduate years. And that is what seems to me most significant in
the Memoir, and most revelatory of the Cambridge-Bloomsbury
ethos.

Of course, Keynes criticises the 'religion' for deficiencies and
errors. But he can't see that, 'seriously' as it took itself, to be in-
imical to the development of any real seriousness was its essence.
Articulateness and unreality cultivated together; callowness disguised from itself in articulateness; conceit casing itself safely in a
confirmed sense of high sophistication; the uncertainty as to
whether one is serious or not taking itself for ironic poise: who
has not at some time observed the process?

It did not prevent us from laughing most of the time and we enjoyed
supreme self-confidence, superiority and contempt towards all the rest
of the unconverted world.

Broadly speaking we all knew for certain what were good states of
mind and that they consisted in communion with objects of love,
beauty and truth.

And Keynes describes the dialectical play ('It was a stringent
education in dialectic', he tells us) that was to merge into, and,
one gathers, was ultimately superseded by, the more 'brittle stuff'
– describes it whimsically, but without in the least realizing that
what he and his friends were illustrating was the power of an
ancient university, in some of its climatic pockets, to arrest development, and that what they were finding in their intellectual
performances was sanction and reinforcement for an undergraduate
immaturity: the more confident they grew in their sophistication,
the less chance had they of discovering what seriousness was like.

The more worldly sophistication that Lawrence encountered in
1914 was not a more genuine maturity. One can readily imagine
how the incontinently flippant talk and the shiny complacency,
snub-proof in its obtuse completeness, infuriated him. He loathed

the flippancy, not because he was an inexperienced prude, but for quite opposite reasons. He had been formed in a working-class culture, in which intellectual interests were bound up with the social life of home and chapel, and never out of touch with the daily business of ensuring the supply of the daily bread. The intellectual interests were not the less real for that: E. T.'s *D. H. Lawrence*, taken together with *Sons and Lovers*, shows what an intense cultivation they had enjoyed during the formative years at Eastwood and Nottingham. Nothing could be more ludicrously wide of the mark than the assumption that Lawrence must have felt inferior and ill-educated when introduced in Russell's rooms to the dazzling civilization of Cambridge. But the thing to stress is his enormous advantage in experience. The young ex-elementary school-teacher was in a position to judge of the most distinguished intellectual among his friends, as he does in a letter of a year or so later:

> What ails Russell is, in matters of life and emotion, the inexperience of youth . . . It isn't that life has been too much for him, but too little.

Keynes, looking back, does of course criticize the 'religion' for certain defects that fall under inexperience. He says that, in its account of human nature, it ignored the formidable part of the irrational forces, and ignored at the same time 'certain powerful and valuable springs of feeling'. But his criticisms have a way of not being able to realize the weight they ought to carry and the depth to which they ought to strike. 'We lacked reverence, as Lawrence observed . . .' Keynes endorses, as he thinks, this radical criticism. But what it means to him is just this and no more (damaging enough by itself, of course):

> We had no respect for traditional wisdom or the restraints of custom . . . It did not occur to any of us to respect the extraordinary accomplishment of our predecessors in the ordering of life (as it now seems to me to have been) or the elaborate framework they had devised to protect this order.

How little Keynes can understand the full force of Lawrence's criticism he shows when he explains what he calls the 'individualism of our philosophy'.

> Now what we got from Moore was by no means entirely what he

offered us. He had one foot on the threshold of the new heaven, but the other foot in Sidgwick and the Benthamite calculus and the general rules of correct behaviour. We accepted Moore's religion, so to speak, and discarded his morals.

. . . we were amongst the first of our generation, perhaps alone amongst our generation, to escape from the Benthamite tradition. In practice, of course, ... the outside world was not forgotten or forsworn.

Moreover, it was this escape from Bentham, joined with the un-surpassable individualism of our philosophy, which has served to protect the whole lot of us from the final *reductio ad absurdum* of Benthamism known as Marxism . . . But we ourselves have remained . . . altogether immune from the virus, as safe in the citadel of our ultimate faith as the Pope of Rome in his.

These extracts illustrate how seriously Keynes takes the 'civilization' that must, he is sure, have impressed the 'ignorant, jealous, irritable' Lawrence. The 'unsurpassable individualism of our philosophy' – call the ethos evoked in the Memoir *that*, while granting that the 'philosophy' had weaknesses, and it becomes possible for Keynes to conclude that 'this religion of ours was a very good one to grow up under'. And it becomes possible for him to suggest that the Club-members would have been more subject to the infection of Marxism if they had been at all seriously affected by the spirit of Sidgwick. But what Lawrence heard was the levity of so many petty egos, each primed with conscious clevernesses and hardened in self-approval:

they talk endlessly, but endlessly – and never, never a good thing said. They are cased each in a hard little shell of his own and out of this they talk words. There is never for one second any outgoing of feeling and no reverence, not a crumb or grain of reverence: I cannot stand it.

The kind of triviality that Lawrence describes here is indeed a worse thing than Keynes was able to conceive it. And the significant fact that emerges unmistakably from the Memoir is that he couldn't really grasp the intention of the criticism he was considering. It is a fact that would seem substantially to confirm Lawrence.

If this judgement seems too severe, let it be remembered that the 'civilization' celebrated by Keynes produced Lytton Strachey, and that the literary world dominated by that 'civilization' made

Lytton Strachey a living Master and a prevailing influence. And if I should seem to be making too much here of facts belonging to the history of taste and literary fashion, I suggest a pondering of these comments which I take from a review by Sir Charles Webster (he is dealing at the moment with the other of the two memoirs in Keynes's book):

Keynes let me read it in 1943, and its facts were then checked against the documents which record – in very different prose – the public incidents which it relates. They were accurate enough, as I told him at the time. But the details were of course selected and distorted to suit his purpose.

These characterizations are of course caricatures. Keynes put down what suited his purpose at the moment. In this ruthless sacrifice of truth to literary purpose he was obviously much influenced by Lytton Strachey, whose popular books depended on little else. The political caricatures of the *Economic Consequences* did as much harm as the economic insight did good.

Keynes was a great representative Cambridge man of his time. Cambridge produced him, as it produced the 'civilization' with which he associated himself and which exercised so strong a sway over the metropolitan centres of taste and fashion. Can we imagine Sidgwick or Leslie Stephen or Maitland being influenced by, or interested in, the equivalent of Lytton Strachey? By what steps, and by the operation of what causes, did so great a change come over Cambridge in so comparatively short a time? These are the questions that we find ourselves once more asking as we put down Keynes's little book. The inquiry into which the second would lead, if seriously pursued, would tell us about a great deal more than Cambridge. That is a reason for thinking it very much worth undertaking.

E. M. FORSTER

THE problem with which E. M. Forster immediately confronts criticism is that of the oddly limited and uncertain quality of his distinction – his real and very fine distinction. It is a problem that Miss Macaulay, in *The Writings of E. M. Forster*, doesn't raise. In fact, she doesn't offer a critique; her book is rather a guide, simply and chattily descriptive, to the not very large corpus of Mr Forster's work. Nor does she provide the biographical information that, however impertinently in one sense of the adverb, we should like to have, and that we might have been led by the publisher's imprint to hope for, however faintly. We should like to have it because it would, there is good reason for supposing, be very pertinent to the problem facing the critic. Still we do, after all, without extra-critical pryings or impartings, know quite a lot about the particular milieu and the phase of English culture with which Mr Forster's work is associated; enough, perhaps, to discuss with some profit the extent to which, highly individual as it is, it is also, in its virtues and its limitations, representative.

The inequality in the early novels – the contrast between maturity and immaturity, the fine and the crude – is extreme; so extreme that a simple formula proposes itself. In his comedy, one might carelessly say, he shows himself the born novelist; but he aims also at making a poetic communication about life, and here he is, by contrast, almost unbelievably crude and weak. Yet, though his strength in these novels, it is true, comes out in an art that suggests comparisons with Jane Austen, while it is in the element, the intention, relating them most obviously to *The Celestial Omnibus* that he incurs disaster, the formula is too simple. For one thing, to lump the four pre-war novels together is clumsy; a distinction has to be made. There is no disastrous weakness in the first of them, *Where Angels fear to tread*, or in *A room with a View* (which, in order of publication, comes third). And the distinction here isn't one of 'comedy' as against 'poetry' or 'comedy-cum-poetry'. For though the art of the 'born novelist' has, in these two novels, a characteristic spinsterly touch, that novelist is at the same time very perceptibly the author of *The Celestial Omnibus*, the tales in which suggest, in their poetic ambition – they may fairly be said to specialize in 'poetry' – no one less than Jane Austen. Italy, in those novels, represents the same bent of interest as Pan and the other symbols do in the tales, and it is a bent that plays an essential part in the novelist's peculiar distinction. Pre-eminently a novelist of civilized personal relations, he has at the same time a radical dissatisfaction with civilization – with the finest civilization of personal intercourse that he knows; a radical dissatisfaction that prompts references to D. H. Lawrence rather than to Jane Austen.

In his treatment of personal relations the bent manifests itself in the manner and accent of his preoccupation with sincerity – a term that takes on, indeed, a different value from that which it would have if we used it in discussing Jane Austen. His preoccupation with emotional vitality, with the problem of living truly and freshly from a centre, leads him, at any rate in intention, outside the limits of consciousness that his comedy, in so far as we can separate it off, might seem to involve – the limits, roughly, that it is Jane Austen's distinction to have kept. The intention is most obvious in his way of bringing in, in association, love and sudden death; as, for instance, in chapter IV of *A Room with a View* (see pp. 54–58). It is still more strikingly manifested in *Where Angels fear to tread*. There Italy figures much more substantially and disturbingly as the critical challenge to the 'civilization' of Mr Forster's cultivated English people, and what may be called for the moment the Lawrencian bent is more pronounced. There is the scene (c.VII) in which passionate paternal love, a kind of elemental hunger for continuance, is enacted in the devotion of the caddish and mercenary Italian husband to the baby; and the baby it is that, in this book, suffers the violent death. There follows the episode in which the Italian tortures Philip Herriton by wrenching his broken arm. Yet none of Mr Forster's books is more notable for his characteristic comedy, with its light, sedate and rather spinsterly poise. And there is, nevertheless, no discrepancy or clash of modes or tones: *Where Angels fear to tread* is decidedly a success. It seems to me the most successful of the pre-war novels.

A Room with a View is far from being a failure, but, though the themes here might seem to be much less dangerous, there are certain weaknesses to be noted. There is, as Miss Macaulay points out, a curious spinsterish inadequacy in the immediate presentation of love (in *Where Angels fear to tread*, significantly, serious love between the sexes doesn't come in, at any rate immediately). And old Mr Emerson, though not a disaster, does lead one to question the substantiality of the wisdom that he seems intended to represent. Nevertheless *A Room with a View* is a charming and very original book – extremely original and personal. Yet decidedly it provokes a comparison with Meredith, for to *The Egoist* it obviously owes its inspiration. *The Egoist* tries only to do something simple (as we are bound to feel if we think of *The Portrait of a Lady*), but, apart from faults of over-writing, over-thronging and prolixity, *The Egoist* is entirely successful. The Lucy-Cecil Vyse-George Emerson trio who replace and imitate Clara Middleton, Sir Willoughby and Vernon Whitford are quite perfunctorily handled and but feebly animated – they are not realized, their emotions are stated but not convincingly conveyed, and the borrowed theme, losing its substance and force, loses also its symbolic strength. Being no longer a parable (though the fashionable term 'myth' could be for once justifiably invoked for *The Egoist*) the Forster version achieves the status only of minor comedy; it is essentially trivial. And if we were unkind enough to bring out the story *Other Kingdom* from *The Celestial Omnibus* volume for similar comparison with its source, which is again *The Egoist*, we should have to make an even more saddening report in which the charge of 'whimsy' would appear.

The reference above to D. H. Lawrence was, of course, an over-emphasis, but as a way of calling attention to Mr Forster's peculiar distinction among Edwardian novelists it can perhaps be justified. The critic who deals so damagingly with Meredith in *Aspects of the Novel* is potentially there in the genuineness of the element in Mr Forster's early novels that sets them apart by themselves in the period of Arnold Bennett, Wells, and Galsworthy. But having credited him with that distinction, one has to admit that in comparison with the *major* contemporary practitioners he appears very differently. Even leaving Conrad out as not inviting comparison, there are the two to whom he owes so much – Henry James and

Meredith. His relation to Meredith we have discussed. And where the other is in question, Forster's art has to be recognized as only too unmistakably mirror. Take even the slightest of James's stories which is fairly comparable: *The Marriages* is, we might say, at first glance entirely a 'Forster' story, with just such characters, plot and setting as Forster chooses. Then we recognize, in its complex ironic pattern and its really startling psychological insight, the art of a master whose depiction of human behaviour is not marginal and whose knowledge of passion is profound.

But Mr Forster's 'poetic' intention is genuine and radical, even if in expression it may manifest itself as a surprising immaturity; and actually, in *Where Angels fear to tread* and *A Room with a View*, it for the most part commands a touch that is hardly to be distinguished from that of the comedy. Or perhaps it would have been better to say 'is commanded by'; for when, coming to the other two pre-war novels, *The Longest Journey* and *Howards End*, we ask how it is that they should be so much less successful, we notice at once how the contrast brings out the sure easy poise, in *Where Angels fear to tread* and *A Room with a View*, of the artist's – the 'born novelist's' – control. The art of the comedy is a distancing art, and it is a tribute to the novelist's skill that we should have no disturbing sense of a change in mode and convention when we pass to effects quite other than those of comedy. That is, the whole action is framed and distanced. Lilia, Gino's silly tragic victim in *Where Angels fear to tread*, Philip Herriton, commissioned to retrieve the baby, Miss Abbott and the rest, are all simplified figures, seen from the outside; it is only in a very qualified way that they engage us (though they engage enough for a measure of poignancy). The complexity of the situation we see as such: though we are interested and sympathetic, we are hardly worried. The critical scenes and episodes towards the end are, of course, not undisturbing; yet we are not immersed in them – the detachment, though modified, still holds. In this effect the Italian setting, exotic and quaint – its people seen as another kind from us, has its part; it lends itself beautifully to the reconciliation of the 'comedy' with the 'poetry' and of tragic intensity with detachment.

The other two novels are much less the artist's: in them the imposing or seeking of any such conditions of a detached and happily poised art has been precluded by the author's essential interest. *The Longest Journey*, perhaps one may without impertinence observe, has plainly a good deal of the autobiographical about it, and it offers, in the presentment of its themes, a fulness and intimacy of realization. True, we find there too the characteristic comedy (notably in all that concerns Mr Herbert Pembroke), but we can no longer say the success of this carries with it a general success. In fact, there are discrepancies, disharmonies and disturbing shifts that go a long way towards justifying the formula thrown out and withdrawn in the second paragraph of this note. The poised success of the comedy in its own mode serves to emphasize the immaturity, the unsureness and sometimes the crudity of the other elements, with which it wouldn't have been easily congruent even if they had in themselves justified the intention they represent.

Passionate love and, close upon it, sudden death, come early in this book:

He had forgotten his sandwiches, and went back to get them. Gerald and Agnes were locked in each other's arms. He only looked for a moment, but the sight burnt into his brain. The man's grip was the stronger. He had drawn the woman on to his knee, was pressing her, with all his strength, against him. Already her hands slipped off him, and she whispered, 'Don't – you – hurt – .' Her face had no expression. It stared at the intruder and never saw him. Then her lover kissed it, and immediately it shone with mysterious beauty, like some star. (p. 51.)

Gerald is a brutal and caddish minor-Public-School Apollo and Agnes a suburban snob, but this glimpse is for Rickie the hero, a revelation:

He thought, 'Do such things actually happen?' and he seemed to be looking down coloured valleys. Brighter they glowed, till gods of pure flame were born in them, and then he was looking at pinnacles of virgin snow. While Mr Pembroke talked, the riot of fair images increased. They invaded his being and lit lamps at unsuspected shrines. Their orchestra commenced in that suburban house, where he had to stand aside for the maid to carry in the luncheon. Music flowed past him like a river. He stood at the springs of creation and heard the primeval monotony. Then an obscure instrument gave out a little phrase. The river continued unheeding. The phrase was repeated, and a listener might know it was a fragment of the Tune of tunes . . . In full unison was love born, flame of the flame, flushing the dark river beneath him and the virgin snows above. His wings were infinite, his youth eternal . . .

Then, a dozen pages later (p. 62):

Gerald died that afternoon. He was broken up in the football match. Rickie and Mr Pembroke were on the ground when the accident took place.

It is a key-experience for Rickie. Its significance is made explicit – perhaps rather too explicit. This memory of pure uncalculating passion as a kind of ultimate, invested by death with an awful finality and something like a religious sanction, becomes for Rickie a criterion or touch for the real, a kind of test for radical sincerity, in his questing among the automatisms, acquiescences, blurs, and blunted indifferences of everyday living:

He has no knowledge of the world . . . He believes in women because he has loved his mother. And his friends are as young and ignorant as himself. They are full of the wine of life. But they have not tasted the cup – let us call it the teacup – of experience, which has made men of Mr Pembroke's type what they are. Oh, that teacup! (p. 74.)

The theme of *The Longest Journey* is Rickie's struggle to live by the truth of the wine while being immersed in the knowledge of the world.

Rickie writes stories like Mr Forster's in *The Celestial Omnibus*. There is a note of ironic indulgence in the references to them: Rickie is very young. The direct and serious expression that the novelist offers us of the bent represented by such stories is in terms of a character, Stephen Wonham,

a man dowered with coarse kindliness and rustic strength, a kind of cynical ploughboy. (p. 217.)

He is the illegitimate child (comes the shattering revelation) of Rickie's mother and a young farmer, of whom we are told

people sometimes took him for a gentleman until they saw his hands.

It is a Lady-Chatterley-and-the-keeper situation that is outlined, though Robert is too much idealized to be called a Lawrencian character. Stephen, product of a perfect passionate love (cut short by death), grows up among the villagers and shepherds a kind of heroic boor, devoid of the civilized graces and refinements, representative of physical and spiritual health:

> . . . looked at the face, which was frank, proud and beautiful, if truth is beauty. Of mercy or tact such a face knew little. It might be coarse, but . . . (p. 243.)

He loves horseplay and can be a drunken blackguard, but he is incapable of anything other than direct sincerity: he would, as Ansell says, 'rather die than take money from people he did not love'. He moves roughshod through the latter part of the action, violating suburban flowerbeds, outraging gentilities, and breaking through the pretences, self-deceptions and timid meannesses of respectability.

> He only held the creed of 'here am I and there are you', and therefore class-distinctions were trivial things to him. (p. 292.)

When Rickie, having suspected him of intent to blackmail, offers apology and atonement, this is how Stephen replies:

> 'Last Sunday week,' interrupted Stephen, his voice suddenly rising, 'I came to call on you. Not as this or that's son. Not to fall on your neck. Nor to live here. Nor – damn your dirty little mind! I meant to say I didn't come for money. Sorry, sorry. I simply came as I was, and I haven't altered since . . .' '*I* haven't altered since last Sunday week. I'm – ' He stuttered again. He could not quite explain what he was . . . His voice broke. 'I mind it – I'm – *I* don't alter – blackguard one week – live here the next – I keep to one or the other – you've hurt something most badly in me I didn't know was there.' (pp. 281–2.)

In short, it isn't easy to feel that the novelist in this essential part of his undertaking has attained a much more advanced maturity than the Rickie of the stories. Of course, what he has undertaken is something incomparably more difficult, and the weakness of the 'poetic' element is made to look its worst by contrast with the distinction of what is strongest in the novel. Still, the contrast is there, and it is disastrous. What Mr Forster offers as the centre of his purpose and intends with the greatest intensity of seriousness plainly cannot face the test of reality it challenges. Uninhibited by the passage about 'knowledge of the world' and the 'cup of experience' quoted above, the reader has to remark that Mr Forster shows himself, for a writer whose touch can be so sure, disconcertingly inexperienced. An offence, even a gross one, against the probabilities, according to 'knowledge of the world', of how people act and talk isn't necessarily very serious. But such a scene as that (c. xxvii) in which Ansell the Cambridge philosopher, defying headmaster, headmaster's wife, and prefects, addresses the assembled boys at Sawston School –

'This man' – he turned to the avenue of faces – 'this man who teaches you has a brother,' etc.

– reflects significantly on the ruling preoccupation that, in the born novelist, could have led to anything so crudely unreal. And of all that in *The Longest Journey* centres in Stephen one has to say that, if not always as absurd, it is, with reference to the appropriate standard, equivalently unreal. The intention remains an intention; nothing adequate in substance or quality is grasped. And the author appears accordingly as the victim, where his own experience is concerned, of disabling immaturities in valuation: his attributions of importance don't justify themselves.

A ready way of satisfying oneself (if there were any doubt) that 'immaturity' is the right word is to take note of the attitude towards Cambridge (after which one of the three parts of the novel is named). Rickie, a very innocent and serious young man, found happiness at Cambridge and left it behind him there, and that this phase of his life should continue to be represented, for him, by an innocent idealization is natural enough. But Rickie in this respect is indistinguishable from the author. And if one doesn't comment that the philosophic Ansell, representative of disinterestedness and intelligence and Cambridge, is seen through the hero-worshipping Rickie's eyes, that is because he is so plainly offered us directly and simply by the novelist himself in perfect good faith.

Howards End (1910), the latest of the pre-war novels and the most ambitious, is, while offering again a fulness and immediacy of experience, more mature in the sense that it is free of the autobiographical (a matter, not of where the material comes from, but of its relation to the author as it stands in the novel) and is at any rate fairly obviously the work of an older man. Yet it exhibits

crudity of a kind to shock and distress the reader as Mr Forster
hasn't shocked or distressed him before.

The main theme of the novel concerns the contrasted Schlegels
and Wilcoxes. The Schlegels represent the humane liberal culture,
the fine civilization of cultivated personal intercourse, that Mr
Forster himself represents; they are the people for whom and in
whom English literature (shall we say? – though the Schlegels are
especially musical) exists. The Wilcoxes have built the Empire;
they represent the 'short-haired executive type' – obtuse, egotistic,
unscrupulous, cowards spiritually, self-deceiving, successful. They
are shown – shown up, one might say – as having hardly a redeem-
ing characteristic, except that they are successful. Yet Margaret,
the elder of the Schlegel sisters and the more mature intelligence,
marries Mr Wilcox, the head of the clan; does it coolly, with open
eyes, and we are meant to sympathize and approve. The novelist's
attitude is quite unambiguous: as a result of the marriage, which
is Margaret's active choice, Helen, who in obeying flightily her
generous impulses has come to disaster, is saved and the book
closes serenely on the promise of a happy future. Nothing in the
exhibition of Margaret's or Henry Wilcox's character makes the
marriage credible or acceptable; even if we were to seize for
motivation on the hint of a panicky flight from spinsterhood in
the already old-maidish Margaret, it might go a little way to
explain her marrying such a man, but it wouldn't in the least
account for the view of the affair the novelist expects us to take.
We are driven to protest, not so much against the unreality in
itself, as against the perversity of intention it expresses: the effect
is of a kind of *trahison des clercs*.

The perversity, of course, has its explanation and is not so bad
as it looks. In Margaret the author expresses his sense of the inadequacy of the culture she stands for – its lack of relation to the
forces shaping the world and its practical impotence. Its weaknesses, dependent as it is on an economic security it cannot provide,
are embodied in the quixotic Helen, who, acting uncompromisingly on her standards, brings nothing but disaster on herself
and the objects of her concern. The novelist's intention in making
Margaret marry Mr Wilcox is not, after all, obscure. One can
only comment that, in letting his intention satisfy itself so, he
unintentionally makes his cause look even more desperate than it

need: intelligence and sensitiveness such as *Howards End* at its finest represents need not be so frustrated by innocence and inexperience as the unrealities of the book suggest. For 'unreality' is the word: the business of Margaret and Henry Wilcox is essentially as unrealized as the business of Helen and the insurance clerk, Leonard Bast – who, with his Jacky, is clearly a mere external grasping at something that lies outside the author's first-hand experience.

And the Wilcoxes themselves, though they are in their way very much more convincingly done, are not adequate to the representative part the author assigns them – for he must be taken as endorsing Margaret's assertion to Helen, that they 'made us possible': with merely Mr Forster's Wilcoxes to represent action and practice as against the culture and the inner life of the Schlegels there could hardly have been civilization. Of course, that an intellectual in the twentieth century should pick on the Wilcox type for the part is natural enough; writing half-a-century earlier Mr Forster would have picked on something different. But the fact remains that the Wilcoxes are not what he takes them to be, and he has not seen his problem rightly: his view of it is far too external and unsubtle.

At the same time it is subtler than has yet been suggested. There is the symbolism that centres in 'Howards End', the house from which the book gets its title. Along with the concern about the practical insignificance of the Schlegels' culture goes a turning of the mind towards the question of ultimate sanctions. Where lie – or should lie – the real sources of strength, the springs of vitality, of this humane and liberal culture, which, the more it aspires to come to terms with 'civilization' in order to escape its sense of impotence, needs the more obviously to find its life, strength, and authority elsewhere?

The general drift of the symbolism appears well enough here:

The sense of flux which had haunted her all the year disappeared for a time. She forgot the luggage and the motor-cars, and the hurrying men who know so much and connect so little. She recaptured the sense of space which is the basis of all earthly beauty, and, starting from Howards End, she attempted to realize England. She failed – visions do not come when we try, though they may come through trying. But an unexpected love of the island awoke in her, connecting on this side with the joys of the flesh, on that with the inconceivable . . . It had certainly come through the house and old Miss Avery. Through them: the notion of 'through' persisted; her mind trembled towards a conclusion which only the unwise have attempted to put into words. (p. 202.)

Yes, but the author's success in the novel is staked on his effectively presenting this 'conclusion' by means of symbols, images and actions created in words. And our criticism must be that, without a more substantial grasp of it than he shows himself to have, he was, as it turns out, hardly wise in so committing himself. The intention represented by Howards End and its associates, the wych-elm, the pig's teeth, Old Miss Avery and the first Mrs Wilcox remains a vague gesturing in a general – too general – direction, and the close of the book can hardly escape being found, in its innocent way, sentimental.

The inherent weakness becomes peculiarly apparent in such prose as this:

There was a long silence during which the tide returned into Poole Harbour. 'One would lose something,' murmured Helen, apparently to herself. The water crept over the mud-flats towards the gorse and the blackened heather. Branksea Island lost its immense foreshores, and became a sombre episode of trees. Frome was forced inward towards Dorchester, Stour against Wimborne, Avon towards Salisbury, and over the immense displacement the sun presided, leading it to triumph ere he sank to rest. England was alive, throbbing through all her estuaries, crying for joy through the mouths of all her gulls, and the north wind, with contrary motion, blew stronger against her rising seas. What did it mean? For what end are her fair complexities, her changes of soil, her sinuous coast? Does she belong to those who have moulded her and made her feared by other lands, or to those who have added nothing to her power, but have somehow seen her, seen the whole island at once, lying as a jewel in a silver sea, sailing as a ship of souls, with all the brave world's fleet accompanying her towards eternity? (p. 172.)

Mr Forster's 'poetic' communication isn't all at this level of poeticality (which, had there been real grasp behind his intention, Mr Forster would have seen to be Wilcox rather than Schlegel), but it nevertheless lapses into such exaltations quite easily. And the 'somehow' in that last sentence may fairly be seized on: the intention that can thus innocently take vagueness of vision in these matters for a virtue proclaims its inadequacy and immaturity there.

In closing on this severe note my commentary on the pre-war novels I had perhaps better add explicitly (in case the implication may seem to have got lost) that they are all, as I see them, clearly the work of a significantly original talent, and they would have deserved to be still read and remembered, even if they had not been the early work of the author of *A Passage to India*.

In *A Passage to India* (1924), which comes fourteen years later (a remarkable abstention in an author who had enjoyed so decided a *succès d'estime*), there are none of these staggering discrepancies. The prevailing mood testifies to the power of time and history. For the earlier lyrical indulgences we have (it may fairly be taken as representative) the evocation of Mrs Moore's reactions to the caves ('Pathos, poetry, courage – they exist, but are identical, and so is filth,' etc. – see pp. 149–151). The tone characterizing the treatment of personal relations is fairly represented by this:

> A friendliness, as of dwarfs shaking hands, was in the air. Both man and woman were at the height of their powers – sensible, honest, even subtle. They spoke the same language, and held the same opinions, and the variety of age and sex did not divide them. Yet they were dissatisfied. When they agreed, 'I want to go on living a bit', or, 'I don't believe in God', the words were followed by a curious backwash as if the universe had displaced itself to fill up a tiny void, or as though they had seen their own gestures from an immense height – dwarfs talking, shaking hands and assuring each other that they stood on the same footing of insight. (p. 265.)

Of course, tone and mood are specifically related to the given theme and setting of the novel. But the Indian sky and the Anglo-Indian circumstances must be taken as giving a particular focus and frame to the author's familiar preoccupations (exhibiting as these naturally do a more advanced maturity).

Fielding, the central figure in the book, who is clearly very close to the author, represents in a maturer way what the Schlegels represented: what may still be called liberal culture – humanity, disinterestedness, tolerance and free intelligence, unassociated with dogma or religion or any very determinate set of traditional forms. He might indeed (if we leave out all that Howards End stood for) be said to represent what was intended by Margaret's marrying Henry Wilcox, for he is level-headed and practical and qualified in the ways of the world. His agnosticism is explicit. Asked

> Is it correct that most people are atheists in England now?

he replies:

> The educated thoughtful people. I should say so, though they don't like the name. The truth is that the West doesn't bother much over belief and disbelief in these days. Fifty years ago, or even when you and I were young, much more fuss was made. (p. 109.)

Nevertheless, though Fielding doesn't share it, the kind of pre-occupation he so easily passes by has its place in *A Passage to India* as in Mr Forster's other novels, and again (though there is no longer the early crudity) its appearances are accompanied by something unsatisfactory in the novelist's art, a curious lack of grasp. The first Mrs Wilcox, that very symbolic person, and Miss Avery may be said to have their equivalents in Mrs Moore and Ralph, the son of her second marriage. Mrs Moore, as a matter of fact, is in the first part of the book an ordinary character, but she becomes, after her death, a vague pervasive suggestion of mystery. It is true that it is she who has the experience in the cave – the experience that concentrates the depressed ethos of the book – and the echo 'undermines her hold on life', but the effect should be to associate her with the reverse of the kind of mysteriousness that after her death is made to invest her name. For she and the odd boy Ralph ('born of too old a mother') are used as means of recognizing possibilities that lie outside Fielding's philosophy – though he is open-minded. There is, too, Ralph's sister Stella, whom Fielding marries:

> She has ideas I don't share – indeed, when I'm away from her I think them ridiculous. When I'm with her, I suppose because I'm fond of her, I feel different, I feel half dead and half blind. My wife's after something. You and I and Miss Quested are, roughly speaking, not after anything. We jog on as decently as we can . . . (p. 320.)

Our objection is that it's all too easy. It amounts to little more than saying, 'There may be something in it', but it has the effect of taking itself for a good deal more. The very poise of Mr

Forster's art has something equivocal about it – it seems to be conditioned by its not knowing what kind of poise it is. The account of the Krishna ceremony, for instance, which is a characteristic piece by the sensitive, sympathetic, and whimsically ironic Mr Forster, slides nevertheless into place in the general effect – there are more things in heaven and earth, Horatio – that claims a proper impersonality. How radical is this uncertainty that takes on the guise of a sureness and personal distinction of touch may be seen in Mr Forster's prose when a real and characteristic distinction is unmistakably there. Here is an instance:

The other smiled, and looked at his watch. They both regretted the death, but they were middle-aged men who had invested their emotions elsewhere, and outbursts of grief could not be expected from them over a slight acquaintance. It's only one's own dead who matter. If for a moment the sense of communion in sorrow came to them, it passed. How indeed it is possible for one human being to be sorry for all the sadness that meets him on the face of the earth, for the pain that is endured not only by men, but by animals and plants, and perhaps by the stones? The soul is tired in a moment, and in fear of losing the little she does understand, she retreats to the permanent lines which habit or chance have dicated, and suffers there.

The touch seems sure in the first three sentences – in fact, but for one phrase, in the whole passage. Consider, for instance, how different an effect the second sentence would have out of its context: one would suppose it to be in satiric tone. Here, however, it is a means to the precise definition of a very different tone, one fatigued and depressed but sympathetic. The lapse, it seems to me, comes in that close of the penultimate sentence: '. . . plants, and perhaps by the stones.' Once one's critical notice has fastened on it (for, significantly too, these things tend to slip by), can one do anything but reflect how extraordinary it is that so fine a writer should be able, in such a place, to be so little certain just how serious he is? For surely that run-out of the sentence cannot be justified in terms of the dramatic mood that Mr Forster is offering to render? I suppose the show of a case might be made out for it as an appropriate irony, or appropriate dramatically in some way, but it wouldn't be a convincing case to anyone who had observed Mr Forster's habit. Such a reader sees merely the easy, natural lapse of the very personal writer whose hand is 'in'. It may seem a not very important instance, but it is representative, and to say that is to pass a radical criticism.

Moreover, a general doubt arises regarding that personal distinction of style – that distinction which might seem to give Mr Forster an advantage over, say, Mr L. H. Myers (to take another novelist who offers some obvious points of comparison). The doubt expresses itself in an emphasis on the 'personal'.

Ronny approved of religion as long as it endorsed the National Anthem, but he objected when it attempted to influence his life.

Sir Gilbert, though not an enlightened man, held enlightened opinions.

Ronny's religion was of the sterilized Public School brand, which never goes bad, even in the tropics.

Incurably inaccurate, he already thought that this was what had occurred. He was inaccurate because he was sensitive. He did not like to remember Miss Quested's remark about polygamy, because it was unworthy of a guest, so he put it away from his mind, and with it the knowledge that he had bolted into a cave to get away from her. He was inaccurate because he desired to honour her, and – facts being entangled – he had to arrange them in her vicinity, as one tidies the ground after extracting a weed.

What had spoken to her in that scoured-out cavity of the granite? What dwelt in the first of the caves? Something very old and very small. Before time, it was before space also. Something snub-nosed, incapable of generosity – the undying worm itself.

A larger assemblage of quotations (there would be no difficulty but that of space in going on indefinitely) would make the point fairly conclusively: Mr Forster's style is personal in the sense that it keeps us very much aware of the personality of the writer, so that even where actions, events and the experiences of characters are supposed to be speaking for themselves the turn of phrase and tone of voice bring the presenter and commentator into the foreground. Mr Forster's felicities and his charm, then, involve limitations. Even where he is not betrayed into lapses of the kind illustrated above, his habit doesn't favour the impersonality, the presentment of themes and experiences as things standing there in themselves, that would be necessary for convincing success at the level of his highest intention.

The comparative reference to Mr L. H. Myers thrown out above suggests a return to the question of Mr Forster's representative significance. When one has recognized the interest and value his work has as representing liberal culture in the early years of the twentieth century, there is perhaps a temptation to see the weaknesses too simply as representative. That the culture has of its very nature grave weaknesses Mr Forster's work itself constitutes an explicit recognition. But it seems worth while insisting at this point on the measure in which Mr Forster's weaknesses are personal ones, qualifying the gifts that have earned him (I believe) a lasting place in English literature. He seems then, for one so perceptive and sensitive, extraordinarily lacking in force, or robustness, of intelligence; it is, perhaps, a general lack of vitality. The deficiencies of his novels must be correlated with the weakness so apparent in his critical and journalistic writings – *Aspects of the Novel*, *Abinger Harvest* – the weakness that makes them representative in so disconcerting a way. They are disconcerting because they exhibit a lively critical mind accepting, it seems, uncritically the very inferior social-intellectual milieu in which it has developed. Mr Forster, we know, has been associated with Bloomsbury – the Bloomsbury which (to confine ourselves to one name) produced Lytton Strachey and took him for a great writer. And these writings of Mr Forster's are, in their amiable way, Bloomsbury. They are Bloomsbury in the valuations they accept (in spite of the showings of real critical perception), in the assumptions they innocently express, and in prevailing ethos.

It might, of course, be said that it is just the weakness of liberal culture – 'bourgeois', the Marxist would say – that is manifested by Bloomsbury (which certainly had claims to some kind of representative status). But there seems no need to deal directly with such a proposition here, or to discuss at any length what significance shall be given to the terms 'liberal' and 'culture'. The necessary point is made by insisting that the weaknesses of Mr Forster's work and of Bloomsbury are placed as such by standards implicit in what is best in that work. That those standards are not complete in themselves or securely based or sufficiently guaranteed by contemporary civilization there is no need to dispute: the recognition has been an essential part of the creative impulse in Mr Forster. But that, in the exploration of the radical problems, more power than he commands may be shown by a creative writer who may equally be said to represent liberal culture appears well enough in *The Root and the Flower* – at least, I throw out this judgement as pretty obviously acceptable. And I cannot see how we can dispense with what they both stand for. They represent, the spokesmen of the finer consciousness of our time, the humane tradition as it emerges from a period of 'bourgeois' security, divorced from dogma and left by social change, the breakdown of traditional forms and the loss of sanctions embarrassingly 'in the air'; no longer serenely confident or self-sufficient, but conscious of being not less than before the custodian of something essential. In these representatives it is far from the complacency of 'freedom of thought', but they stand, nevertheless, for the free play of critical intelligence as a *sine qua non* of any hope for a human future. And it seems to me plain that this tradition really is, for all its weakness, the indispensable transmitter of something that humanity cannot afford to lose.

These rather commonplace observations seemed worth making because of the current fashion of using 'liberal' largely and loosely as a term of derogation: too much is too lightly dismissed with it. To enforce this remark it seems to me enough to point to *A Passage to India* – and it will be an occasion for ensuring that I shall not, in effect, have done Mr Forster a major critical injustice. For I have been assuming, tacitly, a general agreement that *A Passage to India*, all criticisms made, is a classic: not only a most significant document of our age, but a truly memorable work of literature. And that there is point in calling it a classic of the liberal spirit will, I suppose, be granted fairly readily, for the appropriateness of the adjective is obvious. In its touch upon racial and cultural problems, its treatment of personal relations, and in prevailing ethos the book is an expression, undeniably, of the liberal tradition; it has, as such, its fineness, its strength and its impressiveness; and it makes the achievement, the humane, decent and rational – the 'civilized' – habit, of that tradition appear the invaluable thing it is.

On this note I should like to make my parting salute. Mr Forster's is a name that, in these days, we should peculiarly honour.

APPROACHES TO T. S. ELIOT

HERE,[1] edited by a Fellow of Trinity, and contributed to by members of the Cambridge English Faculty and other respectable academics, is a volume of essays on T. S. Eliot, all treating him as a classic and an accepted glory of our language. As one contributor, Miss Bradbrook, indicates, such a thing was, not so very long ago, hardly conceivable; it means that a revolutionary change has been brought about. 'How was it done?' Miss Bradbrook doesn't answer her question; but, while she slights one main part of the answer, her essay seems to me to illustrate the other. Referring back to the Cambridge of the nineteen-twenties, she surmises (exemplifying a tone and an attitude characteristic of her essay – I find them, I had better say outright, very distasteful): '. . . Mr Eliot may be relieved that the incense no longer fumes upon the local altars with quite its old intensity . . .' I can only comment that a pronounced fume, strongly suggesting incense, rises from Miss Bradbrook's own essay, and that it is of such a quality as to give us half the answer to her question. (I find her style, suggesting the influence of Miss Dorothy L. Sayers rather than Mr Eliot, corroborative.)

For it is certain that a marked change in Mr Eliot's standing followed the appearance of *For Lancelot Andrewes* and *Ash-Wednesday*, and that if so difficult and disturbing a poet is so generally accepted as an established institution it is for the kind of reason that makes a great many people (including, one gathers, Miss Bradbrook – see a footnote to p. 21) suppose that *The Rock* and *Murder in the Cathedral* inaugurated a revival of religious poetic drama. The part played by Mr Eliot's association with religious orthodoxy is to be read plainly in at least three of the eight essays presented by Dr Rajan.

Yet Mr Eliot would not have been there for Anglo-Catholic intellectuals as a triumphantly acclaimable major poet, the great living master, nor would the critical apparatus for confidently appraising and elucidating him as such, if there had not been, in

1. T. S. Eliot: *A Study of his Writings by several hands.* Edited by B. Rajan.

the years referred to by Miss Bradbrook, admires capable of something more critical than burning incense. And, I must add, capable of something in the nature of courage that isn't necessary today – an aspect of that forgotten situation not done justice to by Miss Bradbrook, who says:

When *The Sacred Wood* and *Homage to John Dryden* appeared Mr Eliot was still the subject of frightened abuse in the weeklies, and also in some academic circles. But his views percolated downwards, and are now almost common form. How was it done?

That 'still' must appear very odd to anyone who recalls the chronology of Mr Eliot's *œuvre*. *The Sacred Wood* came out in 1920 and *Homage to John Dryden* in 1924 (when in most academic circles Mr Eliot's name would hardly have met with recognition). 'Still', I must testify, having the strongest of grounds for confident insistence, still in 1930 (and later), and in the academic circles that now receive Dr Rajan's enterprise without a flutter, Mr Eliot's mere name, however modestly mentioned, was as a red rag to a bull. I could tell Miss Bradbrook, privately, some piquant and true anecdotes in illustration. I will confine myself here to two reminiscences of sufficiently public fact. When in 1929 an innocent young editor printed an article of mine on Mr Eliot's criticism in *The Cambridge Review* (a reply to a contemptuous dismissal of him by a Cambridge 'English' don in Mr Desmond MacCarthy's *Life and Letters*) he very soon had cause to realize that he had committed a scandalous impropriety, and I myself was left in no doubt as to the unforgivableness of my offence. And when, in 1932, a book of mine came out that made a study of Mr Eliot the centre of an attempt to define the distinctive aspects of significant contemporary poetry, so much worse than imprudent was it found to be that the advanced 'English' intellectual of the day declined (or so the gloating whisper ran) to have anything to do with it, and *The Cambridge Review* could find no reviewer for it in Cambridge. I remember, too, with some amusement, the embarrassed notes I received from correct friends who felt that some form of congratulation on the appearance of a book had to be gone through, but knew also that the offence was rank, disastrous and unpardonable. Yet the matter of that offensive book is seen, in Dr Rajan's symposium, to be now 'common form'. How was it done?

I have thought this note on the development of a literary-critical orthodoxy worth making, not only because history will go on repeating itself and, though it undoubtedly in any case will, there is always some point in insisting on the moral as presented by the nearest striking instance, but because such an orthodoxy naturally tends to discourage true respect for the genius it offers to exalt – to substitute, that is, deference. True respect is inseparable from the concern to see the object as in itself it really is, to insist on the necessary discriminations, and so to make the essential achievement, with the special life and virtue it embodies, effective as influence. Of this respect Miss Bradbrook seems to me to fail.

She is not, among Dr Rajan's contributors, alone in that. I read her first because so much, largely repetitive, had already been written about Mr Eliot's poetry, and the opportunity, I told myself, still lay open for a first-hand attempt to appraise the criticism. My disappointment is the heavier because such an appraisal seems to me very much to be desired. It would involve some firm discriminating and delimiting, and until these are performed, the ambiguity that hangs about the nature and tendency of Mr Eliot's influence must impede the recognition of our debt. It is a debt that I recognize for myself as immense. By some accident (it must have been – I had not come on Mr Eliot's name before) I bought *The Sacred Wood* just after it came out, in 1920. For the next few years I read it through several times a year, pencil in hand. I got from it, of course, orientations, particular illuminations, and critical ideas of general instrumental value. But if I had to characterize the nature of the debt briefly I should say that it was a matter of having had incisively demonstrated, for pattern and incitement, what the disinterested and effective application of intelligence to literature looks like, what is the nature of purity of interest, and what is meant by the principle (as Mr Eliot himself states it) that 'when you judge poetry it is as poetry you must judge it, and not as another thing'.

There are few pieces of his criticism after *For Lancelot Andrewes* to which one would send the student of literature for such demonstration. 'When he stabilized his own style as a poet, some informing power departed from his critical writing. If for example the essay on *In Memoriam* be compared with that on Massinger, or the introduction to the volume of Kipling's verse with the essay on Dryden, it will be seen that Mr Eliot has withdrawn from his subjects: he is no longer so closely engaged . . .' Ah, if that were all. It seems to me, in fact, that Miss Bradbrook's handling of the change isn't free from disingenuousness:

Mr Eliot has apologized for the 'pontifical solemnity' of some of his early writings. Nervous stiffness and defensive irony were inevitable in an age when 'a complete severance between his poetry and all beliefs' could be imputed to him for righteousness. The later criticism exhibits rather a haughty humility – 'The poem *Gethsemane* (by Kipling) which I do not think I understand . . .'; the implication being, 'I expect you think it's simple, but that only shows how superficial your reading is'.

To find the difference between the earlier and the later criticism in the disappearance or diminution of nervousness – that is to me an extremely odd achievement. Mr Eliot's best criticism is remarkable for its directness, its concentrated purity of interest, its intense and rigorous concern to convey the essential perception and the bearing of this as realized by the critic. It exhibits the reverse of hesitation and diffidence; its qualities are intimately related to courage. I don't find these qualities in the Kipling introduction referred to by Miss Bradbrook. On the contrary, in that too characteristic specimen of the later writing the critic seems to me to have misapplied his dangerous gift of subtle statement to the development of a manner (it is surprisingly suggestive in places of G. K. Chesterton) that gainsays the very purpose of criticism, and to have done so because of a radical uncertainty about his intention and its validity. And is what we have here (from *The Use of Poetry and the Use of Criticism*) 'haughty humility'? –

Mr Housman has given us an account of his own experience in writing poetry which is important evidence. Observation leads me to believe that different poets may compose in very different ways; my experience (for what it is worth) leads me to believe that Mr Housman is recounting the authentic process of a real poet. 'I have seldom', he says, 'written poetry unless I was rather out of health'. I believe that I understand that sentence. If I do, it is a guarantee – if any guarantee of that nature is wanted – of the quality of Mr Housman's poetry.

It seems to me also that in Mr Eliot's critical writing from *For Lancelot Andrewes* onwards a limitation that is (on a pondered appraisal) to be predicated of his earlier work asserts itself as a major weakness – a weakness of a kind that might seem to be disqualifying where claims to status as a great critic are in question. That the author of *Selected Essays* is (if not, where shall we find one?) a great critic I don't for a moment doubt. But if he is, it is in spite of lacking a qualification that, sketching the 'idea', one would have postulated as perhaps the prime essential in a great critic. It is a qualification possessed pre-eminently by D. H. Lawrence, though he, clearly, is not to be accounted anything like as important in literary criticism as T. S. Eliot: a sure rightness in what, if one holds any serious view of the relation between literature and life, must appear to be the most radical and important kind of judgement.

As Miss Bradbrook intimates, Mr Eliot's best criticism was related in the closest of ways to his own problems as a poet – a practitioner who has rejected current conventions and modes as inadequate to his needs and so is committed to a labour of thorough-going technical innovation. Questions of technique – versification, convention, relation of diction to the spoken language, and so on – cannot be isolated from considerations of fundamental purpose, essential ethos, and quality of life. That is, one can hardly say where technical questions turn into questions that one wouldn't ordinarily call technical. 'The important critic is he who is absorbed in the present problems of art, and wishes to bring the forces of the past to bear on the solution of those problems'. The attention that Mr Eliot's highly selective kind of interest (the definition just quoted is his own) directs upon Donne, Marvell, Dryden, Jonson, Marlowe, and the others, entails value-judgements. But it doesn't commit him to attempting any comprehensive evaluation or definitive placing. So that, by way of countering one's protests that he over-rates Dryden, one can adduce the very special interest with which he approaches and the strictly limiting end he has in view – one can adduce these, I must add, while deploring both the over-valuation of Dryden that he has certainly helped to establish as a fashion, and the attendant slighting of the incomparably greater Pope (without an appreciation of whom there can't be any but the most incomplete perception of Mr Eliot's seventeenth century – the seventeenth century of Jonson, Donne and Marvell).

But the major instance of the limiting approach, the instance where the limitation is most clearly seen to entail unfortunate consequences, is what we have in Mr Eliot's treatment of Jacobean drama. No one, I think, admires more than I do his contribution in that field, or can be more grateful for it. To approach it one needs to have started reading the Jacobeans when the Lamb-Swinburne tradition was unchallenged, and no better critical equipment for dealing with poetic drama was to hand than that which has its classical exponent in Bradley. No doubt, had one been put on to them, one might have found a tip or two, here and there, in scholarly sources. But only a fine and powerful critical intelligence, informed with the insight got in dealing with its own creative problems, could have brought effective aid, and it was Mr Eliot who brought it. He supplied the equipment of ideas about drama, the enlightenment about convention and verse, that made all the difference. What he did not, however, do, was to attempt any radical revaluation of the Jacobeans. The very marked tendency of his work, in fact (in spite of his admirable asides on Beaumont and Fletcher), has been to endorse the traditional valuations. (It seems to me highly significant that he has gone on reprinting that very unsatisfactory essay on Middleton.) What he hasn't done, no one else has had the courage or the perception to do. So that, though he insisted on the need to distinguish conventions from faults (see 'Four Elizabethan Dramatists'), scholars who, stimulated by him, have undertaken to investigate the conventions have tended to repeat, in inverted form, Archer's failing: that is, to make everything convention, thus emptying the term of its force. To have acted seriously on Mr Eliot's tip, and taken proper cognizance of faults, would have been to face the need for drastic revision of some consecrated valuations.

Here, then, is an unfortunate consequence of the special restricted approach. But restricted approach and special interest are not the whole of the story – this is what we are made to realize when we come to the later criticism. When the critic's technical preoccupations cease to exercise a close direction over his criticism, he gives himself a great deal more to comprehensive and radical value-judgements, and it is then that we have to recognize a fundamental defect. I myself see it in the essay on Tourneur, where he makes what is to me an astonishing reference to Swift: 'We may think as we read Swift, "how loathsome human beings are"; in reading Tourneur we can only think "how horrible to loathe human beings so much as that"'. The phrase used here of Tourneur is precisely what I should have found fitting as applied to Swift. It was D. H. Lawrence who diagnosed Swift's case so well, and who was so quick to perceive, and sure in placing, the signs of such malady as Swift exhibits in that terribly extreme form. And it is Lawrence himself who, as subject, provides the capital instance of Mr Eliot's defect as a great critic. (Mr Eliot himself, in *After Strange Gods*, concedes enough to place the matter above the level of mere difference of judgement.) 'Against the living death of modern material civilization he spoke again and again, and even if these dead could speak, what he said is unanswerable'. Lawrence stood for life, and shows, in his criticism, tossed off as it was, for the most part, in the most marginal way, an extraordinarily quick and sure sense for the difference between that which makes for life and that which makes against it. He exhibits a profound, and for those who come to the criticism knowing only the fiction, perhaps surprising, centrality.

I myself think Lawrence sounder in judgement about the Joyce of *Work in Progress* than Mr Eliot, whose ascription of importance to it doesn't seem to imply importance as representative disintegration-phenomenon. (That the inventor of Basic English should take a keen interest in the *Work* always seemed to me appropriate.) However that may be, I am sure that so distinguished a mind as Mr Eliot's ought not to have been able to take Wyndham Lewis so seriously, or find him so sympathetic. Then there is Djuna Barnes's *Nightwood*: it deals, of course, with Evil – but surely Mr Eliot's estimate of it will stand as one of the curiosities of literature? And to be able to refer favourably to Henry Miller – when I try to believe that some perversity of my imagination has invented this I recall, in detail, an unquestionable fact: the paragraph that finds promise for the future of English fiction in Lawrence Durrell's *Black Book*. The inspiration of these works, in so far as they have any, seems to me to be the desire, in Laurentian idiom, to 'do dirt' on life. And I have to record the conviction that the reaction against the world of William Clissold (shall we say?) represented by Mr Eliot's critical writings is, at any rate largely, of the wrong kind. I put it naïvely no doubt, and I will go on to suggest that Lawrence's reaction against the same world (see his review in *Phoenix* of H. G. Wells and relate it to the *Fantasia of the Unconscious*) has much more of rightness in it.

In general, where contemporary letters have been concerned, Mr Eliot's judgement has, it seems to me, been very much out – deflected by pulls and disturbances of various kinds. Yet in spite of this, and in spite of the radical nature of the major weakness that has been indicated, he remains a great critic. It is not only that he has re-orientated criticism and poetic practice, effecting a profound change in the operative current idea of the English tradition, and that in this achievement his critical writings have played an indispensable part. It is also that the best of these writings represent more powerfully and incisively the idea of literary criticism as a discipline – a special discipline of intelligence – than the work of any other critic in the language (or any in French that I know).

To this high distinction in criticism Miss Bradbrook's intentness on advancing unsustainable claims makes her incapable of doing justice. Thus she writes:

His purely destructive work has sometimes been the result of some temperamental aversion. Milton has survived the attack of Mr Eliot and the Battle of the Critics which it provoked. (Yet how strange that a taste for Landor should accompany a distaste for Milton.)

The taste for Landor always seemed to me strange. I could explain it only as a minor snobbism – one that was peculiarly unfortunate when it led to Landor's being adduced in illustration of impersonality. Landor's impersonality is that of the stiff suit of style that stands up empty – impersonal because there is nothing inside. For Miss Bradbrook, however, it is not the taste for Landor, but the critical attitude towards Milton that has to be deplored. Yet to talk in that way of an 'attack on Milton' ('purely destructive') that Milton has survived is to expose an inappreciation of what Miss Bradbrook admits to be Mr Eliot's most vital criticism, to miss its force, and to deny the essence of that poetic achievement with which the criticism is so closely bound up. For poetry is made of words – words and rhythms, and 'sensibility alters from generation to generation in everyone . . . but expression is only

altered by a man of genius'. It was the informing presence everywhere, in the criticism, of the practitioner's preoccupation with his
problem of putting words together – of inventing the ways of
using words, the rhythms, and the versification, demanded by his
essential interests – that gave his brief asides on Milton their
potency. Milton is indeed still there, an impressive figure (in spite
of some of his defenders), but if you can't see what is meant by
saying that he was a prepotent influence in taste and poetic practice until Mr Eliot's work had its effect, and has since ceased to be,
then you are not really appreciating Mr Eliot's genius or its
achievement. And you make no real restitution by coming with
this kind of offering:

> But in general, Eliot's destructive criticism has also anticipated the
> more general verdict, even as in the poems *Triumphal March* and
> *Difficulties of a Statesman* (1932) he anticipated the spirit of Nazi Ger-
> many and the spirit of Munich with prophetic accuracy.

It is because I admire these poems so immensely, and think they
have not had due recognition, that I feel obliged to say that this
account of them seems to me nonsense – or mere incense.

I have concentrated on Miss Bradbrook's essay because, while
it offers a representative opportunity for underlining what, for
the reader who has (so to speak) lived through the history of
Mr Eliot's reputation, must be the significance and the moral,
there was still, it seemed to me, something that needed to be said
on the criticism. All the other essays are on the poetry. The best of
these are by the two American contributors, Mr Cleanth Brooks
and Mr Philip Wheelwright, together with those by Miss
Gardner and Mr Mankowitz. I was interested by Mr Brooks's
argument against my view that *The Waste Land* 'exhibits no progression' (and touched, I must confess, by his generous acknow-
ledgements to that pioneer book, written nearly twenty years
ago – which has suffered more pillaging than acknowledging).
But it still remains to inquire whether the intention noted by Mr
Brooks (see pp. 129–30) is anything more: is it operative poetically, does it become something realized in the poem? This
kind of question is, in general, not asked by the contributors
to the symposium. They build on the antecedent work of
criticism.

And this is the point at which to mention the general tendency in the literary-academic world today to substitute, the cue having been given, elucidation for criticism. Mr Brooks's kind of elucidation has, I can see, a function, though I can also see dangers in it. The dangers are illustrated by that phrase 'death-in-life' and the part it plays in Mr Brooks's exposition. By the grateful follower of the exposition such a phrase is readily taken as doing more than it does, while, in his sense of having grasped the 'meaning' of the poetry, he has grasped nothing but a phrase. At the risk of seeming egotistic I will say that, for unequivocal aid, one can't, I think, do much more than I tried to do in my own account of *The Waste Land*: commit oneself in clear and challenging terms to the necessary critical judgements, and indicate the nature of the essential organization.

It is when the elucidatory approach is Anglo-Catholic (or made from the point of view of doctrinal acceptance) that the dangers are greatest. They are apparent even in Miss Gardner's scrupulous and sensitive commentary on the *Four Quartets*. There is a clear tendency to frustrate the enormous labour expended by the poet in undercutting mere acceptance, inhibiting inert acquiescence, and circumventing, at every level, what may be called cliché; a tendency, that is, to abet the reader's desire to arrive without having travelled. And the separation from criticism is apparent in the references to *Family Reunion*.

Miss Gardner's essay, however, could for the right reader perform a useful function. But Mrs Duncan Jones's commentary on *Ash-Wednesday* seems to me to do little but justify one's apprehensions about Anglo-Catholic elucidation. Starting with acceptance, it turns the poetry into something like illustrations of acceptances, poetical formulations of antecedently defined attitudes and beliefs. That is, it denies the poet's genius and deprives his poetry of its astonishing (and disturbing) life and its profound general interest and validity. She can say, for instance, of *Salutation* (as it was first called), a poem I intensely admire: 'The second poem ends on a note of absolute assurance and content'. To be able to say that of it you must, I am convinced, have missed something – something essential. And in general it is as if Mrs Duncan Jones were saying what Dr Rajan does actually say (p. 88): 'Mr Eliot means what is meant by any Christian'.

Dr Rajan does not, one gathers, himself write as an Anglo-Catholic. In fact, he intimates that he could, given room, correct Mr Eliot authoritatively about Krishna. And one suspects that the qualification which enables him to do so may be attended with a disadvantage; for after all, the *Four Quartets* are extremely subtle and difficult, and demand for their critical appreciation not only good analytic powers, but as complete an inwardness with the English language as any poetry that was ever written. However that may be, in his essay we have the extreme instance of the divorce of elucidation from criticism. This divorce is not the less apparent for his offering a good deal in the guise of critical and appreciative comment. It is mostly of this kind:

> The confidence of the poetry is superb. It disdains analogies. It will have nothing to do with snapshot imagery. The resonant pride of those polysyllables summons all fact to a defining judgement and then, as the sibilants slow its clash and recoil, the open vowels hush it to repose. Against that liberating assurance the verse speaks again melodious and human. . . .

Surely this kind of commentary is sufficiently placed by Dr Rajan himself when he says:

> Of the tremendous rhymed lyric of section four there is nothing I can say which would not be redundant. People to whom it is not immediately impressive are unlikely to be convinced by a description of its subtleties.

When he does offer comments of a kind that can be checked as tests of sensibility they are usually of this kind:

> The 'fiery rain' which falls here falls also on burning London. Here Mr Eliot, fire-watcher and wanderer in Hades, meets his 'familiar compound ghost' which will provide the backbone for one hundred American theses and which as far as present knowledge can tell is Dante, Mallarmé, and Arnaut Daniel together. The ghost promises Mr Eliot a suitably grisly future, but all that he can say, however terrible, is turned into sweetness by Eliot's *terza rima*.

This passage in *terza rima* is the one about which D. W. Harding (reviewing *Little Gidding* in *Scrutiny*, XI, 3) says:

> The verse in this passage, with its regular measure and insistent alliter-

ation, so effective for combining the macabre with the urbane and the dreary, is a way to indicate and a way to control pressure of urgent misery and self-disgust. The motive power of this passage . . . is repulsion.

I quote Harding by way of emphasizing that it is not just a case of *one* judgement against another. My response corroborates his account very forcibly, and it is a response that is contradicted violently by the description 'sweet'. I can only say that Dr Rajan's account seems to me to betray a striking defect of sensibility. And I can't help associating that defect with the failure in tone and touch (characteristic, I think) represented by such phrases in the commentary as 'The ghost promises Mr Eliot a suitably grisly future'.

Further, I do not think that Dr Rajan could have permitted himself the indulgence of that easy superiority about 'one hundred American theses' (two of the best contributions to his symposium are by Americans)if he had been really responding to the quality of what was in front of him – it is the passage in which (in Harding's words) 'the humanist's ghost sees in his life . . . futility, isolation and guilt on account of his self-assertive prowess', and one would have though it, for the reader exposed to it, destructive of all easy complacencies:

> . . . the laceration
> Of laughter at what ceases to amuse.
> And last, the rending pain of re-enactment
> Of all that you have done, and been; the shame
> Of motives late revealed, and the awareness
> Of things ill done and done to others' harm
> Which once you took for exercise of virtue.
> Then fools' approval stings, and honour stains.
> From wrong to wrong the exasperated spirit
> Proceeds, unless restored by that refining fire
> Where you must move in measure, like a dancer.

Almost always where Dr Rajan commits himself to judgements which can be challenged he seems to me to confirm the suspected defect of sensibility.

His title is *The Unity of the Quartets*, but I cannot see that he adds anything to the extant accounts of the organization of that work. When, for instance, he says, 'What his scheme is I should hesitate to specify, beyond suggesting that *Burnt Norton* is concerned with constructing concepts' we can see that this is D. W. Harding's 'creation of concepts'. But Dr Rajan, as he indeed intimates, does nothing to extend Harding's account, or to explain the borrowed phrase, or to justify in any way the (un-acknowledged) borrowing. His presumptive intention of ex-plaining organization doesn't sufficiently control his commentary, as the large proportion of this which is devoted to a kind of Sitwellian quasi-creative pseudo-analysis betrays. And too often, in the guise of analytic guidance, we have such passages as this:

The words in *Little Gidding* are points of intersection. They join, in the tolerance of a convening insight, the worlds which in common ex-perience are divided and distinguished. Always they bring us back to what is known, but it is the familiar made different by exploration, the 'intimate yet indentifiable', the everyday alchemized into abiding strangeness.

Does this kind of gloss add anything to anyone's understanding or appreciation of the text? It is true that Dr Rajan goes on to say:

It is most difficult to do justice to *Little Gidding*. You have to do the impossible, to say four things at once; and if you try to say them suc-cessively you end up by saying something different.

The moral is that you should be very clear with yourself as to precisely what function you are undertaking to perform. It will hardly be that of 'doing justice' – an aim which would most likely result in the commentator's producing (as Miss Bradbrook puts it) a 'debilitating rehash of what his author may be supposed to "mean" '. What *can* reasonably be undertaken is to point out the nature of the organization, and that task, it should be recognized, is one for a disciplined effort of intelligence. But it cannot be satisfactorily performed except by an analyst with a good sensi-bility. That is, it demands a critic, capable of first-hand response and independent judgement.

It must be said that Miss Anne Ridler, in her chosen mode of commentary, shows herself very much at home. She gives as her subject, 'A Question of Speech', and approaches it as herself an English poet. 'For myself, I should say, it was Eliot who first made me despair of becoming a poet; Auden (with, of course, dead poets, notably Sir Thomas Wyatt) who first made me think I saw how to become one'. She discusses (among other things) the relation between poetry and music, and thinks

the differences more suggestive than the similarities. The elementary fact that poetry has no sustained notes is a big one; 'duration in time' is therefore quite a different thing for her, and she cannot mingle her themes in the way that music does. To compensate for her inability to keep several voices at once, she has her hidden dimension of memory and association: this is the 'Invisible Knight' that is her constant companion.

Miss Ridler doesn't, however, try to give force to these observations (or any others she makes) by any detailed analysis of particular poems or passages. Of Mr Eliot she remarks that 'As a critic, he has kept his preferences while shedding his prejudices', and gives as illustration (among others – one concerns Milton) the difference between his early essay, *The Function of Criticism*, and 'the much less acid *What is a Classic?*' – A classic is what, of its kind, I should myself call *The Function of Criticism*; on the other hand, I couldn't disagree when I heard the less 'acid' performance described as being more like an exercise in tight-rope-walking than a feat of critical thinking. But Miss Ridler has a poise of her own that is in its own way impressive: I suspect it to be very much an Oxford way, and I think I suggest the interest and significance of her essay rightly when I recommend it for study as an Oxford product. I can't, however, see what part it has in a book planned (that is the claim) 'in such a way as to make the consecutive study of the poems possible'.

Mr Mankowitz does a close analysis of that very fine early poem, *Gerontion*. But the contribution I read with some marked pleasure and stimulus was Philip Wheelwright's on *Eliot's Philosophical Themes*, which, it will be noted, doesn't offer a point-by-point elucidation of any poem, and won't, I think, be among the aids most resorted to.

It will be gathered, then, that I shouldn't like to think of this book's being accepted (it very well may be) as a standard introduction and guide-book to Eliot. It contains some respectable things, but it seems to me calculated in sum to promote, not the impact of Eliot's genius – a disturbing force and therefore capable of ministering to life – but his establishment as a safe academic classic.

THE PROGRESS OF POESY

IN 1930, in the shadow of, but not too close to, Mr J. Alfred Prufrock, the *Poems* of Mr W. H. Auden first appeared. Mr T. S. Eliot's *Waste Land* had prepared the way by showing out the Georgians as gracefully but as finally as his Bloomsbury lady pours out tea.

There is a recurrent embarrassment facing anyone who is concerned for the contemporary function of criticism: the call for certain observations and judgements comes endlessly, and certain things have unavoidably to be said again and again, or there is no point in offering to deal with the contemporary scene; yet there is a limit to profitable reiteration, and – is *this* (comes the question) once more an occasion that, after so much abstinence, must not be ignored? The passage quoted above opens a full-page review in the *Times Literary Supplement* (Oct. 23, 1948) of W. H. Auden's *The Age of Anxiety*, and the review does seem an occasion that one must take.

The effect of the passage is not, as might have been supposed, an unfortunate accident of expression. The critic himself doesn't actually say, as the acclaimers of that Poetic Renaissance in which Mr Auden played the leading part did, that Auden superseded Eliot, but his commentary may fairly be said to be in resonance with that view. That is, if we are to grant that what he offers is serious criticism, then the fashionable relegation of Mr Eliot that marked the advancing nineteen-thirties was critically respectable: it was the supersession, as the reigning power in poetry, of one creative genius by another, who understood better how to satisfy the needs of the time.[1]

As a matter of fact, we are left in doubt whether the critic considers Mr Eliot a really major poet: he speaks of his 'grey unruffled language' and his 'gentle and exquisite language'. However, it is hardly worth while to pursue the evaluative

1. It was interesting to observe in the universities how, at senior levels, conventional taste that had continued to resist Eliot was able to leave him behind and achieve a superior advancedness by acclaiming Modern Poetry in Auden.

implications of these astonishing phrases. We need do no more than contemplate the way in which the critic gives as grounds for treating Mr Auden as a great poet the very characteristics that make him so decidedly *not* one – and make him something not seriously to be compared with Mr Eliot. Mr Auden's poetry, we are told,

was philosophy undigested but illuminated by a poet's intuition. It was poetry taken from the same events as those recorded in the daily news-papers. Its range was as sensational, its attitude as unpedantic, its acute-ness in reading the signs of the weather a hundred times greater. . . . For good measure he threw into his verse, like toys, the names of Freud and Rilke; he made the Mother-symbol smart; he made poetry out of dance lyrics. . . .

Of this poetry we are told that it was 'politically honest and self-searching', that it 'could shame a generation into political aware-ness, a personal guilt' and that it 'diagnosed the causes of the struggle correctly and clear-sightedly'. Mr Auden's honesty there is no need to question; it may perhaps be said to manifest itself in the openness with which his poetry admits that it doesn't know how serious it supposes itself to be. He was no doubt 'self-searching', just as a thousand public-school boys going up to the university in those days were 'self-searching'. But to talk of his being 'correct' and 'clear-sighted' in 'diagnosis' is about as absurd a misuse of words as can be imagined. It was not clear-sightedness that made him an irresistible influence. The 'political awareness' and the 'personal guilt' into which he 'shamed a generation' were of a kind that it cost them very little to be shamed into. They asked for nothing better, and his poetry stilled any uncomfortable suspicion that there might be something better (if less comforting) to ask for. There it was, flatteringly modern and sophisticated, offering an intellectual and psychological profundity that didn't challenge them to any painful effort or discipline, and assuring them that in wearing a modish Leftishness they could hold up their heads in a guaranteed rightness – for the play with Depressed Areas, rusty machinery, and the bourgeois Dance of Death had essentially *not* the function of destroying complacency. No wonder they took more kindly to him than to Mr Eliot, who had no such attractions to offer.

The conditions that account for the arrest of Mr Auden's remarkable talent at the stage of undergraduate 'brilliance' are not, we are disconcertingly reminded, less potent now than they were. Our critic says that Mr Auden 'was the Oxford intellectual with a bag of poetic squibs in his pocket', without seeming to realize that he was the undergraduate intellectual – permanently undergraduate and representing an immaturity that the ancient universities, not so long ago, expected their better undergraduates to transcend. It is the more disconcerting in that one can't avoid the suspicion (the signs are strong) that in this criticism we have a voice from the university – and not, of course, a junior one. It judges Mr Auden's last book a failure ('his one dull book, his one failure'), but we get no hint of any perceived relation between this failure and the earlier career that the reviewer has described.

If Mr Auden's successor doesn't become acquainted with serious criticism and the standards of maturity at the university, he will not readily find help towards remedying the lack when he enters the larger literary world. The *Times Literary Supplement* critic's way of seeing in Mr Auden's bright topicality the major poet's kind of authority called to mind a number of *Horizon* (July, 1947) that had been lying by some months among the 'documents' and signs of the times. In an editorial 'Comment' we read:

In order to prepare an edition of essays from *Horizon* for translation into German it was necessary last week to run through all ninety-odd numbers . . . many of the fireworks in earlier numbers which achieved immediate popularity are now inclined to appear superficial and shoddy. One is also conscious of a change of policy which would appear to be justified. This change is expressed in our belief that the honeymoon between literature and action, once so promising, is over. We can see, looking through these old *Horizons*, a left-wing and some-times revolutionary political attitude among writers, heritage of Guernica and Munich, boiling up to a certain aggressive optimism in the war years, gradually declining after D-day and soon after the victorious general election despondently fizzing out. It would be too easy to attribute this to the policy of the editors, their war-weariness and advancing years. The fact remains that a Socialist Government, besides doing practically nothing to help artists and writers (unless the closing down of magazines during the fuel crisis can be interpreted as an aid to incubation), has also quite failed to stir up either intellect or imagination; the English renaissance, whose false dawn we have so enthusiastically greeted, is further away than ever.

Here, in these guileless reflections and avowals, we have an idea of the function of an intellectual literary organ corresponding to the *Times Literary Supplement* writer's idea of the poet. The nature of the 'acuteness in reading the signs of the weather' lauded in both cases is obvious. The consequences for criticism of *Horizon's* idea of its own function are manifested on a large scale in the later pages of the same number. Further on in the 'Comment' we read:

In the light of the comparative failure of the 'progressive' movement of the last few years to rise above intelligent political journalism into the realms of literature, we must look elsewhere, either to the mad and lonely, or to those who have with a certain angry obstinacy meticulously cultivated their garden. Among these the Sitwells shine out, for during the darkest years of the war they managed not only to produce their best work and to grow enormously in stature, but to find time to be of immense help to others. Many poets and writers were consoled by their encouragement as well as by their intransigent example, and so this number, at the risk of the inevitable accusations that we support a literary clique, is wholeheartedly dedicated to them. It includes a new poem by Miss Sitwell, an essay on her later poetry by Sir Kenneth Clark which mentions her most recent work, *The Shadow of Cain* (published by John Lehmann, and among much else a magnificent anti-atomic protest) and a new fragment of Sir Osbert's autobiography in which the Father-Son conflict is treated with his engaging *aigre-douceur de vivre*.

Dr Edith Sitwell, then, is a great poet, with an established acceptance that would have seemed incredible if foretold ten years ago (there are now – Yeats being dead – Edith Sitwell and T. S. Eliot) and Sir Osbert's autobiography is a glory of contemporary English literature.[1]

If a serious attempt should be made to assert a different (and traditional) idea of the function of criticism in a world in which *Horizon's* idea of it reigns, and in which the intransigence of the

1. 'Next week Sir Osbert and Miss Edith Sitwell began a lecture tour in America described as "a lecture-manager's tragedy" on account of its briefness compared with the thirst of the American public to hear and see these two peculiarly English geniuses.' – *Sunday Times*, November 7, 1948.

Sitwells avails to such exemplary effect, then it will appear as it does to the writer of another document that lies to hand: Mr John Hayward. In *Prose Literature since 1939*, published for the British Council, he refers in a passing mention to the 'minority group' of critics (led apparently by the 'cold intellectual', Dr F. R. Leavis), 'whose methodical and uncompromising destruction of reputations periodically enlivens the pages of the hypercritical but bracing magazine *Scrutiny*.'

It would of course be hypercritical to suggest (though Americans and foreigners in the present writer's hearing have said it) that nothing could be worse for the prestige and influence of British Letters abroad than Mr Hayward's presentment of the currency-values of Metropolitan literary society and the associated University milieux as the distinctions and achievements of contemporary England.

No work of the period, at all events, has provoked livelier or more intelligent discussion among the critically-minded. Its merits and faults have been widely debated – to the dismay, doubtless, of its detractors, who, having dismissed the book in its original limited issue as the darling of a coterie, were to see 20,000 copies of two ordinary editions sold out on publication. By that time 'Palinurus' had been identified as Cyril Connolly, editor of the literary monthly *Horizon*, and leader of the intellectual *avant-garde*.

Few contemporary writers care so much about language as Connolly; know so much about its resources; use them with such respect.

Here we have the approach, but no quoting can suggest the completeness and consistency with which the job is done. Among the many names receiving distinguished mention is that of the Warden of Wadham:

Like David Cecil, Bowra is above all concerned with the writer as artist, and with his books as works of art. His criticism is essentially humanistic, deeply rooted in and nourished by the civilization of ancient Greece. It is as unusual as it is welcome to find a professional classical scholar competent to write with authority as well as enthusiasm on subjects as various as the European epic and contemporary European poetry.

The Warden of Wadham, it can now be added, has just applied

his classical scholar's ripeness and percipience to an extended appreciation of the poetry of Edith Sitwell (*Edith Sitwell*, Lyrebird Press).

Mr Hayward's survey ends on this note of uplift:

The integrity of the individual writer can best be defended from all the forces currently arrayed against it, by an attitude of absolute intransigence towards the philistine and all his works. Not only in the immediate post-war era but during the years of man's painful spiritual recovery which lie ahead, such an attitude must be preserved if, out of disintegration, a scheme of values is to arise and out of disillusionment a dynamic faith in the power of the printed word to express the finest operations of human thought and sensibility.

We may rely on the Sitwells to tell us who the philistine is. Can we rely on *Horizon* and Mr Howard's majority array of warm[1] British intellectuals (backed by the British Council) to foster uncompromisingly the necessary attitude of absolute intransigence?

1. The warm intellectual is not, like the cold kind, offensively highbrow: however intransigent, he promotes cosiness.

1948

INDEX

MORE ABOUT PENGUINS
AND PELICANS

Penguinews, which appears every month, contains details of all the new books issued by Penguins as they are published. From time to time it is supplemented by *Penguins in Print*, which is a complete list of all titles available. (There are some five thousand of these.)

A specimen copy of *Penguinews* will be sent to you free on request. For a year's issues (including the complete lists) please send 50p if you live in the British Isles, or 75p if you live elsewhere. Just write to Dept EP, Penguin Books Ltd, Harmondsworth, Middlesex, enclosing a cheque or postal order, and your name will be added to the mailing list.

In the U.S.A.: For a complete list of books available from Penguin in the United States write to Dept CS, Penguin Books Inc., 7110 Ambassador Road, Baltimore, Maryland 21207.

In Canada: For a complete list of books available from Penguin in Canada write to Penguin Books Canada Ltd, 41 Steelcase Road West, Markham, Ontario.

THE PELICAN GUIDE TO
ENGLISH LITERATURE

Edited by Boris Ford

What this work sets out to offer is a guide to the history and
traditions of English literature, a contour-map of the literary
scene in England. It attempts, in other words, to draw up an
ordered account of literature that is concerned, first and fore-
most, with value for the present, and this as direct encouragement
to people to read for themselves.

Each volume presents the reader with four kinds of related
material:

(i) An account of the social context of literature in each
period.

(ii) A literary survey of the period.

(iii) Detailed studies of some of the chief writers and works in
the period.

(iv) An appendix of essential facts for reference purposes.

The *Guide* consists of seven volumes, as follows:

1. *The Age of Chaucer*
2. *The Age of Shakespeare*
3. *From Donne to Marvell*
4. *From Dryden to Johnson*
5. *From Blake to Byron*
6. *From Dickens to Hardy*
7. *The Modern Age*

THE QUEST FOR PROUST

André Maurois

Neither Marcel Proust nor his biographer, André Maurois, needs any introduction. In shaping this magnificent study of the strange, inverted author of *Remembrance of Things Past*, M. Maurois has employed previously unpublished letters and notebooks. It is a book for all to read.

'It is a tremendous apologia for Proust as well as a lively and packed biography, and as a portrait of an extraordinary genius could not be more readable and sympathetic' – V. S. Pritchett in the *Bookman*

'Well-informed, well-translated, and highly readable' – *Guardian*

'M. Maurois obliges us to see Proust . . . not as brilliant eccentric but as a scientific exponent of the great tradition of French literature' – Harold Nicolson in the *Observer*

NOT FOR SALE IN THE U.S.A. OR CANADA

SEVEN TYPES OF AMBIGUITY

William Empson

This is the latest edition of a famous work which has been extensively revised since the original edition of 1930. Professor Empson's analysis of the effects which may be obtained, deliberately or unconsciously, through the use of ambiguity has become a classic of twentieth-century criticism. As Donald Davie has said:

'No feature of the British literary scene since the war is more remarkable than the greatly increased reputation of William Empson ... Developments in British and American criticism cannot be understood except in terms of the key-word, "ambiguity".'

'A work of real originality, the first expression of a genuinely critical intelligence' – *Observer*

JANE AUSTEN'S NOVELS

Andrew H. Wright

Of Jane Austen Sir Walter Scott wrote: 'That young lady had a talent for describing the involvements, and feelings, and characters of ordinary life, which is to me the most wonderful I ever met with.' Coleridge and Southey admired her, 'but Mr Wordsworth used to say that though he admitted that her novels were an admirable copy of life, he could not be interested in productions of that kind'. For him they lacked imagination. Macaulay placed her next to Shakespeare, but Charlotte Brontë wrote: 'Jane Austen was a complete and most sensible lady, but a very incomplete and rather insensible (*not senseless*) woman.' More recently she has been called both a capitalist *bourgeoise* and 'in a sense a Marxist'. At any rate, as Edmund Wilson has said, 'Miss Austen is almost unique among the novelists of her sex in being deeply and steadily concerned ... with the novel as a work of art.'

In this excellent work of modern criticism Andrew Wright, an American scholar, sympathetically examines her materials and themes, her narrative method (with its subtle changes of viewpoint), and finally each of her six great novels, in turn and in detail. His penetrating study adds depth and colour to our appreciation of a great novelist who was wholly alive to her own limitations.

'Mr Wright is keenly appreciative, but not devout ... Confident, and competent, he tackles his subject with zest' – *The Times Literary Supplement*

NOT FOR SALE IN THE U.S.A.

A CRITICAL HISTORY OF
ENGLISH POETRY

Herbert Grierson and J. C. Smith

This famous work was the result of the wartime collaboration
of two Scottish scholars. Their tracing of the course of English
poetry has been described by *The Times Literary Supplement* as
a 'volume of masterly compression'. They deliberately spend
most time on the greatest poets, believing that, significant as
traditions and influences are, the great poet himself affects the
spirit of his age and moulds the tradition he has inherited. At
the same time, enough attention is paid to minor poets to make
the book historically complete, and to fill in the most important
links in the chain of poetic development. Thus Gower is here,
as well as Chaucer; Patmore, as well as Browning. Both in scope
and in detail. *A Critical History of English Poetry* is a distinguished
and valuable work.

'Alive with witty and just appreciation of the best that has been
done in our tongue' – *Scotsman*